A KNOCK AT THE DOOR

A KNOCK AT THE DOOR

A homeless man, a lawyer . . .
and a family changed forever

ROB PARSONS

WILLIAM
COLLINS

William Collins
An imprint of HarperCollins*Publishers*
1 London Bridge Street
London SE1 9GF

WilliamCollinsBooks.com

HarperCollins*Publishers*
Macken House
39/40 Mayor Street Upper
Dublin 1
D01 C9W8, Ireland

First published in Great Britain in 2024 by William Collins

2

A catalogue record for this book is available from the British Library

ISBN: 978-0-00-870866-5

Typeset in Sabon Lt Std by HarperCollins*Publishers* India

Printed and bound in the UK using 100%
Renewable Electricity at CPI Group (UK) Ltd

For Dianne.

My name is on this book but of course this is our story,
and I have loved living it with you.

Contents

Chapter 1 – A Knock at the Door   1

Chapter 2 – Christmas Day   21

Chapter 3 – Two Days of Christmas   39

Chapter 4 – Boxing Day   61

Chapter 5 – Ronnie Grows Up   75

Chapter 6 – People Like Us Don't Become Lawyers   95

Chapter 7 – Ronnie Gets a Job   113

Chapter 8 – Shoe Paint   133

Chapter 9 – A Murder Trial   149

Chapter 10 – The New Car   169

Chapter 11 – The Creaking Stair   193

Chapter 12 – Hard Times   211

Chapter 13 – The Long Winter   227

Chapter 14 – Time for Ronnie to Leave   245

Chapter 15 – A Key in the Door   261

Chapter 16 – Moscow   285

Chapter 17 – Take Me Back   309

Chapter 18 – Sat in Ronnie's Chair   323

Postscript   341

Acknowledgements   347

A Knock at the Door is based on a true story. Some names and locations have been changed but I have relayed as faithfully as I can the account of Ronnie's life with us. The most difficult parts to write, concerned the periods when he was a child in care. In these I have relied on what he told us of his experiences and what I was able to glean from his local authority records. Sadly, his time in those institutions and the effect they had on his life, is mirrored in many other accounts of children in the care system at that time.

Sat on the wall with friends in my childhood street
(I am third from the right).

Chapter 1

A Knock at the Door

23 December 1975.

Two days to Christmas and the doorbell wasn't working properly.

The knock on the door was not loud – not a policeman's knock, but neither was it soft – not the kind of knock you make when you hope nobody will answer. But it was persistent. I sometimes wonder how it would have all turned out if the person standing outside had given up. If, when nobody responded to the constant pressing of the bell push, he had simply shrugged his shoulders and walked away. I imagine how different our lives would have been if he hadn't decided to bang on the door, or we had simply chosen not to answer, believing it to be the return of the small boy we had generously rewarded the previous evening just to stop him murdering 'Once in Royal David's City'.

But answer it we did.

Dianne and I had been married for four years, I was 27 years old, and we had been in our new home on the outskirts of Cardiff for just six months. I was in the living room listening to Prime Minister Harold Wilson talk about his plans for bringing peace to Northern Ireland, when Dianne called from the kitchen, 'See who that is, Rob.'

I moved into the winter chill of the hall and walked past the brown second-hand sideboard; its scratches covered up by a dozen Christmas cards. It had already been dark for over two hours, and as I approached the front door, the frighteningly tall and broad silhouette through the glass made me pause. Opening it slowly, I was relieved to find that the long shadow was cast merely by the lamppost opposite, and an ordinary man stood on my doorstep.

He was of medium height, with several days' stubble on his square chin, and brown hair parted in an indeterminate line. Yet something about him was unusual. At first, I thought it was his clothes – they were creased and dirty, as though he had lived with and in them for a very long time – but it wasn't his clothing that was odd, it was his bearing. In spite of his rough appearance, he looked confident, as if whoever lived at this house would be glad he had called and be sure to show it.

But the owner of this house did not show it. 'How can I help you?' I demanded, with a voice that matched the chill in the air.

He gazed at me as though he felt sorry for me. 'Don't you know who I am? It's Ronnie Lockwood.' Of course – how could I have forgotten him and the mayhem he caused the first time we met?

*   *   *

I was brought up in a street of twenty-eight terraced houses in Cardiff, Wales. It was, in many ways, nondescript, but it did have three things that the surrounding streets did not possess: a laundry, a coal-yard, and a tiny Gospel Hall on the corner. We knew people who worked at the laundry and we got our coal from the yard, but as far as my family was concerned, the church could have been in another country. Then one day, a Sunday-school teacher called Miss Williams came to visit.

Miss Williams was short, with wiry grey hair and replete with a boldness she attributed to the Almighty. When my mother opened the door to her, she smiled and posed the same question she had already asked at the eight houses between us and the Gospel Hall: 'Would any boys or girls in this house like to come to Sunday school? It is every Sunday afternoon at two-thirty. I'll pick them up and be sure to have them home by a quarter to four.'

Whether it was her 4-year-old's spiritual welfare that swayed my mother, or just the prospect of some free childcare for an hour or so, I don't know. But she didn't hesitate. She pulled me out from behind her apron and said, 'He'd like to go.'

And so it was that on the following Sunday afternoon Miss Williams called at our house, took me by the hand and led me down the street, past old Mrs Hughes' place, the Giles', and finally the Morgan's, then into the sombre stone building that would change the course of my life.

Miss Williams was one of the most unusual women I have ever met. She never had any children of her own, yet she possessed an extraordinary gift for dealing with kids. I came to believe that she actually loved me and that if I missed a class, it might well break her heart. And the feeling was mutual, although my affection was not quite so unconditional: I loved her for three reasons. Firstly, once a month she invited us to tea at her house. Tea with the Sunday-school teacher was a big deal. Granted, with our background, it didn't take much to qualify as 'posh', but Miss Williams was. She had a telephone, a fridge and an inside toilet. But best of all, Miss Williams had jelly moulds. If you gave her enough notice, you could have your jelly in just about any shape you wanted. She could do buses, rockets, ships, cars, and any number of animals. My mother took these events seriously. Before I left for tea with Miss Williams, she would slick down my hair, give me a freshly ironed handkerchief, and warn me that if there was only one sandwich left on the plate, under no circumstances was I to take it. And I loved Miss Williams because she gave us stickers. Every time we turned up to Sunday school, we got another one for our album. We cherished those bits of paper – sometimes swapping a 'doubler' of 'Jesus walking on the water' for a rare 'Feeding of the five thousand'. But most of all I loved her for her stories – Miss Williams was a brilliant raconteur. My favourite was 'David and Goliath' and Miss Williams didn't hold back. We gasped when she got to the end, imagining it was Stanley Preston, the street bully, being decapitated instead of the giant.

One Sunday, Miss Williams told us that a new boy would be joining us the following week. She said that his name was Ronnie and explained that he didn't live in a family as we all did, but in something called a children's home, which meant he didn't have a mother or father around. Mr Harker, the Sunday-school superintendent, was going to pick him up from the children's home and bring him to our class. Her explanation ended with a warning of consequences more terrifying than the fires of hell if we were mean to him.

Ronnie obviously hadn't been given any warnings about misbehaviour. The first thing he did when he joined our class a week later was to put Alan Thompson in a headlock, and the second was to hide Miss Williams' handbag under his chair. But it didn't stop there. Ronnie's misdemeanours multiplied until, finally, my friend Peter Clayton had enough and, chancing eternal damnation, told Ronnie that he was ugly and his mother dressed him funny. At first, Ronnie just stared at him, then suddenly all hell broke loose as he flew from his chair and landed on Peter, sending him crashing into the little pedal organ which only moments earlier had been cranking out its accompaniment to 'Yield Not to Temptation'. Peter Clayton got in a lucky shot to Ronnie's head, but before the full wrath of Peter's much stronger rival could descend on him, Miss Williams grabbed both boys and threatened to do all manner of unchristian things to them if they didn't stop fighting. The remarkable thing is that they did stop. The rest of us looked on in wonder. Miss Williams' street cred was at an all-time high.

Over the following years, Ronnie was a regular visitor at our Sunday school. His clothes weren't all that different from ours, but there was something about them that stood out: the invisible uniform of the children's home, which signalled loudly, 'I am not like you.' I'm not sure that we were ever deliberately cruel to him, but the honest truth is that he was so easy to wind up. If you pretended to steal one of his stickers or tapped him on the shoulder and hid, you could really get him going. But he was strong. If he caught you, you were in a lot of trouble, but the problem he had with his knees – he didn't seem able to bend them properly – meant you always had a good chance of being able to outrun him.

One week he didn't turn up for Sunday school. Nobody, not even Miss Williams, seemed to know what had happened to him. I didn't see him again until years later, when I would sometimes run into him in the city centre or at a youth club I ran that he would sometimes drop in on. He was always roughly dressed and looking lost. Our lives were a world apart.

* * *

The man at my door was still smiling even as he waited for a response. I smiled back. 'Of course I remember you, Ronnie. How did you find us?'

He shrugged his shoulders. 'Somebody told me where you live.'

He was holding a black plastic sack in his right hand. I said, 'What have you got in there?'

'Just my stuff. But I've got this, too.' And then he held the package he was holding in his other hand towards me. I took it from him and peeled back the paper: a frozen chicken.

'Where did you get this?'

'Somebody gave it to me for Christmas.'

'Have you got anywhere to cook it?'

He stared at the icy parcel. 'No, and I can't cook anyway.'

'Come in. I'm sure Dianne will pop it in the oven for you.'

He nodded, took the chicken back and stepped through the doorway.

'Di, we've got a visitor,' I shouted in the direction of the kitchen. 'It's Ronnie. You remember Ronnie?' As I began to open the kitchen door, he pushed past me and without saying a word, thrust the chicken into Dianne's hands.

Dianne looked from me to Ronnie to the chicken, as if one of us might offer an explanation.

I repeated my earlier cry from the hall. 'It's Ronnie. You remember Ronnie? Ronnie from the Gospel Hall?'

She narrowed her eyes at me then turned to him. 'Of course. Ronnie, how lovely to see you.' She put the chicken on the worktop and said, 'Why don't you put the kettle on, Rob? Would you like some tea or coffee, Ronnie?'

He shrugged his shoulders, 'Fine.'

We all voted for coffee and Dianne passed Ronnie his cup. 'Would you like some sugar?'

'Fine,' he answered.

The three of us sat around the kitchen table, long periods of silence being punctuated by Dianne or me asking a question. After a minute or two, Ronnie asked if he could use the toilet.

'Sure,' I said, 'it's at the top of the stairs on the right.'

As he passed me to go towards the door, a pungent, acid odour hit me, reminding me of visits to my grandmother in the last weeks of her life. When he had gone upstairs, Dianne said, 'Shall we invite him to stay for a meal? I've got enough for all of us. I can put his chicken in and if it's done, he can take it with him afterwards.'

'Fine,' I said. She kicked me under the table.

Ronnie came back into the kitchen, and I said, 'Stay and have a meal with us, Ronnie, and while you're eating, we'll put your chicken in the oven.'

He smiled. 'Thanks.'

Dianne complains that I'm not much of a conversationalist at dinner parties. Perhaps she's right, but compared to Ronnie, I was in the Champions League. It seemed that he had used up all his available conversation at the front door, and for thirty minutes we sat around the table trying to mine even single syllables out of him.

'Where are you staying, Ronnie?' A shake of the head and silence.

'Have you got a place to live?'

'Not really.'

'So where are you sleeping?' Dianne asked.

'Here and there.'

Ronnie wolfed his meal down then sat looking at his plate, saying nothing. It was excruciating. Finally, with most of her meal unfinished, Dianne put down her knife and fork and said, 'Let's see what's on the telly.' We all trooped into the living room. I turned on the Christmas-tree lights, and Dianne settled Ronnie into an armchair in front of the television. 'What do you like to watch?' she asked.

'Westerns.'

We only had three television channels in the 1970s, and gunslingers were on none of them. We chose *Coronation Street* instead, and although it was immediately obvious that, in Ronnie's opinion, Ken Barlow was no substitute for John Wayne, his full attention was on that screen.

After a short while, Dianne developed a coughing fit. When we got to know him better, we realised she needn't have bothered with this subversive effort to get my attention; Ronnie concentrated on one thing at a time and at that moment he was beamed in on the Rovers Return. Instead of aiming surreptitious gestures towards the door at me, she could just have said, 'We need to talk.'

We left him to Ena Sharples and went into the kitchen. Dianne closed the door. 'What are we going to do?'

'What do you mean, "What are we going to do?"'

'Well, he's got nowhere to stay. And he smells dreadful.'

After a while, one of us said, 'Well, what *are* we going to do?'

There was a moment's silence, each of us with our own thoughts, until the familiar tune wafting in from the living room brought us back to the present. Dianne said, 'We can't let him sleep rough tonight. Let's give him the spare bedroom – I'll have to clear some stuff out of it – then we can talk properly in the morning.'

We went back into the living room. Ronnie was watching the rolling credits with rapt attention. I sat on the settee next to him. 'Would you like to stay with us tonight, Ronnie?'

'Fine,' he said, staring at the Granada Television logo.

Dianne said, 'What have you got in that black sack of yours? Have you got any washing stuff?' He shook his head. Dianne pressed on. 'Any pyjamas?' His eyes fixed on the screen, he bowed his head slightly and shook it again. Dianne looked flustered. 'Don't worry – Rob will find you some.'

The *Corrie* credits had finished and as Ronnie was getting stuck into *The Sweeney*, we went upstairs to get his room ready. I found a pair of pyjamas still in their M&S wrapper, and we added a towel and laid them on the bed. When we got back downstairs, the television was still on but Ronnie was dozing. I tapped him on the shoulder, 'Time to turn in.'

He woke with a start. 'Fine.'

Dianne coughed. 'Would you like a shower before you go to bed?'

'No, thanks.'

She looked at me in a plea for support, but I shrugged my shoulders. We showed him his room for the night and as we closed his door Dianne said, 'We're in the bedroom next door. If you need us for anything, just knock.'

Ronnie said 'Fine.'

*   *   *

I was dropping off to sleep when Dianne whispered, 'Are you still awake?'

'Yes.'

'I was just thinking.'

'What?'

'What if he does something?'

'What did you have in mind?'

'Don't be funny. We've got a man we don't really know from Adam sleeping two feet away from us. He could do anything.'

'So what would you like me to do?'

'Put a chair under the door handle.'

I got out of bed begrudgingly, went downstairs and returned with a dining chair, which I wedged under the handle of our bedroom door. 'There,' I said. 'Safe.'

But she was asleep.

I got back into bed, but I couldn't get to sleep – my mind was racing: how had this happened? One minute I'm answering a knock at the door, the next there's a man sleeping in the bedroom next to us who's practically a stranger. I calmed down after a while: Dianne was right, *We can talk about it in the morning*. But I would not have been calm, if I had known, as I lay in bed that night, that in so many ways that morning would never come: the man would never leave.

* * *

Dianne woke me at 6.45 a.m. 'There's somebody moving around downstairs.'

As I made my way down, I could hear the television. I

opened the living-room door to find Ronnie watching an Open University programme on maths. 'What are you doing up so early, Ronnie?'

'I'm an early bird, I am.'

'What are you watching?'

'I don't know.' He got up from his chair and beckoned me to follow him towards the door. A knowing smile played on his lips. 'I've got a surprise for you.'

I followed him into the kitchen. He had washed up last night's dirty dishes and stacked them away. The kitchen was pristine. 'That's amazing, Ronnie. Thank you.'

'You're welcome.'

Ronnie returned to the living room and settled in front of a bearded lecturer drawing equations on a blackboard. I went upstairs and slid back into bed. Dianne was wide awake. 'What's going on down there?'

'He's watching an Open University programme on calculus.' Dianne laughed out loud.

'And two more things,' I said.

'Don't keep me in suspense.'

'When I passed his room, the door was open.'

'And?'

'My pyjamas are still in the wrapping.'

'And the second thing?'

'He's done the dishes.'

I lay next to Dianne for a while and tried to get back off to sleep but I couldn't settle; I could hear Ronnie moving about downstairs and I wondered what he was doing. I got up and went down. He was in the hall looking at the Christmas cards. When he saw me, he said, 'I wasn't being nosey.'

'It's fine, Ronnie.'

'You've got a lot of friends.'

'Yes, we have. We're very lucky.'

He picked up a card that read: 'To our darling son and daughter-in-law at Christmas.' He seemed to be far away in his mind and then he blurted out, 'I've got five cards.'

'What do you mean?'

He looked at me as if he thought I could have done with a little help from the bearded man teaching calculus. 'I've got five cards,' he repeated.

I lifted my hands in surrender. 'Sorry, Ronnie. I don't get it.'

He smiled sympathetically. 'I'll show you. They're in my bag.' He pushed past me and went upstairs. I heard him rummaging about in his room, and then he descended, clutching a small package wrapped in a cloth. He laid it on the hall table. 'Open it.'

I pulled back the covering and took out a small collection of greetings cards. The first read: 'You are twelve!'

Ronnie said, 'Look inside.'

It read: 'To Ronnie, love Carol.'

I smiled at him. 'It's really nice, Ronnie.'

A huge grin covered his face. 'Look at them all.'

I read each one from twelfth birthday to sixteenth, all bearing exactly the same inscription. 'Who's Carol?'

'She worked in the kitchen in the care home. One day I told her it was my birthday and later that day she gave me a card.'

'And she remembered every year?'

'Yes. Every year until I left.'

'That is really lovely. Have you stayed in touch with her?'

'I went back to the home once. It was a long way away. I asked if I could see her, but they said that she'd left.'

Just then Dianne came down the stairs. We went into the living room together and turned on the television again. It seemed that the gods themselves had felt we needed a helping hand because there was a western on. Ronnie looked as though he had won the football pools and sank into an armchair, transfixed. Dianne and I left him and went to resume the previous night's conversation. As she sat at the kitchen table, I put the kettle on. 'Any ideas?'

She spoke slowly. 'It's Christmas Eve. He can't leave today.' And then she gave me a look of sheer panic. 'We've got your parents coming for lunch tomorrow.'

'You're right. Let's put them off.'

'I'm glad you can see the funny side of all this. You invited Ronnie in in the first place; he was in your Sunday-school class – I hardly know him.'

'So what shall we do?'

Dianne got up from the table and went to the window. She looked down the winter-bare garden. It seemed a long time before she spoke, but finally she asked a question. 'Rob, do you think I'm selfish?'

'Why do you say that? You're one of the least selfish people I know.'

'Because I don't want him here. I want us to have a proper Christmas together – just us.'

She started to cry. I turned the kettle off, walked over to the window and put my arm around her shoulder. 'This is my fault.'

Dianne spoke between sniffles. 'It's not your fault. You had to invite him in. And once he was here, we couldn't not feed him. And then we couldn't just ask him to leave. I know us, Rob, and we both know that he's with us for Christmas.'

'Not necessarily. I can go out with him today and try to find him somewhere for the night.'

'You're kidding yourself. How could we sleep tonight wondering where he is?'

'You decide.'

Dianne looked up. 'No. We decide together. But if we decide that he stays, then we've got to sort his clothes out, and I won't be the one breaking the news to your parents about their new lunch partner.'

Our minds made up, we went back into the living room. Dianne stood next to the TV. 'Ronnie, Rob and I would like you to stay with us for Christmas – you'll be with us until the day after Boxing Day. Would you like to do that?'

Ronnie didn't take his eyes off the cowboys riding out of town. 'Fine.'

Dianne looked crestfallen. I felt cross. 'Ronnie, Di is being really kind – at least look at her when she's talking to you.'

He didn't look offended. He just turned to look at Dianne, smiled, and said, 'Sorry. That's fine.' Then he went back to the film.

Dianne pressed on. 'Could I put some of your clothes in the wash, Ronnie?'

It seemed that Ronnie was a faster learner than I had imagined. He looked up without being prompted. 'Thank you.'

'Can you get them for me, please?'

Ronnie's incursion into politeness was short-lived. This time, he didn't turn away from the television. 'I'll do it later.' Suddenly, *High Noon* was about to be re-enacted; only one person could win. But which one?

In that moment, Dianne moved into one of several roles she would play during our life with Ronnie – not friend this time, nor even older sister. The woman with no kids of her own became a mother. 'Get the bag now, please, Ronnie.'

Ronnie got up from his chair as slowly as he could, left the room and climbed the stairs. I was about to make some comment about a headmistress but thought better of it.

* * *

Almost twelve hours later, we were watching an episode of the prison comedy *Porridge*. As it finished, Dianne said, 'We're going to a midnight carol service later, Ronnie. Would you like to come?'

'Fine,' said Ronnie.

'Perhaps have a shower and a shave and put on some of the clean clothes I've put on your bed?' she coaxed.

'I'll do it after *Kojak*.'

Dianne looked at me as if to say, 'He's smarter than he's letting on.'

Sure enough, the bald-headed champion of American justice was on next. As soon as the programme finished, Ronnie got up and went upstairs. I turned the television off, and Dianne and I sat waiting in the semi-darkness, the room illuminated only by the Christmas-tree lights. Suddenly Dianne shot up. 'We have to get him some presents.'

We began checking the gifts that were piled under the tree, trying to guess what was inside the wrapping paper and factoring in the important condition that whichever ones we chose to be reassigned to Ronnie could not be from anyone who might run into him on Christmas Day. In the end we rewrapped a scarf, a pair of leather gloves and a garish tie that almost made me glad we had invited him to stay.

We had only just finished when we heard him coming down the stairs. Shoving the wrapping paper and Sellotape under a chair, we quickly placed his presents with all the others. And that's when he gave us another surprise. He stood in the doorway clean, shaven, and looking so good I bit my lip. Dianne exclaimed, 'Well, Ronnie Lockwood – you look handsome.'

A huge smile creased his face. 'Not bad.'

It was almost 11 p.m. when we began the short walk to a church around the corner. It was what I have come to call a 'Christmas Eve night' – dry, cold and crisp – and only a dusting of snow could have improved it. I can't say that the church building was attractive. But candles change everything, and inside it was awash with them. It looked magical. Ronnie turned to me and said, 'It's pretty.'

We spoke briefly to Mike and Jean, some old friends of ours, and, having been introduced to Ronnie, they joined us in the few seats still vacant on the back row. As we stood for 'Oh Come, All Ye Faithful', I glanced at him. He was staring nervously at the carol sheet, mouthing sounds and looking around to see if anybody was watching him. It felt good with the three of us sat together like a family in the candlelight. It was a short service and soon the last Bible passage was read: '. . . and she gave birth to her firstborn, a son. She wrapped him in cloths and placed him in a manger, because there was no room in the inn.'

The service was over. Mince pies and drinks were brought out as people milled around chatting and wishing each other 'Happy Christmas!' Ronnie seemed to be surprisingly at ease. When I mentioned it later to Dianne, she said that this may have had something to do with the fact that he had downed at least three glasses of mulled wine before she could get to him. Suddenly, the church leader went back to the microphone. 'Sorry to interrupt, folks.' The church fell silent. 'Mike Shaw has lost his car keys. Can we all have a good look around to see if he's dropped them?'

I'm not sure what made me look at him, but I turned just in time to see Ronnie slip something onto the floor. Ten seconds later he shouted, 'Got them!' I was angry, Dianne was mad as hell, but even if Mike had his suspicions, he was kind. 'That's brilliant, Ronnie. Thank you so much.'

'Pleasure,' said Ronnie. Dianne gave him a look that perfectly expressed what she was going to do to him when she got him home.

An hour later, Ronnie was in bed having had the talking-to of his life, and we were drifting off to sleep. Dianne nudged me. 'Are you awake?'

'I am now.'

'I was just thinking. If tonight was a challenge, wait until we introduce him to your father over lunch.'

'Kill me now.'

Ronnie at Christmas lunch.

Chapter 2

Christmas Day

It was Christmas morning and I could hear a sound. It was not so much threatening as annoying; not that of a menacing intruder, more like a dying bumblebee that had decided to drive two humans crazy before finally expiring. Dianne was asleep and I turned carefully towards the clock radio on my bedside table. The digits confirmed what I already knew instinctively: it was early – very early. I lay in the darkness trying to locate the noise. It was regular, almost rhythmic, and frustratingly hard to pin down. Sometimes it stopped momentarily and then continued, as if finding its stride again. Mostly it was soft, but occasionally it became a low growl. Finally, I nudged Dianne. She woke immediately. 'What's wrong?'

'Listen. What's that noise?'

She listened for all of ten seconds before pulling the sheet around her and turning over. 'It's Ronnie snoring.' This information did not pacify me. *Isn't it enough that we've taken him in, fed him and washed his clothes?* Almost straight away, I felt guilty. He was not snoring to deliberately annoy us and, more importantly, he didn't ask to stay. But the guilt was momentary. It was soon swept aside by another emotion: panic. There was a stranger in our home – in our private space; there was nowhere to hide. The first time I met him he attacked Peter Clayton, and I had no real idea what he had been doing since I last saw him in Sunday school. Had he been in prison? Was he unstable?

Eventually, I drifted back to sleep and then woke again with a start. The early light was finding its way through the cracks in the curtains. For a moment, I just lay there. At first, I felt fine. Dianne was lying next to me. It was Christmas. All was well. But deep in my brain there was a nagging feeling that something was wrong. And then I remembered: Ronnie was in the next bedroom and my parents were coming for lunch. I imagined them contemplating the day with us. My mother would be counting the minutes until I arrived to pick them up; my father simply could not believe he had allowed himself to be talked into coming.

With the exception of Saturday evenings, when he had a couple of beers with some friends, my father didn't do any socialising at all. When I was a child we had no visitors to our home – neither friends nor relatives, and I can't recall my parents ever going out alone together without us kids in tow – not once. It wasn't just social occasions he shunned: wherever possible, he avoided meeting people at all. We had sacks of coal delivered once a month from the yard at the

end of our street. The lorry would pull up outside our door
and the coalmen would hoist a sack onto their back, carry
it along the passage, through the living room, and dump
the contents in the coal house in our back yard. When it
was coal-delivery time, my father would either go out or sit
nervously waiting for the knock at the door. As soon as he
heard it, he would rush upstairs and stay there until the job
was done and the men had gone.

If one was being kind, one could say my father epitomised
the spirit of 'Keep calm and carry on'. But it would be more
accurate to say that he was detached. He spoke little, and
whereas my mother would attempt to kiss me in front of my
friends, no matter what my age, my father never displayed
any affection. I can't remember him hugging me, praising
me or saying that he loved me. He used to say, 'A mother for
love, a father for discipline.'

As I lay in bed thinking of him and listening to the rhythm
of Ronnie's snores, in my imagination I found myself back
in my childhood street, filled with working-class families –
railway labourers, factory hands, shopworkers. Some of the
wives worked outside the home, but not many; my mother
wanted to, but my father forbade it. Our terraced, three-up-
two-down house had no running hot water, bathroom, inside
toilet, or even toilet paper. (Even now, I can't look at the *South
Wales Echo* without imagining it cut into squares and hanging
on a nail behind the toilet door.) With me and my older
sisters, Val and Joan, it was cramped, but as my mother used
to say, 'You could eat your dinner off that front doorstep.'

Mr Glover, the landlord, called every week, and my
mother would hand over the money she had set aside in the
large cup with the piece of paper marked 'Rent' Sellotaped
onto it. My father insisted that what we lacked in terms
of house ownership – not to mention washing machines,
telephones, fridges and televisions – we made up for in pride.
He told us that lots of the people in the fancy houses where
he delivered letters were up to their eyes in debt and that it
was all for show – 'Lace curtains and no tablecloth,' as he
would sometimes say in a rare moment of levity. Joan would
giggle each time he said it and whisper to me, 'Cavalry twill
trousers and no underpants.' My father said we were different
from the people in the big houses. We never missed a rent
payment and paid the grocer and baker on time. He had a
saying that guided his financial life and which he repeated to
us all at least once a week: 'Out of debt, out of danger.'

He was short and slightly built with a bulbous nose and
heavily brilliantined brown hair parted neatly to the side. He
would never fail to raise his hat when he passed a woman
from our street, often accompanied with a smile and a cheery,
'Good morning – lovely day today.' But when the front door
closed behind him, he often darkened. My auntie used to say
he was 'street angel, house devil'.

On my first day at grammar school, the form teacher
asked each of us to shout out what our fathers did for a
living – just the fathers. One by one, kids yelled out various
professions, the boy next to me saying, 'Company director,'
even though I later discovered that his father was a bookie.

When my turn came, I was flummoxed. I considered inventing a prestigious job, but in the event I simply froze. The teacher looked annoyed. 'You, boy.' His eyes scanned a list of names on his desk. 'Parsons, isn't it?'

'Yes, sir.'

'Well, Parsons?'

I mumbled, 'Postman,' as quietly as I could.

When I got home, my father was shaving. I said, 'Do you ever get bored just sticking letters through doors?'

If I hurt him, he didn't show it. He said, 'Your father delivers the Royal Mail.' You'd have thought the Queen herself had asked if my old man would be so kind as to deliver some of her correspondence. He went on, 'Businesses depend on me, armies depend on me, families depend on me. You should see somebody waiting to get one of my letters. No, son, I don't get bored.'

Before he set off to work, he would put on a fresh white shirt, black tie, and trousers with parade-ground creases. But before getting dressed, he would shine his shoes. I have never seen shoes so bright. One day I caught him cleaning the soles. 'Don't do that, Dad,' I urged. 'Nobody will ever know.'

Without looking up, he replied, 'I'll know.'

In the evenings, he would sit in our living room. It had faded wallpaper and a ceiling stained by nicotine. Three ducks flew up the wall over the fireplace, as if trying to make for the window and freedom. There was a settee, an easy chair and my father's armchair, to the left of which was a radio tuned to BBC Home Service (which would later be replaced by Radio 4). He would listen to it while working his way through a packet of Player's untipped cigarettes and filling in the football pools. Whenever the national anthem was played, he would stand until it had finished. Occasionally, he would fiddle with the knobs on the wireless until he picked up somebody using Morse code and then decode it and write it down. One day I asked him how he had learned to do that. He gave me a withering look and said, 'Careless talk costs lives.' After he died, I was going through his old papers and came across his army discharge documents from the Second World War. He was described as a 'Special Operator' – part of the Special Operations Executive that Churchill set up to work with the Resistance in France and Belgium. My mother knew none of that; my father never spoke of it. She only knew that whatever he had gone through in the war, he was a changed man when he came back – more nervous, quiet and unpredictable.

As my mind continued back down the years, a hundred memories of my father came back, but clearest of all was the showdown he had with one of our neighbours, Mrs Coulter. Every kid in the street was involved in either making up new games or taking part in old staples. My favourite was Rat-Tat Ginger. It wasn't complicated: you knocked somebody's door, ran away and hid. But there was a variation to the game that was so terrifying that at 7 years old I wet myself the first time I played it. You had to hide in the *front* of the house you knocked at. Bear in mind that these were small houses with very little frontage to the pavement. The best you could do was to crouch behind a bay window, or if you were lucky, be partially hidden by a bush. The character of each householder was a big consideration when deciding on whose door to knock, especially if you were playing the extreme version. The possibility of getting caught by Miss Palmer was only concerning in that she might tell your mother, but other houses had occupants who threatened terrors that were too awful for a kid to imagine.

Nobody in the whole history of my childhood had ever attempted to knock and hide in the front of Mrs Coulter's house. I say 'Mrs Coulter's house' rather than 'Mr and Mrs Coulter's house' not because there was no Mr Coulter. There was. It is just that he was so mild and his wife so terrifying that it seemed appropriate to give her the honour of total ownership. The Coulters didn't have children of their own. Thinking back, they must have only been in their fifties, but in our minds Mrs Coulter was as old as the antediluvian strata that lay beneath our feet.

The fact that Mrs Coulter had little experience of children did not stop her attempting to exercise complete control over the small brood that dared to inhabit the same street as her. Her appearance wasn't distinctive: she was short and thin with tightly curled, white hair. But her voice was special: high pitched and screeching, a scraping of her vocal cords like fingernails along a blackboard. It was with that terrifying voice, ramped up to maximum volume, that Mrs Coulter issued her warnings, and none more heartfelt than those relating to the iron railings on top of the dwarf wall that surrounded the frontage of her house. Every house in our street used to have railings once, but they were requisitioned in the war and ended up as bits of tanks and other armoury. Only the wealthiest could afford to replace them. Although, like us, Mrs Coulter had neither an inside toilet or bathroom, she did have railings, and these set her apart. She would sometimes line us up to receive the admonition, 'Do not dare to think of running pieces of wood along my railings.'

But Mrs Coulter understood that if you are to exercise complete control, the carrot is sometimes as necessary as the stick, so once in a while, she would hand us all a threepenny bit. These occasions were like Maundy Thursday: we kids were the serfs, grateful to be so honoured, and Mrs Coulter was the queen.

The mutual fear/respect, carrot/stick routine would no doubt have continued uninterrupted if a new family had not moved into the corner house. The O'Briens had three children. Two were well into their teens and way beyond wanting to be part of our gang, but Anne, aged nine, was a perfect fit – except for the fact that in Mrs Coulter's eyes, the whole family had a fundamental flaw: they were Catholics. We didn't care what religion or non-religion they were; none of our parents went to church and this wasn't a sectarian area. As far as we were concerned, the O'Briens could have been part of the murderous Manson family. But it mattered to Mrs Coulter.

One day she took me aside and said, 'Robert, if I were you, I wouldn't play with the O'Brien family. They are not like us.' There was much my parents couldn't teach me academically, but they had taught me many other things, including drumming into me how important it was to respect other people, whether it was the Giles (the Black family that lived two doors down from us), the women who streamed red-faced out of the laundry at 5 p.m. each day, or the coalmen from the yard. In a burst of indignation, I puffed out my chest and answered her with more courage than I actually felt: 'I'll play with who I want.' And then I ran away.

Activism and protest are necessary but there is sometimes a price to pay, and so it turned out for me. From that moment on, Mrs Coulter made every effort to ostracise me, not only from her beneficence but from the other kids. They could sit on the little bit of wall in front of her house, but I was banned from doing so. On one occasion she lined us up and gave everyone threepence except me.

Every time Mrs Coulter exercised some form of warfare against me, I told my mother, and my mother told my father. At first, she might just as well have told the statue of the Marquis of Bute that stood in the square not far from our home, given his response. My father didn't court trouble, but as well as that, he was incredibly deferential. He had an inherent sense of one's place in society, he knew that Mr Coulter's job as a senior guard on the railways outgunned his as a postman, and the truth is that even he was probably a little overawed by the railings. Which is why what happened one Wednesday afternoon in the middle of the summer holidays was such a surprise to everybody – perhaps even to my father. It was lunchtime and he had just got up from bed, having done the previous night shift. He sat at the dining table and my mother put his lunch in front of him. Thirty minutes before, I had complained to her that Mrs Coulter had ordered me off her wall again in front of all the other kids.

As my father started his meal, my mother said, 'Mrs Coulter has been having a go at our Robert again.' As she spoke, his body stiffened. He stopped eating and put down his knife and fork. He had trousers on, but his upper body was covered only in a white singlet, over which he wore a pair of braces. He got up from the table, walked along the passage, and we heard him open the front door. None of us dared to follow. It was no more than five minutes before he returned, and when he did, he made no attempt to explain what had happened. He simply sat at the table, said, 'That should do it,' and carried on with his meal.

Three days later, while my father was at work, we found out what *That* was. We didn't get many letters, so the expensive-looking envelope addressed to him caught my mother's attention straight away. On the front, the name of a firm was imprinted from a rubber stamp: 'Davidson and Price, Solicitors and Commissioners for Oaths'. My mother boiled a kettle and steamed the envelope open, took out the letter and read it out loud. According to them, my father had 'hammered on the door of my client's house and threatened that if she upset his son again, he would shoot her'. The letter went on to warn of all manner of repercussions if this offence were to be repeated.

My mother looked concerned at first, but then she smiled. She had been brought up in the country in a community of poachers and worse, people who were used to living off their wits and had frequent run-ins with the law. It would take more than fancy notepaper to scare her. She used to say, 'I've lived too near the wood to be afraid of the owl.' She folded the letter up carefully, put it back in the envelope and threw it on the fire.

She was different from my father. People sometimes say they can't remember the faces of loved ones who have died. That's mainly true for me too – except for my mother; I can recall every part of her appearance. When I was very young, she would pick me up and I would bury my head in her neck and search for the wart at the top of her back, as if needing proof that it really was her. I remember her black hair, olive skin, deep brown eyes, and the way she wore her pinafore wrapped tightly around her ample frame. In a photograph that stood on the dresser, my 18-year-old mother looked like a 1920s movie star.

Whatever beauty she had back then wasn't down to expensive cosmetics or clothes. She was one of six children, and they were poor, my grandfather's low wage from the quarry barely enough to feed the family. But things were to become worse. On 9 September 1909, when my mother was twelve weeks old, my grandfather made a tragic mistake. He used a metal ram instead of a wooden one to push the explosive into the rockface and the metal sparked and caused a blast that threw him forty feet down the quarry. A huge piece of rock that had been dislodged by the explosion followed him to the bottom. He died instantly. The headline in the *Evening Express* screamed: 'QUARRY BLAST. 1 MAN KILLED. TWO INJURED.'

My grandmother was left to bring up six children in a two-bedroomed house with no sanitation, in Wenvoe, a rural village on the outskirts of Cardiff. The only offer of help came from the nuns at the local convent, who said they could take my mother and her sister into care. My grandmother said she would rather die.

When my mother left school at fourteen, there was no work around her village, so she became a live-in housemaid in a large house in Ely, Cardiff. The work was hard, her employers were unkind, but most of all she missed the countryside and her mother. When she was eighteen, her older sister got her a job at Ely Paper Mill, and it was while walking home from there one day that she started talking to the young postman.

I'm honestly not sure if she was in love with my father, but being pregnant out of wedlock in 1934 didn't leave much room for talk of romance, and within seven months of meeting, they were married. But I have no doubt that she loved us kids, and told us so every chance she had. Our mother was soft, but not in a shallow, sentimental way; she was warm and safe, forgiving and unselfish. And kind. Yes, that's the best word for it – our mother was kind.

* * *

I have always found it hard to describe my parents' relationship with each other, but one event in particular defines it better than any other. My mother wanted a new three-piece suite for the 'best room' – the room at the front of our terraced house that was kept for best, in case we had visitors. Which we never did. My father wouldn't even allow relatives to visit, let alone anyone else. Nevertheless, no effort was spared with regard to its condition, just in case that situation ever suddenly changed. To be honest, I'm not exactly sure why she wanted the suite; there was nobody to impress. We had seen our mother give her own food to us if we were still hungry, so you would have thought that replacing the old brown leatherette settee and accompanying chairs was pretty far down her list of priorities. Nevertheless, unusually for her, she not only *wanted* a new three-piece suite, but one day decided she was going to *have* one.

In the row of shops across the railway bridge from our home was Harrison's Furnishings. Mr Harrison knew his customers well, including the fact that most people surrounding his store couldn't possibly afford to purchase his furniture outright, so he offered a weekly scheme – the affectionately known 'never-never'. One day my mother was shopping near Harrison's when she happened to glance into his window and saw it: the three-piece suite of her dreams.

It was cream with brown piping around the edges – to her eye at once totally impractical and utterly beautiful. She went into the shop and enquired as to the price. It would cost seven shillings a week for four years: impossible.

My mother smiled, thanked the salesman and walked out. She had only reached the post office at the corner of the street when she stopped and turned back.

The following Wednesday, having borrowed a pound from my older sister Val, who had just started a job as a telephone operator, my mother walked into Harrison's, paid a £2 deposit and her first weekly instalment. In return, Mr Harrison gave her a receipt for the money and a card to record each time she made her payment. The suite was to be delivered the following Monday morning when she knew my father would be on the day shift. When she got home, my mother had two problems: where to hide the card and, more importantly, how to break the news to my father. She pushed the card under the mattress on Joan's bed and waited for the right moment.

When my father went out each week with his friends, he never came home drunk, but he always came back with a different personality: he was nicer. The man who would hardly say two words during the week became a raconteur on a Saturday night. And it was at a quarter to midnight on one of those nights that my mother broke the news of her purchase to him. She told him that she had been saving a bit and had had the chance to buy a nearly new suite from a woman in the next street who was moving to a smaller house.

With the scene set, Mr Harrison turned up in his van on the Monday morning and, as arranged, delivered the suite and took the old one away. With no visitors allowed, there was only one other adult with whom my mother could share her excitement. By the time his shift ended, she was bursting to show him, and as soon as he came through the door, she ushered my father into the front room. 'What do you think?'

He sniffed and said, 'Is dinner ready?'

My mother said, 'Five minutes.'

I suppose she wasn't expecting a great reaction. She knew that as far as he was concerned, the new furniture was in the 'best room', and as long as it didn't interfere with where he normally sat in his battered leather chair next to the radio in the living room, he couldn't care less.

And that would have been the end of it if, four months later, my mother had not left her payment card in Harrison's shop when she made the weekly instalment. The second she got home she realised what she had done and asked my sister to go straight away to the telephone kiosk at the end of the next street, ring the shop and tell Mr Harrison she would pick up the card when she called the next week. 'Be sure to tell him not to bring it to the house,' she added. When my sister rang the shop, Mr Harrison was out, so she gave the message to his daughter.

The next day, when Mr Harrison noticed my mother's card lying on the shop counter, he thought he had better return it. At his first attempt, he got the wrong house, knocking next door at Mrs Grey's place. When he called at the right house, my father opened the door and smiled.

'How can I help you, sir?'

'I've brought your weekly payment card back. Mrs Parsons left it in the shop yesterday. I called next door by mistake and Mrs Grey kindly put me right.'

My father shook his head. 'You must be mistaken. We don't have anything like that in this house.' He started to close the door.

Mr Harrison wedged his foot in it. 'It's for the three-piece suite.'

My father glanced up and down the street, grabbed the card and slammed the door. When he came back into the living room, his face was ashen. He sent my sister and me upstairs. My mother looked more scared than I have ever seen her, and as I was putting my foot on the first stair, I heard her start to cry. The shouting went on for a long time and when my father left later for his night shift, the atmosphere was still tense.

But she kept the suite.

My mother.

Chapter 3

Two Days of Christmas

The alarm went off. I leant across, pressed the button to silence it, and as I did, I remembered what was going to happen in less than six hours – my parents would join us for lunch, where there would be a homeless man sat next to them at the table. As my head sank back onto the pillow, my mind immediately went to thoughts of my mother and the row with my father over her secret purchase. Dianne stirred and turned over. 'Did I ever tell you about my mother and the three-piece suite?' I asked.

Before she could answer, there was a crashing sound from the kitchen underneath us. Dianne pulled the sheets up over her face and replied from underneath them. 'Ronnie's up and wrecking the kitchen, your parents are coming for lunch, and you want to tell me about your mother and a three-piece suite? Merry Christmas!'

My father didn't like cars; they made him nervous. He preferred to catch a bus, but as there were none running, he agreed to my picking him and my mother up at 1 p.m. I glanced at the clock on the kitchen wall as we ate breakfast. Four hours to D-Day. Ronnie had finished his toast and was sitting silently looking out of the window.

'My parents are joining us for lunch today, Ronnie.'

'Di told me.'

'I don't think you've ever met my father, have you?'

'Don't think so.'

'He's a nice bloke, but he finds it a bit hard to make conversation.'

Ronnie nodded.

I pressed on. 'You'll like my mum, Ronnie – it will be such a surprise for them both to meet you.'

'It'll be fine,' he replied.

Dianne said, 'I think it would be good if you had a shower and shave this morning, Ronnie.'

'I had one yesterday.'

'I know. But you looked so smart afterwards, and it would be nice for Rob's mum and dad to see you at your best.'

'Fine,' said Ronnie. He got up from the table and made his way upstairs.

I reached across the table and took Di's hand. 'That went well.'

Dianne said, 'It's not Ronnie I'm worried about.'

'My father will be OK. Anyway, I've had a brainwave. I'm going to erect that little snooker table we've got in the garage. Apparently, he used to be a pretty good player when he was young and it will help to break the ice.'

'Where are you going to put it?'

'I thought we could use the living room if I put the chairs in the hall. And you and Mum can chat for a bit in the kitchen.'

'Just when I thought my day couldn't get any better,' she groaned.

*   *   *

I rang the bell of my childhood home. My father opened the door wearing his suit, a collar and tie, and gleaming shoes. He rarely smiled and Christmas Day was no exception. 'Your mother's just coming.'

'OK, Dad. Do you want to get in the car?'

He approached my old Hillman Hunter as though at any moment it might swallow him. I opened the passenger door and he got in. As I helped him fix his seat belt, he looked worried. 'How do I get this thing off if I need to?' he asked.

'Push that little button.' I tried to keep the impatience from my voice as I showed him.

Just then my mother came out of the house, slammed the front door behind her and walked to the car. I went to her. 'Hi, Mum. This is going to be fun.'

She hugged me. 'Yes, my love. I can't wait.' She smiled. 'What a treat.'

I helped her into the back of the car, then moved off. 'Slow down,' said my father, 'there's no rush.'

'I'm doing twenty-five, Dad.'

'Well, do twenty.'

There was no point arguing. I glanced in my mirror and saw a long trail of cars on the road behind us. This was going to be a long day.

'Are these new seat covers, love?' my mother asked.

'No, Mum, they're the same ones.'

'Well, they look lovely. There's lot of room in this car, isn't there?'

I turned to my father, 'Have you got enough room, Dad? That seat can go back a bit.'

'Don't look at me when you're talking to me. Keep your eyes on the road. Talk through the windscreen.'

'Have you got enough room?' I repeated, this time without moving a neck muscle.

'I'm fine.'

As we neared our house I said, 'We've got somebody else joining us for lunch.'

My father wriggled in his seat, but my mother asked, 'Who's that, love?'

'He's called Ronnie. He used to go to the Sunday school in the Gospel Hall. He has no family of his own – spent all his childhood in care – and now he's going through a bit of a rough time.'

'How old is he, love?'

'He's a bit older than me – not much.'

'Well, it will be nice to meet him. Won't it, Bill?'

My father nodded.

Dianne had left the front door on the latch, and we walked straight into the hall.

'I love this house. Isn't it lovely, Bill?' my mother exclaimed, as if she'd never visited before.

My father scowled. 'I wouldn't leave the front door open like that if I were you. You never know who's around.'

'You're right, Dad,' I said as I closed it firmly. I shouted, 'Di – we're here.'

Dianne came out of the kitchen with Ronnie trailing behind her. She kissed my parents and ushered Ronnie forward. 'This is Ronnie. He's a friend of ours. He's staying with us over Christmas.'

My father put out his hand, shook Ronnie's hand firmly and smiled. 'It's nice to meet you, Ronnie.' I was staggered.

'Nice to meet you, too,' said Ronnie.

My mother stepped up to Ronnie, hugged him and kissed him on the cheek. 'It's lovely to see you, Ronnie. You look just like Rob. You could be brothers.'

Dianne stifled a laugh and said, 'Why don't we go straight in to eat? It's all ready.'

The table looked amazing – simple things made magical by the addition of some tinsel, candles, and serviettes fitted stylishly into wine glasses. Dianne sat at the head, with Ronnie and my father either side, and I sat next to my father with my mother next to Ronnie. Dianne lifted a cracker from the table and held it towards my father. 'Come on, Bill. Let's see how strong you are.'

Dianne and my father tussled back and forth a little until, finally, there was a small bang and he was left holding a pair of nail clippers and a red party hat. By now Ronnie and I were also engaged in a cracker battle. I tried to lose with every fibre in my body, but I didn't – and Ronnie looked crestfallen. He threw his empty half of cracker on the table. 'Just like me to lose.'

My mother came to the rescue. She held a cracker across the table to Ronnie. 'Come on, Ronnie – pull hard.'

He almost fell backwards with the force of his tug and to everybody's relief held up a miniature pack of playing cards and a yellow hat. 'I'm strong, I am,' he said, glowing as if he was on the podium at the Olympics.

Once everybody had a prize of sorts, Dianne insisted that everybody put their hats on. She positioned hers carefully on her hairdo and my mother and I followed suit. But my father and Ronnie looked dubious and made no move to comply. Finally, my father said, 'Come on, Ronnie,' and almost in unison, they both donned their headgear. I wasn't sure I could handle too many more surprises.

*   *   *

Lunch was over and it was time to unwrap our presents. Pretty soon the floor was strewn with wrapping paper. Ronnie opened every one of his gifts with wonder, like a child. My mother noticed it first. 'Are you all right, Ronnie?'

He sniffed. When he spoke, his voice cracked. 'I haven't got any presents for you.' Dianne went to him and put her arm on his shoulder. 'You've tidied the kitchen twice since you came – that's my present.'

Gift-giving over, we all helped clear the dishes and then

Ronnie, my father and I made our way into the living room to play snooker. It was only a six-foot table, but when my father saw it, he brightened as he realised that potting balls was going to be a lot easier than making conversation. As we were going in, my mother pulled me back into the hall. She put her hand to my face and posed a question that would take us almost half a century to answer: 'Ronnie's lovely, but what are you going to do with him, love?'

*   *   *

It was 8 p.m., my parents were safely home, the snooker table was back in the garage and Dianne was on her second gin and tonic. The day had gone better than we had dared hope. With the television temporarily set up in the kitchen for Dianne and my mother, Ronnie and my father had taken over the living room and played snooker most of the afternoon, with me as referee. It turned out that my father was a pretty good player. Ronnie, on the other hand, could hardly pot a thing. And then, after twenty minutes or so, he had suddenly got better. Before long, he was sinking balls as if he was in the final of the Masters. At first, I couldn't work out how he had improved so quickly, and then it dawned on me: my father was setting the shots up for him. And as Ronnie downed another red ball, my father looked across at me and winked.

Later, as I drove my parents home, my father said, 'Nice chap, that Ronnie.'

My mother said, 'I hate leaving Di and Ronnie to do all the clearing up.'

I glanced at her in the rear-view mirror. 'They'll be fine, Mum – chatting ten to the dozen, I expect.'

She smiled back at me. 'I doubt that, my love. But he is a very nice man.'

* * *

Now the three of us were in front of the television, Dianne dozing while Ronnie and I watched Sean Connery doing his best to stop the world economy being brought to its knees. We didn't need a James Bond film to keep us in the festive mood; the wrapping paper still on the floor, a tin of Quality Street on the coffee table, and a dish filled with uncracked Brazil nuts was enough to establish that this was indeed Christmas. Like *Morecambe & Wise*, a Bond movie was a firm Christmas tradition, and Ronnie was absorbed in it – until the moment when Pussy Galore unzipped her leather suit and began to roll on a bed with the hero. Just as she was about to slip out of what little she still had on, Ronnie said, 'I think I'll go on up.'

Dianne opened her eyes. 'Early night, Ronnie?'

'I'm a bit tired.'

'Have you had a nice day?' she asked.

'Yes. Very nice, thank you.'

I looked away from the television and up at him. 'You were brilliant at snooker, Ronnie.'

He shrugged his shoulders and smiled. 'Not bad.'

'I can't believe you potted that last black – it looked impossible.'

Ronnie lifted his eyebrows. 'I surprised you, didn't I?'

'You did. Where did you learn to play snooker?'

'In the homes.'

'Well, sleep well, you snooker champion,' I said.

He smiled. 'I'll do the kitchen when I get up tomorrow.'

Dianne started to protest. 'No, it's fine Ronnie we'll—'

'No arguments,' said Ronnie, wagging his finger. 'Goodnight.'

I watched him shuffle towards the door. 'Have you hurt your leg?'

He shook his head. 'It's fine. Di will tell you about it.'

When he had gone, I turned off the television. 'What was that Ronnie said about his leg? What happened?'

'It was an initiation ceremony in the children's home that went wrong. He hurt his knees so badly he had to have two operations on each of them. He was in hospital for six weeks. He can't bend them properly and said they play up when he's been standing too long.'

A sadness wedged in the pit of my stomach. 'I didn't know about that,' I said. 'I'm going to open a bottle of red. Will you have a glass?' I fetched the wine from the kitchen and put a match to the fire. We sat in silence, sipping our drinks in the light of the Christmas tree. 'What else did you talk about?' I asked, breaking the stillness. Dianne put her glass on the coffee table and leant back into me on the settee. 'He didn't say an awful lot – no surprise there – but he did tell me about the day he was taken into care.'

I said, 'Tell me about it.'

Of course we weren't there when Ronnie was in care, but over his many years with us, he told us bit by bit what happened to him; at times it was as if he could only bear to tell it piecemeal.

Dianne took a chocolate out of the tin and opened the wrapper as she spoke: 'He was eight years old . . .'

*   *   *

Janet, the social worker, came for Ronnie at 4 p.m. on a rainy Tuesday in March 1953. When he had gone to bed the evening before, his mother had said, 'You're going on a little holiday tomorrow, Ronnie.'

'Are we all going together?' he asked.

His mother said, 'No, it's just you at the moment. And I want you to be brave – for me.'

He had never been on holiday, but the thought of being without his mum had emptied him of all sense of excitement. And all that Tuesday, Ronnie had waited, fear subduing his appetite and dulling his usual mischievousness. When, finally, there was a knock on the door, he ran upstairs and hid behind an old wooden chest in his bedroom. Low voices were broken by the thud of footsteps and thumps on his bedroom door. 'Ronnie, come out now,' his father growled. 'The lady's here to take you on holiday.'

'I don't want to go on holiday.'

The door burst open and the shape of Ronnie's father filled the frame. 'You get downstairs now.'

Fighting back tears, Ronnie asked, 'Where's Mum?'

'She's busy. Now get a move on, the nice lady in the car is waiting for you.'

Outside, a small crowd of children and adults had gathered, and Ronnie kept his head down as his father marched him to the car. He slid into the back seat and clutched his black hold-all close to his chest, trying hard not to cry. As he glanced out of the window, he watched his father go back to the house. He could see his mum standing at the front door. She started to walk down the path, but his father held her back. Tears welled up in his eyes and he couldn't hold them back any longer; his whole body was racked with silent sobs.

Suddenly his mother broke free of his father and ran down the path. 'It's just for a few days, Ronnie,' she shouted. 'You'll be home soon.' Before she could reach the car, Janet turned the ignition key and they lurched away from the kerbside. Ronnie turned to look at his mum through the rear window, unable to see her clearly through a blur of tears. She was standing in the middle of the road with her hands up to her face. Just behind her, the small crowd of people who had come to see him off were waving; waving to Ronnie Lockwood going on his holidays.

*   *   *

As Janet drove through the gates of the children's home, Ronnie clutched his bag tightly towards him. She pulled into a parking space in front of a huge, austere-looking building. 'This is your new home for a while, Ronnie,' she explained. 'There's lots of other children here – they play football, rugby and have their own snooker table. Shall we go in and have a look around?'

Ronnie shook his head violently. 'No, thanks. I want to go home.'

Janet turned in her seat, reached back and touched his arm. 'Come on, Ronnie. It's just for a short while.' He started to cry again. Janet got out of the car, walked round the bonnet and tried to pull Ronnie's door, but he was holding the handle from the inside and wouldn't let go. She rapped hard on the window, suddenly becoming stern. 'Let go now or I'll get one of the carers.' Ronnie looked at her and shook his head.

With a last futile pull at the handle, she turned and marched up the steps to the huge brown front door. Ronnie watched her go inside. As he sat in the car, he looked around. A small group of boys were standing near a high wall that ran around the edge of the grounds. One of them caught his eye and made a cutting gesture across his throat. Ronnie felt something wet on his legs and pulled his bag lower to cover the stain.

Suddenly there was a banging on the car window. A tall man with a huge barrel chest started tugging at the door. Ronnie held on for as long as he could, but the man was strong and finally the door flew open. The man grabbed him by the collar and yanked him out. He fell onto the gravel drive with his bag landing next to him. The man looked down at him. 'We've got a clever clogs here, have we?' He turned to Janet. 'You go on, love. I'll look after him now.'

Ronnie watched as the social worker did a three-point turn and made her way down the drive. 'Well, come on,' the man said. 'We haven't got all day. Let's get you settled in.' He bent and picked up Ronnie's bag. 'Follow me.'

As soon as they got through the front door he said, 'Let's get those trousers changed before the other boys see them. Have you got another pair in your bag?' Ronnie nodded. The man waited outside the toilet while Ronnie changed. He wasn't sure what to do with his wet trousers, but the man shouted through the door, 'Don't worry about the dirty ones. Just bundle them up and I'll take them to the laundry.' It was the first kindness Ronnie had known that day.

When he had changed, Ronnie opened the toilet door, handed his soiled trousers to the man, and followed him along a wide corridor and up a huge staircase. The man led him into a long room with beds down both sides. As they went in, he flung Ronnie's trousers into a corner and began fumbling in his pocket. He pulled out a crumpled sheet of paper, unfolded it and scanned it, looking up occasionally at the lines of beds. 'Now where are you, Mr Lockwood?' Suddenly he strode forward and banged the end of a bed with his hand. 'Here we are. Primo position – near the door. Put your bag on the bed, then we'll go back downstairs and I'll introduce you to some of the other kids.'

When they approached the boys that Ronnie had seen near the wall earlier, he started to feel sick. He willed himself not to let the wet come. The man walked up to the tallest boy, pointed at Ronnie and said, 'This is Ronnie Lockwood. He's in the same dorm as most of you lot. Show him the ropes.'

The tall boy smiled. 'Leave him with us, sir.'

The man clipped the boy gently around the head, 'And be nice to him.' Then he turned and began walking back towards the big house. 'I'll see you later, Ronnie,' he shouted over his shoulder.

Ronnie shouted back, 'See you later.'

'See you later, *sir*,' the tall boy said.

Ronnie echoed, 'See you later, sir.'

As soon as the man disappeared into the building, the boys made a circle around Ronnie. With all eyes fixed on him, he wondered what he should do, but then one of the boys broke the silence with a command, 'Walk the wall!' The others quickly joined in and began dancing around him, their words becoming a chant, 'Walk the wall! Walk the wall!'

The tall boy put his hand in the air and the chanting came to a stop. 'Let the walk begin,' he announced. He bent and whispered in Ronnie's ear, 'It's just a little test to prove that you've got balls.' Two boys grabbed Ronnie by his arms and led him to the foot of the ten-foot-high wall. It was built of rough stones. As he looked up at it, Ronnie could see bits of glass cemented into the top.

The tall boy spoke. 'All you have to do is to walk along the top, the whole way around – then you'll be one of us.' Ronnie looked up at the wall and nodded.

'Let's give him a bunk-up,' one of the boys said. Three of them started to help him clamber to the top, but before he could find the first foothold, a small boy with thick spectacles and ginger hair shouted, 'Make him take his shoes off.'

The tall boy turned to Ronnie and whispered in his ear again. 'Some really brave kids do it with their shoes off – do you want to try?' Ronnie felt his chest tighten.

Bending down, he undid his laces and eased his shoes off. 'And your socks,' the ginger-haired boy shouted. Ronnie bent and took them off. The three boys came forward again and boosted him up the wall. As he stood on the top, they all cheered. Ronnie gazed at the six-inch-wide path snaking into the distance and then looked down at the boys watching. Now he was standing on top of it, the wall seemed much higher. The cement under his feet felt cold, and he could see a large piece of jagged green glass embedded in the surface just in front of him. He didn't want to move. Then one of the boys started chanting. 'Ten, nine . . .' and they all joined in, '. . . eight, seven, six, five, four, three, two, one – go!' Ronnie inched his left foot forward and lifted his right one to avoid the glass.

He had almost finished – just six feet to go. One of the boys had yelled, 'Good job!' and Ronnie looked down to smile at him. But then someone picked up a long stick and started prodding Ronnie's leg with it. 'Come on, Lockwood – get a move on.' Ronnie stepped forward in panic and as he put his foot down, he felt a searing pain. Yanking it up, he saw blood pouring from a wound where the glass had ripped into his skin. And then he started to wobble. He tried hard to balance on one foot. And then he fell.

At first it seemed as if he was going to be all right – he landed on his feet. But milliseconds after, there was a sickening cracking sound. Ronnie put his hands to his knees and fell over.

* * *

As Dianne and I worked our way through a bottle of Rioja and wondered about a man we hardly knew but who already felt part of our home, he was in bed in the room above us, reliving other events that he had long ago pushed into the furthest corners of his mind. It was years later when he shared with us the memories that flooded his mind on that Christmas night. Pandora's box had been opened.

It was his ninth birthday, he had been in the children's home for almost a year, and he had wet the bed – again. He looked across the dormitory at the clock on the wall by the door. Five past seven. As far as he could tell, the other twelve boys were asleep and there was still twenty-five minutes before Mr Anderson came in to wake them. Ronnie had time – if he was quick and quiet.

His feet were curled high in the bed away from the wet. He moved them slowly back down and tried to dislodge the bottom sheet from where it was tucked in, careful not to move too quickly and attract the attention of the older boys. He tried to squeeze the sheet between his toes and pull hard, but it wouldn't move. He lifted his backside, grabbed the sheet with his hands and yanked. It finally came away and he began to pull it upwards, scrunching it into a ball. And then he heard somebody laugh. It was Carl Davies in the next bed, lying on his side and watching him. Ronnie let go of the bottom sheet, pulled the top one over his chin and turned away from the prying eyes. He lay still.

At exactly 7.30 a.m., the dormitory door flew open and Mr Anderson began his normal wake-up routine. 'Wakey-wakey, wasters.' He went around each bed, hitting its occupant's feet with his rolled-up newspaper. Various cries of 'Knock it off, sir' went round the room, as well as less polite things said more quietly, but the boys began to get up. All except one.

Ronnie couldn't move. He knew that if he did, somebody might see or even smell what he'd done. Mr Anderson had almost reached the door when he realised that one boy hadn't got out of bed. He made his way back down the aisle. Ronnie was terrified. The mouse knew the falcon was coming, but still it just waited, transfixed. Anderson stood at the end of the bed and glared down.

'What's wrong with you, Lockwood? Become paralysed during the night?'

Ronnie pulled the sheet higher around him. 'I don't feel well, sir.'

'What is it? Heavy session on the pop last night?'

'No, sir.'

'Well, what's wrong with you, boy?'

Carl Davies shot his hand in the air. 'Please, sir, he's pissed the bed.'

Anderson's face darkened. He caught hold of the bedclothes and threw them off. Ronnie's pyjamas and the bed were soaking. 'Get out now. Get this bed stripped and take those filthy sheets to the laundry.' He held his nose. 'You stink, Lockwood.' And with that, he walked out of the dorm.

As Anderson marched along the corridor towards his office, he did not hear the chant that filled the boy's dormitory: 'Pisser Lockwood. Pisser Lockwood. Pisser Lockwood.'

*   *   *

I have often tried to imagine Ronnie in the children's home, as he wondered why his life was so very different from the lives of other children he had left behind on the day he was taken into care. But, perhaps, after some years, life in the institution began to feel normal; maybe, as he played football, snooker and got to know the carers, he began to feel that he belonged, even in that austere setting. But as he neared his eleventh birthday, he had no idea what was about to occur.

Ronnie had just finished playing football in the yard with the other boys. Mr Tompkins, the home's supervisor, had pulled him aside and said, 'Come into the office. I've got some exciting news for you.' A few minutes later Ronnie sat down in the large office. It wasn't excitement he felt but fear. With the wisdom born of experience, he knew that words such as 'exciting', 'enjoyable' or 'fun' were best treated with suspicion.

Mr Tompkins didn't waste any time coming to the point. 'You have been selected to go to a special school for boys,' he announced with satisfaction. It had, after all, taken him several minutes to think of a term he could use instead of the one in the letter that lay on his desk: 'A school for subnormal boys.'

And so it was that a small boy with learning difficulties, taken from his parents at the age of eight and placed in a local children's home, was sent hundreds of miles away to a place where he had no family or friends, and no teachers or social workers who knew him. Several decades later, three of the carers from that school were incarcerated after being found guilty of the systematic abuse of the children there over a period of thirty years. One small boy who was abused within two days of arriving was told by a carer: 'There's no point crying – it won't help you. And it's not worth telling anyone because nobody's going to believe you.'

Dianne and I knew nothing of the memories Ronnie was reliving as we finished off the red and made our way upstairs. When we got to the landing, we were surprised to see a light under his door. I knocked on it gently. 'Come in,' he shouted. Ronnie was sat up in bed and his eyes were swollen.

'Are you OK?' I asked.

'I'm fine.'

'Are you sure?'

'I had a bit of a bad dream, that's all.'

'Do you want to talk about it?' I asked.

He lowered his head and shook it slowly.

I persisted. 'Are you sure?'

'It was nothing. I just dreamt they were making me walk the wall again.'

'Well, you're safe now, Ronnie – with us.'

'I know.'

'Knock on our door if you need us.'

Dianne and I got into bed and as I turned off my bedside light I said, 'Do you want me to put a chair under the door handle?'

'No, of course not. But I really don't understand what's happening to us.'

I put my arm around her. 'Let's not try to work that out now. I've got another idea.' She started laughing.

'We'll have to be quiet.'

I pulled her closer. 'As two mice.'

Early carefree days.

Chapter 4

Boxing Day

I woke on Boxing Day to see Dianne with a pillow over her head. I glanced at the clock: 07:25.

She spoke in muffled tones. 'He's been crashing around the kitchen since six o'clock.'

'You should have woken me up. I'd have gone down and stopped him.'

Dianne emerged from underneath the pillow, sat up and ran a hand through her hair. 'We can't yell at him for trying to be kind.'

I kissed her cheek. 'I'll go and make a cup of tea. Do you want some toast?'

'No, tea would be great. Don't have a go at him. Let's talk about it later.'

I made my way downstairs and was about to go through the kitchen door when Ronnie shouted, 'Stop! Close your eyes.' I did as I was told. After a minute or so he came into the hall, took me by the arm and led me forward. 'Keep your eyes closed.' I could hear his breathing. 'Open them now!' I did.

At first, I didn't spot it but then I saw the dishwasher open – and empty. 'Wow! You've stacked away all the dishes.'

A huge smile creased his face. 'I'm good in the kitchen, I am.'

Teas made, I got back into bed and, propped up against the pillows, we sipped our drinks. For a while neither of us said anything, until the tension was finally broken by Dianne. 'Ugh – you've left the tea bag in.'

'Sorry. I was trying to stop Ronnie stacking all the plates in the wrong cupboard.'

A smile lifted her cheeks. 'I don't know what we did before we had Ronnie to blame for everything.'

I offered my cup to her. 'Finish mine off.'

'No, you're fine. What are we going to do tomorrow?'

I bit my lower lip and said nothing.

The smile had disappeared and Dianne pressed on. 'We said until the day after Boxing Day, didn't we?'

'Yes, we did. But we didn't know him then.'

'That's crazy. He's only been with us for two days – we hardly know him at all.'

'I know, but don't you feel as if he needs us?'

'He needs somebody.' She leant her head against my shoulder. 'We've been kind to him, and the truth is, I'm sure he's loved being with us, but the longer we leave it, the harder it'll make it when he has to go.'

'But where would he go? We can't send him back onto the street.' I bit my fingernail.

Dianne slapped the back of my hand. 'Don't start that or I'll think we're really in trouble.'

As we talked, we could hear Ronnie clattering dishes and saucepans in the kitchen underneath us. Dianne turned to me. 'Let's get some advice. For goodness' sake, the church has that great contact with a homeless centre. As soon as Christmas is over, we'll go and talk to them. See what they suggest.'

I said, 'They could find him a place.'

* * *

When we got downstairs, we went straight into the kitchen. It was unnaturally tidy. Not only were the worktops clean and clear, but the tea towels were folded exactly in half and hanging on the bar in front of the oven. The washing-up liquid, sponge and pot scourer were lined up on the windowsill, and the chairs around the table were all placed with exactly the same gap between them, like soldiers waiting for inspection. But no Ronnie.

He was in the living room watching television.

'Good morning, Ronnie,' Dianne said as she went in. She pointed at the screen. 'Is that good?'

'It's fine,' said Ronnie.

Dianne watched for a moment and then said, 'Oh, this is *The Little Mermaid*. Do you know this story, Ronnie?'

Ronnie shook his head, his eyes still on the screen.

Dianne went on, 'It's a story about somebody who gives their life for the one they love. What do you think of that – isn't that romantic?'

'It's fine,' said Ronnie.

Dianne was on a roll. 'And that's Richard Chamberlain's voice telling the story. He used to be Dr Kildare – he's gorgeous – and so caring.' She shot me a look. 'I'll bet he wouldn't have left the tea bag in. I wouldn't mind being a mermaid around him.'

Ronnie laughed. 'He wouldn't be as good as Rob.'

Dianne tapped him on the head. 'You're beginning to sound like his mother, Ronnie.'

His laughter stopped and he looked down. 'Only joking.'

I quickly put on a voice of mock hurt. 'What do you mean that you're only joking. Do you think I wouldn't be as good as Richard Chamberlain?'

'I don't know what I mean.' He shook his head slowly. 'Just change the subject.'

Dianne shot a glance at me. 'Hey, Ronnie, the kitchen is amazing. Thank you.'

'Pleasure.' Ronnie kept staring at the television and for a moment we thought we'd lost his attention, then without looking at us, he said, 'You'll miss me tomorrow.'

Dianne gazed at Ronnie as if she was about to say something and changed her mind.

I stepped in. 'We will, Ronnie, but we're firm friends now and you'll be visiting us lots.'

Dianne gave a strained laugh. 'You're not getting out of doing the kitchen that easily.'

Ronnie turned away from the screen and looked at us. 'It's best if I go tomorrow, isn't it?'

'I need to . . .' Dianne turned and left the room.

'I'm not being rude, mind. I hope I didn't offend you,' said Ronnie.

I said, 'No, Ronnie. You haven't offended us and you're not being rude. Let's chat about it later, OK? I just need to help Dianne.' I went into the kitchen, but Dianne wasn't there. I found her upstairs, sitting on the edge of the bed. As I came in, she looked up at me. 'Can we go for a drive – on our own?'

'Sure.'

She stood up. 'Will Ronnie be all right in the house?'

'Unless he tries to steal the silver – if we had any.'

Dianne smiled. 'I just need some space. And we need to talk.'

On the way out, I put my head around the living-room door. 'We're just going out for an hour, Ronnie. Will you be OK? There's some turkey in the fridge and bread in the cupboard. Make yourself a sandwich.'

Ronnie kept his eyes on the television. 'I didn't offend you, did I?'

'No, of course not, Ronnie.'

He turned, 'Good. You two go out and have a good time.'

As I was closing the front door, it struck me how strange it was to be leaving somebody we hardly knew in charge of our new home. And yet I completely trusted him. But how could I be so sure after just two days? I wasn't naïve. My job as a lawyer brought me into contact with conmen, blaggers and the downright criminal – some of them within the profession; I wasn't a walkover.

As I walked away from the house on that Boxing Day, it

dawned on me that there was definitely something remarkable about Ronnie. He was at once the most frustrating guest we had ever had in our home, and the easiest. He demanded nothing – not even conversation. I thought back to how I had felt as the three of us had gone to church together on Christmas Eve. Like the battered and scratched sideboard in our newly decorated hallway, he, surprisingly, fitted.

*   *   *

The day was perfect, the air crisp and the winter sun welcoming. As we got out of the car and entered Roath Park, I breathed in deeply, the air filling my lungs, relaxing my shoulders. Over a hundred years ago, the Cardiff city fathers decided that if they were to build thousands of houses in the north of the city, they should put a spine of parks through the middle of them. Seven parks, one after another – and all different. And if it wasn't enough to reclaim vast areas of bogland, they had created a thirty-acre lake in the heart of this one. Every year, thousands of families rowed its boats, fed its ducks, or simply meandered around its circumference.

Today was no exception. The winter sun had lured hundreds of families away from Christmas presents and larders stocked with brandy butter and mince pies. Seagulls screamed and swooped, trying to steal the bread that toddlers were throwing to the ducks, children wobbled along the path on gleaming new bicycles, and an ice-cream van, unused to such brisk winter trade, sang out its lure.

We found an empty bench overlooking the children's

playground, sat down and lifted our faces to the sun. Dianne put her hand in mine. 'I can't remember when we last came here. It's lovely, isn't it? I feel free – as if I'm mitching from school.'

'Would you like an ice lolly?'

She turned and faced me. Her eyes were wide. 'No, but I'll tell you what I *would* like: a cone with a massive Cadbury's Flake in it.'

When I returned with two enormous 99s topped with sweet, sticky red sauce, I found Dianne gazing at the kids in the playground. As she took her cone, she asked, 'Do you think we'll ever have children?'

I took a bite of my 99. 'What – in addition to the one we've got?'

She brushed ice cream off the tip of my nose. 'Don't. It's not funny. Do you?'

'You know I do. We talked about it loads before we got married. Don't you remember we used to imagine that we had six and try to find names for them all?'

'Of course I remember, but I never really knew if you were serious. You'd have said anything to lure me into your web of love.'

We sat for a long time saying nothing, just watching the kids on the roundabout and swings and eating our ice creams. As Dianne put the last piece into her mouth she leant back and put her feet across my lap. 'So. What are we going to do?'

'What – about having kids?'

'No – about Ronnie.'

A middle-aged man was coming towards us, his bright red sweater distracting Dianne. She said, 'When we were kids, my mum and dad would bring us all here on Boxing Day and we'd try to guess if any of the people walking towards us on the path were wearing Christmas presents. You got one point for a bobble hat, two for a jumper and three for a scarf. This one coming is a surefire two points.' We watched as the man passed then Dianne stood and stretched. 'Let's walk around the lake.'

As we strolled hand in hand, she asked, 'What was the name of that film where some kids find a homeless man in a barn at Christmas and mistake him for Jesus?'

'No idea.'

'Come on, try a bit harder. They always used to show it at school as a treat on the last afternoon. It had Hayley Mills in it.'

'*Black Beauty.*'

'Don't be silly.'

'Honestly, I haven't got a clue.'

'Oh, it's a lovely film. I know: *Whistle Down the Wind.*'

'I don't think anybody would mistake Ronnie for Jesus.'

Dianne laughed. 'Not before he had a shower, they wouldn't.' Her face became serious. 'You know he won't be going tomorrow, don't you?'

'Well, not until we've spoken with the guys at the centre. The truth is, it'll take a couple of days to find him somewhere.'

Dianne stopped walking and turned to me. 'We can't slide into this, Rob. We're already in way above our heads.'

I put my arm around her shoulder and we carried on

past the lighthouse that commemorated Captain Scott's expedition on the *Terra Nova* to find the South Pole. None of the team survived, and although the sun was on my back, I shivered.

* * *

Back home, I opened the front door. The house was quiet. In the living room the television was off. I went to the foot of the stairs and shouted up. 'Ronnie. Ronnie?'

Dianne came out of the kitchen. 'Where is he?'

I ran upstairs and knocked on his door. No answer. I pushed it open. Nobody.

I walked down the stairs slowly. Dianne was in the hall looking up at me.

'He's gone,' I said.

She paled, went into the living room and sat on the settee. 'I can't believe he'd just go like that. I feel really let down. I suppose we should feel glad, but I don't – I feel gutted.' She sat staring at the Christmas tree, then looked up. 'Was his room empty? What about his stuff? I think some of his clothes are still in the tumble dryer?'

I took the stairs two at a time and burst into Ronnie's room. It looked empty, but then I opened his chest of drawers. His few clothes were laid out perfectly, each folded to the same size. I pulled back the drawer beneath; there was just one thing in there, a small package wrapped in cloth. I shouted down. 'All his stuff is here.'

Dianne came to the foot of the stairs and was about to

come up when there was a thump at the door. As she opened
it, a smiling Ronnie pushed a large block of Cadbury's
chocolate towards her. 'Happy Christmas!'

Dianne put her hands on her hips. 'We thought you'd
gone, Ronnie. Where have you been? Why did you go out?
You don't have a key. What if we'd been a long time?'

He said, 'I went to the shop. I waited on the corner for
you to come back.' He looked crestfallen. 'Have I done a
bad thing?'

Dianne pulled him into the hall and hugged him. 'No,
Ronnie, you haven't done a bad thing. We were just worried
about you.'

With a deep sigh Ronnie shrugged off his coat. He
looked pained, and for a moment I thought he might cry.
'I'm always getting things wrong.'

I touched him on the arm. 'It's fine, Ronnie. You didn't do
anything wrong. We were a bit concerned, that's all. What if
we hadn't come home until midnight?'

Ronnie looked at me as though I was a little slow. 'I'd
have waited.'

'How about a cup of tea?' Dianne suggested. 'I could
certainly do with one.' When we got to the kitchen,
Dianne said, 'Would you mind making it, please, Ronnie?
Rob and I need to have a quick chat about something. We
won't be long.'

As if he'd lived in our home for ever, Ronnie went straight
to the cupboard where we kept the china. He took out three
mugs and lined them up equidistantly along the worktop,

with handles to the right. We left him to it and stepped into the living room. Dianne closed the door and blew out her cheeks, letting the air escape slowly before saying, 'I think we should tell him that we've decided to ask him to stay a few more nights; that we're going to talk to some people who may be able to help him find a place.'

I said, 'That's good. Then he can stop worrying for the moment. Are you sure?'

'Sure.'

Ronnie walked in with a cup of tea in each hand.

As I took them from him, Dianne said, 'Bring your tea in here with us. We want to have a bit of a chat.'

Ronnie looked panicked. 'I've done a bad thing, haven't I?'

Dianne smiled at him. 'No. You haven't done a bad thing.' She sat down and tapped the seat beside her. 'Sit by me. Rob will get your tea.'

When I came back into the room, Ronnie's head was down and Dianne had her arm around him. He looked up and as soon as I'd given him his tea, I blurted out, 'We just want to say that we don't want you to leave tomorrow, Ronnie. We're going to talk to some people who may be able to help you find a good place to live, but it may take a few days to do that.'

Ronnie put his tea on a side table. He said nothing.

'Is that OK, Ronnie?' Dianne asked. 'To stay with us for a few more days while we sort out somewhere proper for you to live?'

Ronnie looked at her. 'It's fine.' He dropped his head, his

stillness silencing the room. When he lifted his face he said,
'Can I ask something?'

'Of course,' said Dianne.

'You won't be cross, will you?'

I touched him on his arm. 'We won't be cross.'

'Can we have the television on?'

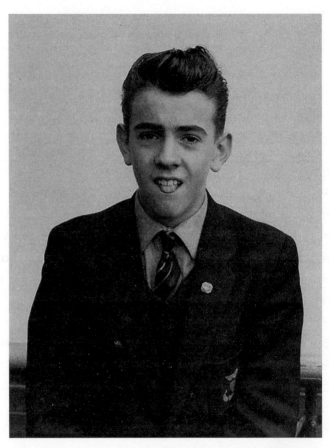

Grammar School.

Chapter 5

Ronnie Grows Up

I was 14 when I saw an advert that promised to change my life. I had saved my pocket money, sent off a postal order, and the shipment had arrived that morning. We had very few parcels delivered to our house, and when I got home from school, my mother broke the news to me as soon as I put a foot inside the door. 'It's come. It's in the best room.'

The best room had faded floral wallpaper, the hints of green matching the huge aspidistra that stood in the corner. We didn't have a single fitted carpet in the house, but the large rug in the front room came closest: the bare floorboards could only just be seen around the edges. There was the three-piece suite from Harrison's, and over the backs of its settee and chairs were white embroidered covers in case the imaginary visitors ever leant back and soiled the suite with their greasy hair. A light hung from the ceiling – a large, upturned opaque bowl suspended on bronze chains, which dared any illumination to try to penetrate its denseness. And there were brown slatted blinds, held together by strips of fawn material and cream strings. They were only ever closed a few times a year. If any of our neighbours died, everybody in the street would close their blinds or curtains as a mark of respect. It was true that only Mrs Coulter had railings, but our house did have blinds – and with those we were at least in the game.

As I opened the best-room door, a stale odour mixed with the fragrance of polish played around my nostrils. The box was on a small, low table. I approached it slowly and then lifted it gently. My mother had already placed a pair of scissors on the table, and I began to gingerly slide the edge of one of the blades along the brown sticky tape that secured the edges.

I lifted one of the flaps and peered inside: it was stuffed with newspaper. I took out sheet after sheet of the *Surrey Advertiser*. And finally, I saw it. At the bottom of the box a small furry thing was lying as if curled up asleep. I removed it carefully, cupped it in my hands and gazed at it.

Over the fireplace was a mirror, cracked around the edges and hanging on two chrome chains. I turned to check the door was closed, carefully spread out the furry object and placed it on my head. A little adjustment here and there, a tweak at the corners, and then a stepping forward to get right up to the mirror. I peered at my reflection, looked at myself full-on, then turned to get a sideways perspective. I smiled and sighed with satisfaction; the 'Lifelike Beatles Wig' had worked. It was 1963. The best band in the world were at number one with 'She Loves You'. And I was Paul McCartney.

There was a lot riding on that small furry bundle. As far as I was concerned, the life-changing attributes promised by the advert could not come a moment too soon: life was not going well. As a child I dreamt of passing the Eleven Plus examination and going to grammar school; after all, no kid in my street had ever done it. I would sometimes sit in front of the coal fire in our living room and dream of what I might become if I ever achieved that goal. But the odds weren't good. I was sick a lot when I was a child and missed a lot of primary school. It was obvious that I was lagging behind. That's when my mother decided to make an appointment to see the headmaster. He told her that I had a chance of passing but I had fallen behind in maths. He suggested that I miss swimming lessons and instead do an extra maths class. My mother agreed. When she told my father, he exploded. 'Just leave him be. Let him be like the other boys.' And then he added, 'And what if he drowns when he grows up?'

My mother got her way, and I swapped the breaststroke for fractions. I passed the exam and with the letter that brought the news came a list of uniform items I would need. It said there were some second-hand blazers for families that couldn't afford new ones. My mother wouldn't hear of it. She made my father agree to her having a temporary job clearing tables in a department-store restaurant. I wore my brand-new blazer in the street before I had even started at the grammar. Stanley Preston said that if I didn't stop wearing it, he would hit me.

It was Oscar Wilde who said there are two tragedies in life: 'One is not getting what one wants, and the other is getting it.' On my first day at the grammar school for boys, I felt like a refugee in a foreign country. As the months went by, I not only felt inadequate academically but in every other way as well. In primary school, I had just about held my own, but the kids in this school were from another planet. They had cars, telephones, went on holidays, and had homes filled with literature.

We only had three books in our family: a Bible, an atlas and something called *The Doctor's Book*. This latter tome was so designed that you discovered you were suffering from whatever disease you'd looked up, and probably the one on the facing page as well. Nevertheless, it was more well-thumbed than either of its rivals. And it wasn't just the lack of books that was the problem; I'm sure that my parents did their best to help me with my homework, but the truth is they really didn't know how to. Perhaps those are excuses and I was slow or just downright lazy, but for whatever reason, my academic life could be summed up by a comment that I was to hear many times during my school career: 'Weak, at best.'

And it wasn't just in academic subjects that I struggled. In a cruel twist of fate, I was hopeless at practical skills as well. For the woodwork examination, we had the choice of either making a coffee table or a potato plunger. The teacher explained that the latter was essentially a piece of wood with a handle like a spade, but with a pointed shaft which could be plunged into the ground to make a hole into which a potato could be dropped. I have sometimes wondered if he invented it as a way of giving the less able kids something they had a cat in hell's chance of making.

The day of the inspection came, and we were asked to lay out our offerings in the woodwork room. I got there late, and by the time I arrived, the floor was practically covered with coffee tables. I laid my potato plunger on a bench. The teacher began at the end of the room, inspecting each boy's work, and finally reached me. He looked down, grimaced, and barked, 'What is it?'

I thought that unfair; it obviously wasn't the coffee table. I said, 'Please, sir, it's a potato plunger.'

He said, 'It should be taken out and shot.'

I pleaded, 'Please, sir, I did my best.'

He didn't hesitate in his answer; perhaps if he had done, he would have realised the nuclear effect of his comment. 'Parsons, your best is not good enough.'

Unfortunately, it seemed that his judgement was not just true of potato plungers, but chemistry, geography and a host of other subjects. Things did not improve, and the nadir of my grammar school performance was reached in the Easter exams in April 1963.

When you joined the grammar, they gave you a hard-backed black book containing twenty-one blank reports – three for each term, including the sixth form. I still have that book in my study. It is filled with comments such as 'Weak',

'Must try harder' and 'Could do better'. In one subject in July 1962 the teacher wrote 'Very Good' and then crossed out 'Good' and replaced it with 'Satisfactory'. I have sometimes thought I might look him up and ask, 'Why did you bother?'

The school policy was for form teachers to read out the exam results, beginning with the boy in the class who had come top. It was a system designed to honour and humiliate. There were thirty-four of us, and as the names droned out, my heart began to beat faster. *Was it possible that I'd be in the teens?* It wasn't. By the time we were into the late twenties my head had sunk onto my chest. Our form teacher knew how to play to the gallery, and he slowed in his delivery as he got into the thirties. Eventually, there were just two names left. I glanced across at Bernard Harries and he shrugged his shoulders back at me. The class was hushed. This was the Colosseum, the crowd were baying for blood, and the teacher was Nero. I thought I might be sick. And then I heard it: Bernard's name. Thirty-three kids turned to stare at me.

When my teacher wrote his comments in my report that term, he decided to expand his criticism so that it went beyond a cataloguing of my academic failures. He shared also his view of what talent I had accumulated in my short life, either from nature or nurture. He wrote: 'A disgraceful report. He is making no use of what little ability he has.'

It is perhaps unsurprising that we are so deeply affected by the judgements of those whom we feel matter when we are young. When he wrote those words in my report that day, he created a box covered in labels: 'Disgraceful', 'No use' and 'Little ability'. And because he was a teacher and I was a child, I assumed that was my place. I climbed into that box and lived in it for years. Too many years.

Fortunately, I had other irons in the fire, ways of making money, attracting girls, and generally having a great life that my teacher could only dream of. And that's why the wig mattered. It mattered because of the Blue Jets.

The wig was, in fact, my second major purchase of that year. For my Christmas present, my parents had bought me a cheap guitar, and a few months later I had bought a copy of a manual to which almost every British guitarist of the Sixties (including Eric Clapton) acknowledges at least some debt: Bert Weedon's *Play in a Day*. Rather like the marketing blurb for the wig, the title contained a bold claim. Nevertheless, a combination of three simple chords allowed many budding Claptons to belt out the first song in the book, 'Bobby Shaftoe Went to Sea', if not in a day, then at least in a week.

On my fifteenth birthday I got together with three of my friends and we took a step that was destined to change one of our lives for ever: we started a band – the Blue Jets. It was decided that Paul Dixon, who had mastered ten chords in addition to Bert's staple three, would be lead guitar; having got 'Bobby Shaftoe' and a couple more numbers worthy of a rock icon under my belt, I would play rhythm, and Roger Joslin, whose father owned a pub and who had bought him a bass guitar, would provide the sonic link between Paul's melody and my rhythm.

But as it turned out, it was none of those whose life was to be changed by our decision to go into the music business; that touch of fate fell to Dennis Bryon. Dennis's parents owned a bed-and-breakfast business, and one day a member of a pop group stayed there. Dennis offered to help clear away the breakfast dishes and got his wish of a few moments with the ageing rocker. Dennis told the guest that he wanted to be in a band and intended to learn the guitar. The musician was dismissive. 'Guitarists are two a penny; get yourself some drums.' He took his advice, begged his parents to buy him some, and vowed he would pay them back when he was famous. I was with him when he and his father walked into Barratt's music store in the Wyndham Arcade in Cardiff. Dennis asked the assistant if he could try some drums and was pointed towards a silver set in the centre of the store. He just gazed at them in silence until his father said, 'Well, go on – you're not going to get on *Six-Five Special* by looking at them.'

Dennis sat on the small black plastic stool behind the bass drum, picked up a pair of drumsticks, and held them above the skins. He said, 'I don't know what to do.'

His father by now was both losing interest and wondering whether giving in to the purchase was wise after all. 'Just hit them,' he said. And Dennis did. In fact, he hit them so well that pretty soon he left the Blue Jets behind and was snapped up by a band that could really play. And eight years after the birth of the Blue Jets, and while Paul, Roger and I were still working on *Play in a Day*, Dennis was drumming for a group called Amen Corner and topping the UK music charts. The big music show at that time on British television was *Top of the Pops*. I remember watching, transfixed by the screen, as Dennis belted out 'Bend Me, Shape Me'. After he left Amen Corner, he joined the Bee Gees.

A few years ago, I discovered he had written an autobiography: *You Should Be Dancing: My Life with the Bee Gees*. I bought it and straight away turned to the index to see if I was mentioned: nothing. Surely the Blue Jets must have got a mention somewhere. I found it on page two.

> Initially the plan was to get together with three or four friends . . . and form a band. But the band thing didn't really work out. I was keen to play and getting better at the drums, but my mates weren't doing so well with their guitars. They got sick of practising and sounding awful, so one by one they gave up.

Thanks a lot, Dennis.

I was poor academically, the Blue Jets were struggling, and the girl I fancied had told me that my Paul wig looked like a dead cat. Life was challenging. But things were about to improve and from a very unexpected quarter. As I strolled down the street one day, dressed in a leather jacket, ice-blue jeans and with ten Embassy Tipped in my back pocket, I had no idea that walking towards me was a man who had passed fewer exams than me, was worse at practical skills than me, and might well have been the only man in the universe who either hadn't heard of the Beatles or, if he had, didn't care: Arthur Tovey.

* * *

As I grappled with the disappointment of my Beatles wig, Ronnie was facing bigger issues. As he was walking out of breakfast one day in the home to which he had been sent when he was eleven – the one for 'subnormal boys' – one of the carers, Mr Dancey, had collared him. 'Mr Stephenson wants to see you in his office.'

Ronnie paled. 'Have I done a bad thing?'

Dancey laughed and mimicked Ronnie's voice. 'No, Lockwood, you haven't done a bad thing. You've just grown up.'

Ronnie shrugged his shoulders and began to make his way back down the corridor towards the principal's office. He had never been in Mr Stephenson's room. He knocked as quietly as he could on the large brown door: no answer. He waited, then knocked again a little louder. He heard a bellow. 'All right, all right. I heard you the first time. Come in.' Ronnie opened the door slowly. Even before he stepped in, he could smell cigarette smoke, and as he entered the room, he saw it hanging like a low cloud above Mr Stephenson's head. The principal was in a suit but had loosened the tie around the collar of his shirt. He was a huge man, red-faced, with a stomach that hung over the edge of the desk, as if it was battling for space with the papers scattered all across its surface.

Ronnie stood, hands clasped in front of him, and with his head bowed. Mr Stephenson gestured impatiently to a chair. 'Sit down. Nobody is going to eat you.' Ronnie slid tentatively onto a dining chair placed directly in front of the desk.

Mr Stephenson looked up at him. 'So, you're leaving us today?'

Ronnie leant forward, looking puzzled. Mr Stephenson said, 'Has nobody told you?'

Ronnie shook his head.

Mr Stephenson picked up a packet of Senior Service, tapped out a cigarette and lit it. He threw his head back and began blowing rings of smoke above Ronnie's head. Ronnie watched, transfixed, as the rings played in the air, disappeared and were then replaced by new ones. Ronnie smiled. 'Clever.'

Mr Stephenson held out the packet. 'Do you want one? You're allowed to, now you're sixteen. No need to huddle behind the gym thinking nobody can see you.'

Ronnie shook his head, 'No, thank you.'

The principal reached across his desk and lifted a buff-coloured folder from a pile of papers stacked to his left. He flicked it open. 'Now let's see.' His eyes ran down the sheet of paper at the front of the file. 'You were sixteen last week, on March sixth?'

Ronnie nodded slowly, as if afraid to admit to a birthday.

Mr Stephenson's eyes continued to wander down the page. 'You're being picked up at two-thirty.' He closed the file and put it back on the stack of papers. 'Be in the main hall with your stuff by a quarter past.'

Ronnie scratched his head. 'Where am I going?'

Mr Stephenson reached for the file again and opened it. He turned over several pages and then said, 'Number 5a, Moss Road, Cardiff.' He tore off a scrap of paper from the bottom of a letter, wrote on it and passed it to Ronnie. 'Here. Your social worker knows the address anyway.'

Ronnie took the paper and shuffled in his seat. 'How will I get there?'

'Camel,' said Mr Stephenson and then saw the puzzled look on Ronnie's face. 'How do you think you'll be getting there? They're sending a social worker in a car to get you. You'll be like royalty.'

Ronnie said, 'When will I be coming back?'

At first Mr Stephenson looked as if he was cross, then puzzled, but finally he leant back in his chair, blew a ring of smoke into the air, and laughed out loud. 'After running this place for five years I finally meet a boy who wants to come back.' He stretched a hand across the desk. 'Goodbye, Ronnie.'

Ronnie closed Mr Stephenson's door behind him and started to run down the main corridor, left at the toilet block, past the dining hall and to the kitchen. He banged on the door. Charlie, one of the cooks, opened it. Ronnie was breathless. 'Can I see Carol?'

Charlie started to close the door. 'Carol is busy.'

Ronnie put his foot in the door. 'It's important.'

Something about Ronnie's manner caused Charlie not to argue. 'Wait here.'

When Carol came to the door, she was wiping her hands on her pinafore. Before she could say a word, Ronnie started to cry. Carol stepped into the corridor and closed the kitchen door behind her. 'Ronnie, whatever is the matter?'

He sniffed.

Carol pressed on. 'Ronnie – what's happened?'

Ronnie lifted his shoulders and then let them fall suddenly. 'I've got to leave the home.'

Carol pursed her lips. She put a hand on his shoulder. 'Oh, Ronnie. Of course. You were sixteen last week, weren't you?'

Ronnie nodded.

Carol looked along the corridor and then turned her eyes back to him. 'When are you leaving?'

'At half-past two.'

'What . . . today?'

'Yes.'

'Do you know where you're going?'

Ronnie pulled a piece of paper from his trouser pocket and handed it to her. As he watched Carol read it, he thought that she was about to cry as well. Suddenly, she hugged him and said, 'Now you be brave and make sure you come back and see us soon.' Her eyes began to fill. Perhaps she thought he looked betrayed – even by her. She drew the back of her hand across her eyes. 'Do you want me to help you pack?'

'Yes, please.'

Carol opened the kitchen door and went inside. Soon she was out again and they made their way together towards the dormitory. They stood at the end of Ronnie's bed. 'Have you got a case or something?' Ronnie shook his head. Carol suddenly looked angry. 'Wait here. I won't be long.'

She returned with Dancey, who was carrying a battered brown suitcase. He threw it on the bed. 'There you are, Lockwood. Harrods' finest.' He glared at Carol, turned on his heels and he was gone.

* * *

The social worker, Claire Hodges, arrived ten minutes early. She could have been two hours early. Ronnie had been sitting in the reception hall since midday. In that time, two boys and one member of staff had found him and said goodbye. He had been in this home for five years. Everything he had was packed into that suitcase, except for a small bundle, wrapped in cloth and which he placed on the chair beside him.

Claire stretched out her hand. 'You must be Ronnie.'

Ronnie shook her hand. 'Yes.'

Claire said, 'The car's outside,' and went to pick up Ronnie's case.

Ronnie grabbed the handle. 'It's fine.'

As they reached the door, Ronnie suddenly put the case down and rushed back to the line of chairs in reception. He came back clutching a small package. Claire looked intrigued. 'What have you got in there, Ronnie?'

Ronnie laid the package on his hand and carefully pulled back the cloth. He looked at Claire, waiting for a response. She went for one that she felt was safe. 'Birthday cards?'

Ronnie smiled as he folded the cloth back into place. 'There are five of them.'

'That's great, Ronnie.'

'They're from Carol – she's my friend.'

'Who's Carol, Ronnie?'

Ronnie gave Claire an exasperated look. 'Carol. Carol from the kitchen.'

'Ah,' said Claire. 'Perhaps I'll meet her someday.'

Ronnie smiled. 'She won't send you cards, mind.'

Claire lifted her eyebrows. 'I'm sure she won't.'

Ronnie followed Claire out of the building and towards a pale blue car parked near the front doors. Ronnie said, 'A Ford Prefect.'

Claire turned and smiled, 'You're clever.'

Ronnie laughed out loud. 'Mr Tompkins had one.'

'I just hope it will get us there. It overheated twice on the way down.'

'How far is it to Cardiff?'

'It's a long way. It's going to take us about five hours.'

Ronnie put his case in the boot and got into the front seat. As they were edging out of the drive onto the main road, Claire tried to make conversation. 'You used to live in Cardiff, didn't you?'

Ronnie started chewing the inside of his mouth, then he answered, 'Yes, I lived there until I was eleven.'

'Were you in a care home there?'

'Yes.'

'What school did you go to?' This was hard work, and they were only just out of the drive.

Ronnie fiddled with the knob on the glove compartment. 'I can't remember.'

'You can't remember? Come on, Ronnie – have a think.'

Ronnie screwed up his eyes and tilted his head to one side. 'I think it was called the Backward School.'

Claire frowned. 'Have you got any family or friends in Cardiff?'

'I've got some brothers and sisters, but I haven't seen them for a long time.'

'What about friends?'

'I used to have some friends in the Sunday school and Mr Harker was my friend.'

'Who is he?'

'I don't know who he is, but he used to come to the homes and give me a lift to the Sunday school.'

'Well, perhaps you'll be able to look them up when you get back.'

'I don't know where they live now.'

'Try to have a little sleep, Ronnie – it's a long way.'

'I'm fine.'

*   *   *

It was 8 p.m. and dark when Claire finally reached Cardiff. There had been moments on the journey when she had thought she might scream, but mercifully, Ronnie had fallen asleep just past Guildford and now at last they were back. She pulled into a side street lined with fast-food outlets and restaurants that seemed to represent every nation on the planet. She parked outside a kebab shop, turned off the engine and nudged Ronnie. He opened his eyes and blinked.

She said, 'Well, this is exciting.' They got out of the car, and she pointed to a house two down from the kebab shop. 'That one is yours.' She dived into her handbag and started fumbling around. 'The keys are in here somewhere.'

Ronnie retrieved his case from the boot and made his way past a group of teenagers lounging outside the kebab shop. He stopped at the house that Claire had pointed out. It was four storeys high with grey bricks that reminded him of his first children's home. Between the front wall and the street was a small forecourt in which a soiled mattress lounged against a broken gas cooker. Torn and stained net curtains hung in some windows, but others had none, and one on the ground floor was boarded up and covered in graffiti.

Ronnie turned and started back towards the car. He shouted to Claire 'I don't want to live here. I want to go back.' He opened the boot, put his suitcase in and started to open the passenger door.

Claire was still fumbling for the keys in her handbag. And then, as if she had only just heard him, 'No Ronnie. This is your new home. You're grown up now.'

Ronnie hesitated for a moment and Claire thought that he might run down the street. Then he sighed deeply and took his hand off the door handle; he went to the back of the car, got his case out of the boot and began walking towards the front door.

Claire waved a small bunch of keys in the air. She shouted 'Eureka!' and made her way towards the house. A pile of mail lay on the passage floor, and as she opened the door some of it wedged underneath. She gave a shove and they were in. She turned and handed the keys to Ronnie. 'Welcome to your new home. You have a look around while I get the boxes from the car.'

The basement bedsit was dark. The only window looked out onto steps that led up to the street. Ronnie flicked a switch on the wall. A single light bulb with no shade cast a thin light across the room.

There was a table with three dining chairs, a settee, and in one corner a small sink next to an electric stove. Lying on the floor was a single, heavily stained mattress, with no sheets, just a grey blanket strewn across it, as if the previous sleeper had left in haste.

Claire came into the room carrying two boxes. 'I think this is everything you need. The bathroom is upstairs in the main house. You'll need the bronze-coloured key for that.' She put the boxes on the table. 'Now let's see what we've got here for you.' She pulled out a frying pan and two saucepans and laid them on the table. 'Are you a good cook, Ronnie?'

Ronnie sat on one of the dining chairs, looked at her blankly and shook his head.

Claire handed him a packet with two single bed sheets and a pillowcase. Next out was a knife, fork and a soup spoon. She peered inside the second box. 'Here's your crockery.' She placed a plate, a cereal bowl and a mug on the table. 'It's like your birthday, Ronnie.' Two tea towels, a tin-opener, a used colander and the presentation was over. Ronnie looked down at the table and then up at Claire. He thought she looked sad. He smiled. 'I'll be fine.'

Ronnie Lockwood was grown up now.

* * *

Some may ask, 'Why did Ronnie allow people to treat him like that – as if he had no dignity, no say in his own life, as if he was not worth consulting?' I found at least part of the answer to that quite recently. While writing *A Knock at the Door*, I have been running creative-writing classes in a high-security prison. It's been an incredible experience. Most of the men in my class have had little experience of writing, and certainly not of sharing their work with others. But many of them seem to have found the experience richly rewarding. One inmate said to me, 'In my cell at night I can write and go anywhere I want to.' As the class progressed, I read them portions of what I had written about our life with Ronnie; like him, many of them had a background in care. As they listened to his story, one of them said, 'Ronnie comes over as a little person: somebody in the hold of the system who had no power and was tossed back and forth by its whims.' I think he was right. It reminded me of something said by Maya Angelou in *I Know Why the Caged Bird Sings*. As a child, she was pushed from pillar to post by people who had power over her and she had learnt a survival strategy: 'At fifteen, life had taught me undeniably that surrender, in its place, was as honourable as resistance, especially if one had no choice.'

A page from my grammar school report – 'He is making no use of what little ability he has.'

Chapter 6

People Like Us Don't Become Lawyers

Arthur Tovey and his wife Margaret lived in two rooms in Arthur's mother's house in a small terrace just around the corner from the Gospel Hall. As the church had no paid leaders, Arthur and Margaret were part of a small cohort of volunteers that looked after the older teenagers who attended.

I was on my way to a Blue Jets band practice when I ran into Arthur in the street. He was an unremarkable-looking man: middle-aged, short and balding – his small amount of thinning, sandy-coloured hair looked as though it might develop at any minute into a comb-over.

'It's Robert, isn't it?' he said.

I didn't want to get into a lengthy conversation. I had a long evening in front of me practising 'Johnny B. Goode'. 'Yes,' I said.

He screwed his eyes up in a gesture that I later came to

recognise as a precursor to his saying something he thought profound. 'I've been praying that I'd bump into you.'

I only just stopped myself saying that we both went to the same church and if he'd prayed he'd meet me on a Sunday, he'd have made it a lot easier for the Almighty. 'Wow!' I said.

'Yes. Margaret and I are starting a weekly study group for older teenagers – boys and girls. I'll make sure I don't bore you and we'll play table tennis and have fish and chips to finish with. We start next Wednesday evening at seven p.m. Will you come?'

My ambition at that time was to parade on stages playing my way through the Beatles' repertoire and having security to protect me from the baying masses. A discussion group on a Wednesday night wasn't exactly top of my agenda. For a moment I said nothing, and then I realised that he was waiting for my reply as though I had the power to make his day. I said, 'Yes.'

I have often wondered what it was that made a teenage kid agree to join the group and – even more – keep attending Wednesday after Wednesday. Perhaps it was that I would be with kids slightly older than me, or that there would be girls there. Maybe it was that I scored seventy per cent plus in the little tests at the end of every session – a number I had never seen next to my name at school. It could have been the table tennis or the fish and chips that did it, but it was many years later that I got an answer that seemed to make at least some sense. I was having dinner with a friend who is a professor of psychology at Oxford University. We'd been talking about people who had come into our lives and changed our trajectories. I asked him, 'What was it about those evenings that made them so special for me?'

He thought for a while. 'Arthur made you feel not only cared for and supported, but as if you belonged.' He reached across the table to top up my glass and continued. 'We all want to belong – whether it's at the high table in the Great Hall, or as a member of a gang in the East End of London. You just got lucky.'

*   *   *

I only ever saw one of the two rooms that Arthur and Margaret rented from his mother. It was a downstairs middle room with a conservatory that housed a tiny kitchen. And it was in that room that four of us gathered on that first Wednesday night: two boys, both called Robert, and two girls, Sandra and Dianne.

It is true that Arthur had never passed an academic exam, but that didn't stop him being a brilliant youth worker. True to his promise, he knew we'd get bored quickly with the religious stuff, so after twenty-five minutes he would announce, 'Time for table tennis.' The room was so small that tiddlywinks would have taken some organisation, but table tennis?

Arthur and Margaret disappeared from the room and, after some banging and clattering on the stairs, reappeared with two pieces of hardboard which they placed on top of the dining table. A net, two bats and a ball were produced and the game began. We played with the bats up against our chests. If the ball went underneath the table, it was a feat of contortion to retrieve it.

Table tennis over, Arthur declared, 'Time for fish and chips. The boys and I will go and get them. Girls, help Margaret lay the table.'

I can still smell the vinegar seeping through the newspaper as we carried the fish and chips home to Arthur's. By the time we got back, the table was laid, the tea brewing, and the room filled with chatter. When I walked into that home, I felt special. If ever I missed a night, he would come looking for me the next day.

I had been going to Arthur's class for a while when he asked, 'Do you ever take part in drama or debates at school?'

I said, 'I don't even put my hand up in class if I can help it.'

He screwed up his eyes. 'Well, I think God has given you a gift of public speaking and I'm going to help you develop it.'

The offer was kind; nevertheless, there were at least two things wrong with it: not only was it the last thing I wanted to do, but Arthur was one of the worst public speakers I have ever heard. However, despite strong protestations on my part, he would not be moved, and communication classes were fixed for Sunday afternoons, when he taught me to tell stories to the kids in the Sunday school.

One night during the discussion group, I caught Dianne looking at me intently. I began to dream of possibilities. Arthur's group not only provided me with the prospect of a girlfriend, but with something that, hitherto, had seemed even less likely: a certificate. But the award was not destined to rest alone on the mantlepiece in the best room. It was eventually joined by some others I had accumulated: six and a half O Levels, admittedly achieved in a somewhat piecemeal fashion. Three and a half were gained at my first attempt: English language, English literature and history. The half was for 'special arithmetic', which was for kids that couldn't pass O Level maths but could at least count. The fourth was a resit. To help me pass my French O Level, my mother got a job cleaning other people's houses and saved enough money to get me a French tutor. It wasn't just the extra tuition that got me that qualification, though: some weird logic meant my November resit didn't include an oral exam. This was a relief given my earlier effort.

The examiner had begun by saying, *'Qu'as-tu mangé au petit déjeuner?'*

I replied, *'Je ne comprends pas, monsieur.'*

He repeated, *'Qu'as-tu mangé au petit déjeuner?'* Again, I gave the same response, and again, until finally he said in English, 'What did you have for breakfast, son?'

For some reason the correct phrase for toast (*pain grillé*) eluded me, and I proffered, *'Le toast.'*

O Levels five and six were collected a year later, and I was admitted to the sixth form into stream Six T. This was for boys with an insufficient number of O Levels to do three A Levels, but who could try for one or two instead, and attempt to pick up some extra O Levels on the way. The 'T' stood for the Latin word *Trans*, which essentially means 'a journey'. Presumably this was towards the promised land of the sixth form proper. But every kid in the school knew it stood for 'Thick'.

Life at school changed for me with a whisper when one day, Dewi Williams, the English teacher, paused by my desk and picked up part of a short story I was working on. He read it, then leant down and put his mouth close to my ear. 'This is good. We should try to get it into the school magazine.'

A teacher had praised me.

It had been a good eight years since that had happened: in primary school when Mr Thomas asked me to go to the front and hold the paper in the guillotine while he sliced. It was the first time I had stood at the front of the class. As I gazed at the other kids watching me standing next to him, I felt more special than at any time of my life. Mr Thomas liked a good edge on the paper, so I kept my head down and concentrated on holding that paper completely still. The next week he did something he had never done before: he asked the same child to hold the paper again. And he did the same the next week and the week after that.

After four weeks of my fulfilling that role, Mr Thomas turned to my class and said, 'Robert Parsons is the best holder of guillotine paper in the whole of the class.' I have often imagined him waking one morning and thinking to himself, 'The kid must be able to do something. I know . . .'

Since holding that paper, I have been a senior partner in an eleven-office law practice, lectured across the world to thousands of lawyers, more blue-chip companies than I can recall, and even to governments. But 'Robert Parsons is the best holder of guillotine paper' still sticks in my mind. It's as if a seed of hope was planted at that moment that there may be something else out there I could achieve.

And with Dewi Williams a new seed was planted. With his encouragement I got into teacher-training college, where I studied English literature and thrived. The mysteries of trigonometry, geometry and algebra were left behind. All I had to do was read novels, plays, write poetry, learn what made kids tick and how to connect with them.

I was 21 years old. I had finished college and was about to go for my first job interview – teaching English to secondary-school children – but a few days before, I was giving a talk to a group of teenagers at church. While the kids feigned interest, a man sat at the back listening intently. John Loosemore had recently started his own law practice, but he occasionally volunteered at the youth club. When the talk was over, the class disbanded, but instead of leaving, John walked down the aisle towards me.

He reached the end of the aisle just as I had finished putting my notes away. He spoke with a drawl. 'That was a very interesting talk you gave to those kids. You're pretty good on your feet.'

I shrugged my shoulders in what I hoped was a gesture of humility, but the second I'd done it, I realised it might have smacked of arrogance. I stumbled out, 'Thanks. Arthur Tovey taught me.'

John smiled. 'Ah. I've come across Arthur. Well, he did a good job.'

'Thanks.'

John hesitated. 'You're about to become a teacher, aren't you?'

'Hopefully.'

'My father used to be a teacher.'

I've never claimed to be the sharpest tool in the shed, but I have always had a sixth sense that has rarely let me down. Something was going on here.

He went on, 'I'm sure you'll make a great teacher, but I need a trainee solicitor and I'd like you to join my practice.'

Even now as I type the words, my stomach churns. I shook my head slowly. 'I'm not even sure my qualifications are enough to get me into law and I haven't got any money to pay for college.'

'I'll pay for you to go through law school, and don't worry about the qualifications, you've got enough. You'll have to do it the long way – it'll take you five years altogether – but you'll be a solicitor at the end of it.'

I suddenly imagined becoming the kind of lawyer that took on huge corporations in the High Court and won, the sort of man who could sway juries with his rhetoric, the type with a fierce independence: in short – a fighter. One might have thought that with those images swimming in my brain, I would have given John a decisive response. The sentence that actually came out of my mouth was anything but: 'I'll have to ask my mother.'

The moment I had spoken, I wished I could pull the words back, but they hung in the air as if taunting me.

John smiled.

'And my father,' I added, as if that somehow made me look less pathetic.

'If your parents want to chat to me, I'll pop round and see them. Ring me at the office.'

I didn't trust myself to produce another speech that would impress him, so as he extended his hand towards me, I said simply, 'Thank you. I'll get back to you soon.'

I left the church and walked down the street towards my house. I had reached Mrs Webster's when the reality of what had just happened hit me. I would like to think that I was captivated by the prospect of fighting for justice for the poor and oppressed, but the truth is, as I passed the Giles', Mrs Hughes', and finally banged the knocker of our front door, all I could think about was the money. I was going to be a lawyer. We were going to have an inside toilet.

My mother was preparing the tea and my father was shaving, ready to go on the night shift. I knew my mother wouldn't be a problem. If I'd come home and said, 'They've asked me to become prime minister,' she would have wondered, 'What kept them?' But when I told my father the news, he was not impressed; in fact, he seemed downright annoyed. Perhaps that is understandable; he was coming to the end of his life as a postman. He had been with the General Post Office since he was fourteen – forty-six years in all. In all that time he had only had twelve days' absence from work due to sickness. His job mattered to him. I would sometimes see him on his rounds as I cycled back and forth to school. If it was raining, he would have his cape around his mailbag. He would rather have wet clothes than sodden letters. And now his son had a chance to become a teacher and he was thinking of throwing it away. He simply couldn't understand it.

We talked for half an hour. The discussion was only ended by my father's need to leave for work and my relaying John Loosemore's offer to call at the house and chat with my parents. My father had no desire to meet a stranger, let alone spend time discussing what he considered to be a frivolous job offer with him. He eventually agreed, but not before barking out his basic objection to the whole foolish venture: 'People like us don't become lawyers.'

* * *

When Dianne and I woke that morning, two days after Christmas, we had no idea that by the end of the day we would have taken a step that would change our lives for ever. The man at the heart of that decision was already at work in the kitchen below us. If the sound he made as he washed and stacked the crockery had any correlation with cleanliness, this kitchen was on track for a five-star hygiene rating.

Dianne turned over in bed and propped herself up on her elbow. 'We're seeing Kevin and Caroline today, aren't we?'

I said, 'Half past eleven, I think. It's on the calendar in the kitchen.'

Kevin and Caroline worked in the homeless shelter and we were pinning our hopes on them providing a way out. I lay back on the pillow, saying nothing.

She touched my arm. 'You're quiet.'

'Oh, I've got a hundred thoughts fighting for space in my brain. I was just thinking how brilliant you've been in this. I love the way you deal with Ronnie – part friend, part mother, part headmistress.'

She laughed. 'I might try the headmistress thing with you.'

'I find that prospect strangely attractive.'

She looked exasperated. 'I really like him, Rob. He's so vulnerable and what you see is what you get. I know we don't really know him – he's only lived with us for a couple of days, for goodness' sake – but part of me thinks that in some ways we've already seen the essence of him: this is how he is.'

'Ah – as opposed to the voyage of discovery that you've embarked upon in trying to uncover the many layers of my mysterious personality.'

She poked me in the ribs. 'Come on. Let's get up before he scrubs the colour out of the worktops.'

When we got downstairs the kitchen was empty, but the television was on in the living room. I popped my head around the door. Ronnie was transfixed by the children's programme the *Flower Pot Men*.

He spoke without taking his eyes off the screen. 'Kitchen's done.'

'We've seen. Thanks. You're the kitchen supremo.'

He turned towards me and smiled. 'Not bad.'

'Would you like a cup of tea? I'm doing one for Di and me.'

But Ronnie was engrossed again. With his eyes firmly on the screen, he shook his head. 'No, thanks.'

When I went back into the kitchen, Dianne was holding up two empty lager cans. 'Look what I've just spotted in the rubbish.' She handed me one of them.

I turned it over in my hand. 'Well, well.'

I passed it back to her and she put them back in the bin. 'Do you think we should ask him about them?'

I have often wondered why that scene in the kitchen with Dianne holding the cans has remained in my memory. I think it may be because it so clearly sums up many of the dilemmas we faced with Ronnie over the years. It is true that he was 30 years old and that it was only two cans of lager, so hardly wild living. Nevertheless, it felt as if there was a subterfuge about it – and that surprised us.

'He didn't tell us he'd bought them,' I said. 'Or offer to share them.'

Dianne's forehead wrinkled. 'Mmm. Just as we didn't tell him we'd bought the bottle of red or offer to share it.'

'That's different. He—'

Dianne held up her hands. 'Just kidding. Yes, it is different. Why don't you ask him about it?'

'Fine.'

Dianne laughed out loud. 'You're beginning to sound like him.'

I went into the living room to see Ronnie watching Bill and Ben dancing around a large weed. 'Hey, Ronnie.'

No response.

'Ronnie!'

He turned reluctantly to face me.

I asked, 'Did you have a drink last night?'

His face fell. 'I didn't mean to.'

'What do you mean, you didn't mean to?'

'I don't know. I just didn't, that's all.'

'When did you buy the cans?'

'When I went to the shop to get Di's chocolate.'

'When did you drink them?'

'In bed last night.'

'Why didn't you drink them with us?'

Ronnie shook his head, as if impatient with himself for not being able to give a convincing answer. 'I just didn't, that's all.'

I turned the television off and sat in a chair opposite him. 'Ronnie, it's fine for you to have a couple of beers now and again. We just don't want you to do it secretly.'

He shook his head in place of words. But eventually he spoke slowly. 'I'll be gone soon anyway.'

'Have you got any more cans in your room?'

'Only two.'

'Where are they?'

'In my bottom drawer.'

'Bring them down and put them in the fridge.'

He got up and made his way to the door, his shoulders slumped. 'I'm always getting things wrong.'

I remember a doctor telling Dianne and I that parents so often feel guilty as to whether or not they are doing a good job of raising their children. She said, 'Guilt is an occupational hazard of having kids.' I think I felt something of that guilt just then with Ronnie. Was I right to have mentioned it? Did I deal with it badly? What was the big deal anyway?

With the benefit of many years of hindsight I know what the big deal was. There is another emotion that comes with the role of parenthood: fear. And it was fear I felt that day. Fear that the two innocent, battered cans nestling underneath the discarded sleeve of the lasagne carton were actually the faintest sound of a distant warning bell.

* * *

When we got to the homeless shelter the place was alive with the sound of frying and the smell of onions cooking. Behind the kitchen hatch, Kevin, Caroline and two other helpers were serving food to a haphazard queue, and around the tables people sat eating – some still wearing their overcoats and hats.

Kevin put down his ladle and shouted across at us. 'We're just about done here.' He turned to a woman working alongside him. 'Sally, will you finish up? Caroline and I need to speak with these folks. We'll be in the office if you need us.'

The 'office' was a room no more than eight feet square with packets of soup, pasta and toilet rolls piled up against the walls. Kevin was mid-forties, tall and with a ponytail that made him by far the coolest volunteer youth leader at our church. Caroline was in her early twenties with a Cambridge First in psychology and was working at the shelter while doing her master's.

We sat on old dining chairs and Kevin spoke as he plugged in the kettle and got some mugs out of a cupboard. 'Tea or coffee?' I'd had the pleasure of the shelter's coffee before, so joined the others with tea. As Kevin opened a carton of milk, he smiled. 'I understand you two are trying to put us out of business.'

Dianne laughed. 'Hardly. It's good of you both to see us. We're in way above our heads.'

Caroline smiled. 'Was that Ronnie with you at the carol service – who helped find Mike's car keys?'

I said, 'It was indeed. Although I have to say, it was made easier by the fact that it was Ronnie who had hidden them in the first place.'

Kevin chuckled, 'Sounds like a couple of the characters we have with us here. Now, how can we help?'

Dianne shifted a little on her chair. 'Just some advice, really. We don't know Ronnie very well. Rob used to know him a bit when they were kids – from Sunday school.' She spoke quickly. 'But he was in care, and I think he has some learning challenges. He just turned up on our doorstep on Christmas Eve and he's still with us.'

'That's amazing,' said Caroline.

Dianne said, 'I'm not so sure. I mean, he's a lovely man . . .'

She hesitated and looked across at me, '. . . and we really want to help him. But how can we do that?'

'Presumably he has no home of his own or a job?' Kevin asked.

I said, 'All his possessions were in a black sack.'

'And you say he has some learning difficulties?'

Dianne answered. 'When we asked him which school he attended, he said it was called the Backward School.'

Kevin said, 'That's really sad, isn't it? Well, look, we could find him a bed here for a night or two, but that doesn't really help in the long term. The problem is, to find decent accommodation he really needs to be in some kind of employment.' Kevin took a pen out of his pocket and reached across a desk to get a sticky note. He spoke as he wrote. 'Here's the name of a contact at the Jobcentre. He's pretty sympathetic to our kind of guys.' He handed it to me. 'The only problem is that even with all the good will in the world, to get a job, you need an address. But to get an address, you need money – and that normally means a job. Ronnie's in the Catch-22 situation that affects most of the people here.'

Caroline said, 'And the care-home thing is massive. Almost a quarter of the people here have been in care, and many seem to never recover from the experience. Their self-esteem and confidence have gone through the floor. They believe they'll fail at anything they try.'

Dianne was thoughtful. When she spoke, it was almost a syllable at a time. 'What if we could keep him with us while he tried to get a job?'

Kevin breathed in deeply and his shoulders lifted. He let the air out in a huge puff. 'Well, that would be brilliant for Ronnie, but there's no knowing how long that would take, and even if he does get a job, how long he would stay in it.'

Dianne looked at me, and then back at Kevin as she said, 'But it would give him a chance, wouldn't it?'

'Yes,' Kevin said. 'It would give him a chance.'

John Loosemore.

Chapter 7

Ronnie Gets a Job

The second my father had left for work, I walked to the telephone kiosk on the corner of the next street and called the number John had given me. Even as I put my finger in the dial, I felt an imposter.

The phone rang and rang, then there was a brusque, 'John Loosemore.'

I considered hanging up, but I managed to say quietly, 'Hello, John. It's me – Robert. We talked at the church.'

His voice brightened. 'Oh, hi Rob – that was quick.'

Was I too fast in my response? Should I have left it a week or so? I pressed on anyway. 'I spoke with my mother and father, and they'd really like to talk with you about your kind offer.' Even as I mouthed the words, it struck me that I was already trying to sound like a solicitor.

'Great,' said John, 'let me check my diary.' As I waited, I made a mental note to get myself a diary. He was soon back with a date. I thanked him, said goodbye, and put the receiver down gently, as if out of respect. As I turned to leave the telephone kiosk, there was a woman waiting to use the phone. I opened the door, stepped out and said, 'Sorry to have kept you – business.' She smiled as if to say, 'What business, love? Lost your homework?'

When I got home, my mother was sat at the kitchen table. I had hardly got through the door before she said, 'What did he say?'

'He's coming next Sunday afternoon at four o'clock.'

She looked pleased at first but quickly became agitated. She started counting on her fingers, looked up at me and said, 'That's good. Your father will be on night shift. He'll be here then.' She stood, smoothed the front of her apron, lifted her shoulders, exhaled loudly and said, 'Well, we'd better get ready for him.'

'Mum, it's a week away.'

'It will go quickly. There's a lot to be done. I'll start on the front room.'

* * *

Our best room, the one kept for the visitors which we never had, was about to step into its moment of destiny. The three-piece suite, the lace chair-backs that adorned it and the aspidistra in the corner were to form a stage set onto which would stride a handsome, six-foot-tall, jet-black-haired lawyer who would arrive in an Alfa Romeo. He would be interviewed by an office cleaner and a five-foot-six postman who had recently bought himself a second-hand girl's bicycle because it was going cheap.

Just as when a town or village prepares for a visit from royalty and potholes are repaired, lampposts painted, and brown patches of grass sprayed green, so it was in the seven days before the visit. My mother began at the front of the house: the little forecourt was weeded and the brass knocker polished, then polished again. She then moved into the passageway through which John would have to walk to reach the best room. My father's bicycle was carried to an upstairs bedroom lest the lawyer bang his shin on the pedals as he passed through; the floor tiles were scrubbed and the selection of overcoats that hung on hooks thinned so that only our newest ones were on display. The best room itself was subjected to a tsunami of cleaning, disinfecting and endless titivating, plumping and turning over of cushions. But it was not until the evening before D-Day that a realisation hit my mother that caused her to pale. We were watching *Dad's Army* when she suddenly put down her knitting and said, 'What if he wants to go to the toilet?'

Our toilet was in a lean-to in the garden. We had got used to the cold in the winter, the roughness of the *South Wales Echo* on our backsides, and sitting at the right angle to avoid our buttocks being pinched by the crack down the centre of the wooden seat. But how would John Loosemore negotiate these challenges? The remedial works required seemed impossible to carry out in so short a time. But by the time he arrived less than twenty-four hours later, the toilet door and walls had had a fresh coat of paint and a new seat was fitted. And for the first time in the history of our family, that bastion of journalism, the *South Wales Echo*, was discarded and replaced by something worthy of the posterior of a member of the legal profession: real toilet paper.

* * *

It was a rainy Sunday afternoon when John came to our house. It's fair to say that Mrs Webster's door curtain, Mrs Coulter's railings and even Mr Sullivan's Austin A35 couldn't compete with the Alfa Romeo parked outside our front door. We'd hit the street top spot – if only for an hour.

As my mother ushered John into the front room, she had on her best dress and the smell of polish was in the air. John was offered tea and a plate with eight of my mother's Welsh cakes arranged in a circle. My father entered the room wearing his suit with a collar and tie. My mother looked surprisingly comfortable, but not my father. It is only in thinking back on that day that I realise what a major effort he made in seeing John. For the man who ran upstairs when the coalmen came, this was not a simple task. I think what may have made it possible for him to even contemplate doing it was that although John was much younger than him, he represented an authority figure, and my father felt comfortable with structure. He believed his place was to be polite, deferential even. What was more surprising was that as the conversation developed, his boldness in asking probing questions grew. At one stage he turned to me and said, 'What about becoming a teacher?'

I hesitated. I knew how secretly pleased my father was that

I had achieved that qualification. 'Dad, I work with kids a lot in the youth club – most nights a week, actually. I'm not going to lose that connection. And perhaps I could go back to teaching if it doesn't work out with John. But I think I'd like to give it a try.'

Finally, with only two Welsh cakes left on the plate (which my mother thought a respectable result), the meeting came to an end. John stood, shook my father's hand, kissed my mother on the cheek and said he very much hoped that I would join his practice.

The second the front door closed, my mother was effusive. 'What a lovely man. And what a wonderful opportunity.'

My father didn't say much. I have never seen him, before or since, as he looked that afternoon. He seemed defeated, but willingly so. He was silent for a long time and then he muttered, 'A very nice chap.'

Just four words, but all three of us knew that in that brief phrase was implied consent. John Loosemore had passed the interview. I was going to be a lawyer.

I looked across at my mother. Her excitement had died down and she was staring at the aspidistra. 'What are you thinking, Mum?'

She shook herself out of her musing. 'Oh, nothing really, love.' She hesitated and smiled at me. 'He didn't use the toilet, did he?'

*　*　*

When we got back from the homeless centre, Ronnie was out. We walked into the kitchen and as Dianne sat at the table, I put the kettle on. I went to get a couple of mugs out of the cupboard, but it was filled with packets of cereal standing like soldiers, end to end in a line.

'Who moved the crockery?' I began opening cupboard doors and banging them shut.

Dianne lifted an eyebrow. 'Well, let me see? It wasn't me, and presumably, as you can't find it, it wasn't you? Now who does that leave?'

I slammed another door shut. 'Don't be funny. He'll drive us crazy.'

'Calm down. He's moved a couple of cups and plates – nobody's died. They're in the cupboard in the dresser. I found them this morning when I was hunting for the toaster.'

'You'll have to talk to him.'

'*I'll* have to talk to him?'

'We'll have to talk to him.'

Dianne started giggling and I joined in. Neither of us knew exactly what we were laughing at, but it didn't matter. We were now laughing at laughing, and it got increasingly noisy, until Dianne said, 'Stop, or I'm going to be sick.'

I put my arm around her. 'What are we going to do?'

She kissed the back of my hand. 'Do you realise how many times we've said that in the last three days?' Of course, neither of us knew that those six words would become a mantra for us in our life with Ronnie. I got two mugs out of their new resting place and tossed a tea bag in each. As I poured on the boiling water I said, 'What do you think about the Jobcentre?'

Dianne giggled again. 'By the way, the milk is in the chest of drawers on the landing.' As I threw my arms in the air, she added quickly, 'Just joking.'

'Don't start us off again,' I said. 'Seriously – what do you think?'

'I think it's a good idea. But one of us will have to go with him. I'm back in work tomorrow, but if we can get him an appointment, can you go with him?'

I shrugged my shoulders. 'I've got the day off, so I suppose so. But what about that business of his needing a permanent address?'

I have scoured my memory to ascertain the moment that the line was crossed: the point at which, not so much that there was no going back, but that it all moved onto another level. The conversation in the kitchen that day may well be that moment. The decision was so fast and open-ended, neither of us paused to consider an important question: if Ronnie's ability to get and keep a job depended on his being able to live with us, how long would he have to stay?

'Why don't we suggest he stay for a couple of weeks to help him get a job, then find somewhere to live?'

I never got to answer. There was a knock at the front door. I walked towards the hall still talking over my shoulder. 'How can he go out when he hasn't got a key? He could be on the street all day.'

Dianne shouted after me. 'I think he's used to that.'

I let Ronnie in and he followed me into the kitchen clutching a plastic Co-op bag. Before Dianne could say a word, he reached into it, took out a giant-sized bar of Cadbury's chocolate and thrust it into her face.

She put a hand up. 'Steady on, Ronnie. You nearly had my eye out with that.'

He hunched his shoulders. 'Sorry.'

Dianne smiled. 'It's really kind of you, but you mustn't buy me any more. I haven't finished the last bar.'

'No problem,' said Ronnie and reaching into the bag again, he pulled out a can and held it out to me. 'And this is for you.'

It was a cold can of Coke. 'Wow! Thanks, Ronnie.'

'And I've got two for myself. No more beers.'

'You can have a beer, Ronnie. Just don't do it secretly.'

'Do you like the kitchen?'

Dianne dived in. 'Yes, Ronnie. You've made it look lovely.'

I coughed. 'You've done a great job on it, Ronnie. But we've got used to things in certain cupboards, so it may be best to keep them there.'

He looked as if I had lanced his soul.

Dianne glared at me. 'Let's leave the stuff where Ronnie has put it for now. We might get to like it there.' She patted the chair next to her. 'Sit down. We've got a bit of news for you.'

He sat reluctantly.

'We've been chatting to some people we know,' I said. 'They've got a contact at the Jobcentre and said if we make an appointment, they'll try to find you a job. What do you think?'

Ronnie's face brightened. 'I've had a job.'

'What job did you have?'

Ronnie screwed up his eyes and tilted his head to one side as if the task of recalling his past employment was taking some effort. After a few moments he spoke. 'In a warehouse.'

'What did you do there?' Dianne coaxed.

Ronnie's eyes screwed up again. 'Just things. That's all.'

I sat down next to him. 'Why did you leave?'

He spoke slowly as if it hurt him to say the words. 'They said a bad thing about me.'

'What did they say, Ronnie?'

'They said that I smelled.'

I fiddled with the can of Coke. 'Where were you living then?'

'Just here and there.'

Dianne touched Ronnie on the arm. 'It's hard to smell good when you haven't got anywhere proper to wash. You should have smelt Rob before I met him.'

Ronnie looked up. 'Rob wouldn't smell.'

Dianne laughed. 'You really are like his mother, Ronnie. She thinks he's perfect. Now is it OK if Rob makes an appointment for you to go to the Jobcentre? If they can see you tomorrow, he's going to go with you.'

Ronnie lifted his shoulders. 'Fine.'

'And one more thing. We'd like you to stay with us for a couple of weeks until you get settled in your new job.'

'Fine.'

* * *

The Jobcentre was crowded, the red plastic chairs filled with people waiting for their name to be called. Ronnie and I had to sit on opposite sides of the room. As I sat, I looked across at him; he was twisting a piece of paper over and over in his hand and glancing around as if at any moment an attack might come. He looked as if he might cry.

I left my seat and went to stand next to him. 'You OK, Ronnie?'

He looked up at me. 'Bit nervous.'

'Nothing to be nervous about. It's just a chat, and I'll be with you.'

'I'm not good at meetings.'

'It's not a meeting, Ronnie. Just a chat about jobs.'

He lowered his head and shook it, as though this had been the worst decision of his life.

The contact that Kevin had given us was on holiday, but after a while Ronnie's name was called. We made our way towards a nearby cubicle where a woman in her mid-fifties with peroxide-blonde hair and bright, rouged cheeks over-filled an office chair. A cigarette played at the corner of her lips. She looked up at Ronnie and waved a nicotine-stained finger towards the single chair in front of her desk. I grabbed one of the red chairs from the waiting room and placed it next to his. She looked at me as though I had defecated on her Christmas pudding. 'And who are you?'

'I'm a friend of Ronnie's.'

'I'm a friend of Ronnie's,' she mimicked. 'And what do you do?'

In just thirty seconds this woman had annoyed me out of all proportion. I toyed with the idea of telling her to mind her own business, but I knew there was a lot more mileage in a different answer. 'I'm a solicitor. Ronnie lives with us.'

I was dressed in faded jeans, an open-necked shirt and a much-loved Puffa jacket that had long since passed the point of risking consignment to a charity shop. She looked at Ronnie then back at me, the cigarette dangling precariously. The way she chewed her mouth, I half-expected her to retort, 'And I'm Diana Dors,' but to press home the advantage, I took a business card out of my wallet and slid it across the desk towards her. She picked it up, studied it and placed it carefully in her desk drawer as if she might need it someday. She smiled at Ronnie.

'Now. How can I help you, Mr Lockwood?'

And suddenly, Ronnie twisted in his chair like he was 8 years old, looking as terrified as if he had wet the bed and Mr Anderson was coming for him; a mouse transfixed again before the eyes of the falcon. He said nothing.

'Ronnie's a little nervous,' I explained.

Transmorphing from the Wicked Queen to Snow White, the woman smiled sweetly. 'Nothing to be nervous about, Mr Lockwood. I'm here to help you. Now what do you like to do?'

'I like to tidy things.'

'Well, that's good. Do you have any qualifications?'

Ronnie shook his head.

'What school did you go to?'

Ronnie seemed pleased to know an answer. 'The Backward School.'

Snow White smiled, but underneath the veneer it was obvious that the Wicked Queen was losing patience. She stared at Ronnie and said, 'I think I can help.' She pulled a dog-eared directory from her drawer and began thumbing through it. 'I'm looking for the number of the City Cleansing Department. I've had three calls from them this week. They're desperate.'

I shot her a look that was designed to explode on impact. It worked.

'What I mean, Mr Lockwood, is that I think this would be a very good fit for somebody who likes tidying things.'

She was on the call less than a minute. When she put the phone down, she beamed at Ronnie, scribbled on a scrap of paper, and passed it to him. 'Ask for Brian Clarkson. They'll try you out for a week. Would you like a copy of it, Mr . . .' She opened her top drawer and retrieved my business card. She examined it as if it were a holy relic. '. . . Parsons. Of course. Would you like a copy, Mr Parsons?'

* * *

As soon as Dianne came in from work she asked, 'Well, boys, how was the job hunt?'

Ronnie beamed at her. 'I've got a job.'

'Wow, Ronnie, that's amazing! What is it?'

Ronnie took a piece of paper out of his pocket and began to laboriously read what was written on it before handing it to me. 'You read it. You're brainier than me.'

'Ronnie is going to be . . .' I held the paper in the air, '. . . a waste operative.'

Dianne clapped. 'That sounds very important. We are very proud of you Ronnie. We must celebrate later. But now I'm gasping for a cup of tea; put the kettle on, Rob.'

Before I could move, Ronnie stood and headed for the kitchen. 'I'll do it.'

Dianne closed the living-room door and, raising her hands to the air, wrinkled her forehead and mouthed silently, 'What's a waste operative?'

I walked across and whispered in her ear, 'He's going to be a dustman.'

* * *

On the following Sunday the three of us went to church together. Before the start of the service, people were mingling in the foyer, drinking coffee together. We introduced our friend Andrew to Ronnie. Andrew is a firefighter and went on to tell us about a bad house fire he'd been called to the day before. Ronnie listened intently, then suddenly broke in with, 'I was in a fire once.'

'When was that?' Andrew asked.

'When I was in the homes.'

'What happened?'

'Some boys did a bad thing.'

'What did they do?' Andrew probed.

'They got grounded for drinking in the dormitory, so they set fire to one of the beds.'

Andrew said. 'Was it a bad fire?'

'Not really. Mr Beeston came in and put it out.'

'What happened to the boys?' I asked.

He shrugged. 'They were put on punishment.'

'What kind?'

I waited for Ronnie to tell us, but as Mike and Jean Shaw came in, he said, 'Just stuff, that's all,' and turned away from us.

Ronnie went over to Mike and put his arm around him. 'I hope I didn't offend you?'

Mike looked puzzled. 'Hi, Ronnie. How could you have offended me?'

Ronnie shook his head impatiently, 'You know, with what I did.'

'What did you do, Ronnie?'

'You know, with the car keys.'

'You didn't offend me, Ronnie. You found them for us.'

'Di told me off when we got home.'

'Why did she tell you off?'

'Because it was me who hid them.'

A smile played on Mike's lips. 'Well, well.'

'I was just joking, mind. No offence.'

Mike patted Ronnie's back. 'Well, you certainly fooled us. And no offence taken at all.'

'I've been in a fire,' Ronnie blurted.

The smile fell from Mike. 'When was that?'

'When I was nine.'

'When you were . . .'

But Ronnie had moved on.

As Dianne and I continued to talk with Andrew, we were joined by Chris, who taught at a local university. Chris had his back to Ronnie as he chatted with us. Suddenly I glimpsed Ronnie coming up behind him. My memory of what happened next is conflicting: on the one hand it happened very quickly, and yet in my mind's eye the whole thing played out in slow motion. It began in an innocent, if not socially acceptable, way. Ronnie put his hands over Chris's shoulders and covered Chris's eyes. 'Guess who?'

Not many people sandbagged the professor in church that way, and connecting the perpetrator with Dianne and me, he said, 'Now, let me see . . . Ronnie?' If he thought that his powers of deduction would impress, he was wrong. Ronnie liked to tease, to enjoy brief moments of control, and Chris was not playing the game. He paid the price for that. The next moment, Ronnie had him in a headlock and was rubbing the top of his balding pate with his knuckles. I froze, but Dianne yelled and at the same time leapt forward. She managed to extricate the academic from Ronnie's grasp and, in the tone of a mother who has just caught her child flicking bogies at other shoppers in Asda, yelled, 'Ronnie! That's not nice.'

Her intervention and admonition seemed not to bother Ronnie. Instead, he put an arm around Chris, who was by now looking exceedingly nervous, and said, 'He knows I'm joking. Don't you?'

'Yes,' said the professor.

A huge smile broke out on Ronnie's face. Chris looked as though he had never been so glad to get the right answer to a question in his life.

'There we are,' said Ronnie, ruffling Chris's hair. 'We're friends.'

Dianne looked at Ronnie as though, any minute, judgement could be unleashed. We were all saved by Andrew announcing, 'Service is about to start.' As we trooped into the main hall, Ronnie was in the lead. I glanced back at Chris. He was rubbing his head.

It was many years later that a psychologist explained to us that Ronnie's habit of hiding keys, handbags and coats was an effort to exercise some control in a life that had almost none, and tapping people on the shoulder and yelling, 'Caught you,' when they turned around (as if such a reaction was solely down to Ronnie's cleverness), was his way of trying to connect; even the placing of various heads in the vice-like grip of his arms (he was exceptionally strong) was his cry for touch.

The service had just started and James, the church leader, was working his way through announcements for the week to come. As the notices were drawing to an end, he said, 'We have a special guest with us today – Ronnie Lockwood. Ronnie is going to be living with Rob and Di for a while, so hopefully we'll be seeing a lot of him. Let's give him a massive welcome.' James had obviously tipped a few people off, because applause swept through the place as though it was the Last Night of the Proms. I whispered to Ronnie, 'Give people a wave.'

Ronnie lifted his hand in a brief gesture of acknowledgement. I couldn't work out whether this was the worst moment of his life or so special he never wanted it to end. When the clapping had finished, he turned to me and in a whisper you could hear three rows back, said, 'I'm famous, I am.'

When we were about to head for home, Ronnie was nowhere to be seen. I left Dianne to look for him and bumped into James. 'Thanks for doing that for Ronnie earlier. It will have meant a lot to him. He hasn't had much of that in his life.'

James smiled. 'The look on his face as we were clapping was worth it all.'

'You haven't seen him around, have you?'

James pointed towards the main hall. 'He's in there helping put the chairs away. And I can tell you he's pretty good at it. I've got a couple of the kids from the youth club trying to keep up with him.'

When Ronnie eventually appeared, he was wearing a smile so wide it belonged on a sweatshirt. 'Matthew and Connor and me had a race to see who could stack most chairs away the fastest.'

'Well – who won?' Dianne asked.

'I did. I beat both of them. And I've got some news for you.'

I moved us towards the exit. 'Tell us as we walk, Ronnie. They're waiting to lock up.'

Ronnie practically pushed us through the doors and started speaking the second we were outside. 'James has asked me to join the chair team. I have to be here on Sunday at ten o'clock to put them out and then help put them away afterwards.'

I smiled at him. At least for now, the hunched figure who had knocked at our door in the darkness just a few days before was gone. He was more erect and looked healthier and more confident. Over the years that he lived with us, we noticed that whether it was household tasks like tidying the kitchen, gifts at birthdays and Christmas, or volunteering in the church, like helping with the chairs, Ronnie came alive when he had the opportunity to give. I think that when he gave, he felt special, and needed; for somebody with a past like his, that was like rain in the desert.

Young love.

Chapter 8

Shoe Paint

Arthur was in his element running the Wednesday-night course, and I'm pretty sure he thought that my almost perfect attendance record was due to my deep spirituality. Maybe he was right, but there was also a much baser urge, the evidence of which emerged at Christmas in 1964; I was 16 years old. The carol service was a highlight in the chapel's calendar, but each year there were several older members who were too infirm to attend. For these select few there was a treat in store (although some had been heard to describe it as a punishment for not making enough effort to get to the service): kids from the youth club would sing outside their homes. On this particular Christmas, Arthur decided his discussion group would join in to bolster the choir numbers.

Fifteen of us met outside the church at 7.30 p.m. It had snowed during the afternoon, and although it had stopped, there was enough of a veneer of white to make even the drab grey stone and roof of the Gospel Hall look Christmassy. And it was cold; the road alongside us glistened where the snow had melted and frozen, as if somebody had carelessly scattered diamonds across its tarmac.

Dianne isn't tall – just five feet one inch – but I spotted her standing at the back of the group straight away. She had on a long black overcoat, a red scarf, and her blonde hair was tucked into a white fur bonnet. I was pretty sure that whatever falling in love was, I was doing it, but I just wasn't sure what she thought of me. Any hint of a romantic spark would have had to have occurred either over table tennis, or perhaps on the occasion when Arthur and Margaret were out of the room and the four of us had discussed whether the end of the world was likely to happen before any of us had had sex.

And I wasn't exactly experienced in the art of the amorous. The only girl I had ever dated was Lesley Gordon, for whom I saved my pocket money and taken to a Craig Douglas concert at Cardiff's New Theatre when I was twelve. It didn't go well, but that may have had something to do with the fact that I was so nervous that I asked my friend Roger Simons to come as well.

But now I was in love. I knew it for certain when Arthur was in the middle of a discourse as to whether movies were out of bounds for the righteous (as another church leader had so aptly put it: 'It's not called a *sin*-ema for nothing'). Dianne had curled her slim frame into one of the armchairs and was looking intently at him as he spoke. As I gazed at her, my sole desire was to entice her into the back seat of a cinema as soon as possible.

But now it was time for carolling and Arthur was delayed. He worked as an assistant in a technical college and had to work late. As we milled around, stamping our feet against the cold, I worked my way nonchalantly towards the back of the group – and the desire of my heart.

When he arrived, Arthur seemed somewhat agitated and although he knew that we were joining in with the youth-club kids, he seemed thrown by their presence – as if the Manchester United bus had been invaded by the Leyton Orient second team. With a solemn face, and obviously cognisant of the evils that lay before a group of young carollers, he whispered to us as we set off, 'Stay together.'

* * *

The standard of our singing wasn't high, and with only two torches between us (the third had given up at the first house), we struggled to read the carol sheets. But we were fast movers and within an hour we had already tormented four old couples on Arthur's list.

As we walked, it began to snow again, but we continued through the streets, ticking off the houses until we finally came to our last engagement; a few more carols and we'd be finished. As we assembled in the front garden of Mr and Mrs Prothero's semi-detached, our spirits were high as we began 'Hark the Herald Angels Sing'.

Entertaining the old people could be dispiriting, as they

rarely showed themselves. Once in a while they would brave the cold to stand briefly at their front door, but more often it was only the twitch of a curtain that assured us that we weren't performing to ourselves. But this was not the case at the Prothero's. We were only just coming to the end of the first verse when Arthur pointed upwards into the darkness and shouted, 'Look – the upstairs window on the left. They're waving at us.'

The prospect of audience appreciation seemed to seize the group with tremendous excitement and we all shuffled backwards to get a better look. And that's when it happened: just as we reached the line 'Born to raise the sons of earth', Brian Peters, who was standing next to Dianne and I, stepped into the fishpond. At first it was just his left foot, but then, in struggling, he lost his balance and his right foot went in as well. There was no real danger to him – he was a lanky teenager and the pond was only four feet deep at most – but he yelled and thrashed about as though he had fallen out of a plane over the Atlantic.

Arthur, who was at the front of the group, at first thought the rumpus was due to some troublemakers from the youth club messing about and showing a grave disrespect to both angels and the Protheros. 'Quiet back there.' It didn't take long for some kids in a burst of *Schadenfreude* to break the news to him of Brian's plight. As Arthur pushed his way towards the back of the group, Mrs Prothero, seemingly imagining that Brian was enjoying his dip, opened the window and yelled, 'Get out of our pond!'

And it was in the middle of the mayhem that the baser urge of which I spoke earlier emerged. Dianne was standing next to me and now I saw my chance. Ostensibly to save her from the same fate as our fellow choir member, I grabbed her hand. This was an empty gesture: the pool was small and with both the fish and Brian Peters in it, there was no room at all for further visitors. She looked a little surprised but then smiled at me. By the time Brian was safe and sat turning his shoes upside down, dispelling the contents of the Prothero's pond, we had not let go of each other.

Dianne's smile, the fact that we were still holding hands, the almost complete darkness, and the mayhem distracting the group filled me with confidence. I turned towards her. She had snowflakes on her face which was framed by her fur bonnet. I leant forward and kissed her. Her lips felt hot against the snow. As my eyes were closed in bliss, I heard a voice somewhere near me say, 'Brian's killed a fish.'

It is to Arthur's credit that even in the midst of the pandemonium, he picked up that something was occurring in the group that related more to the lusts of the flesh than harking heralding angels, and his voice rang out above the clamour: 'No kissing in the youth group!' Dianne and I quickly turned to see him standing with his arms folded and shaking his head. Even the Protheros moved their attention briefly away from their fishpond and towards us. We let go of each other's hands as though we'd been caught *in flagrante delicto* in a convent and stepped away from each other.

When we got back to Arthur's house, Margaret had hot

drinks ready, but before Dianne and I could take a sip, Arthur screwed up his eyes and delivered a stern lecture, warning us how quickly things could 'lead from one thing to another'. I find it almost inexplicable, but also moving, that two people in their mid-teens allowed him to talk to them in that way. But the truth is that by now we not only respected him but loved him. And anyway, I could still sense the heat of Dianne's lips on mine, so behind my mock repentance there was an enormous smile. We dutifully listened and looked suitably penitent, but even as I sipped my hot chocolate, I hoped with all my heart that Arthur was right about one thing leading to another. I was sixteen and at last I had a girlfriend.

But the course of love was not destined to run smoothly. I knew the old saying 'Better to have loved and lost than never to have loved at all' – I just never envisaged actually *losing*.

*   *   *

The homeless centre was in a small terrace of buildings just off City Road in Cardiff. When she was a child, Dianne used to live near the top of that road and near the bottom end of it was a newly built prestigious office block, one of the first in Cardiff; a towering edifice that housed the Sun Alliance Insurance Company.

And in 1964 there was a desk in that auspicious building occupied by a 16-year-old office junior. It was her first job. She was slim, blonde, funny, and I was in love with her.

As Dianne and I had driven along City Road on our way to our meeting about Ronnie with Kevin and Caroline at the homeless centre, I had punched her softly on her leg and pointed to a grocer's shop. I said, 'Remember that corner?' She laughed. 'I do. You came crawling.' I smiled, but the truth is that she was right.

We were 21 when it happened, and we had been boyfriend and girlfriend since the night we kissed in the Prothero's front garden. Dianne was keen to get married, but I was not so sure. How would my mother cope without me around?

Dianne took it into her own hands to help me decide. She went on a week's training course to Croydon, where she met and promptly fell in love with one Phillip Bowden. When she broke the news to me that my mother could have me to herself, I was heartbroken. I cried and was sick for a solid month. In fact, my grief was so apparent that it eventually came to the attention of a man in our church called Barrie Cirel. Barrie was in his mid-thirties and owned one of the most exclusive (and expensive) clothes shops in Wales. One Sunday after church he said, 'You look down in the dumps. Call at the shop on Wednesday afternoon and we'll see if we can cheer you up a bit.'

Wednesday afternoon came and I made my way to Barrie's shop. I felt nervous. Something was going on, but I wasn't sure what. When I got there, I hung around for a few minutes looking in the windows. It all looked so classy – and there were no prices on anything. Suddenly, Barrie was at my side. 'Come on in. Let's see if we can sort you out with something.'

I walked into the most amazing shop. Ties, shirts and knitwear were laid out in colour-coordinated blocks. There were rows of trousers, jackets and suits along two long walls. Barrie walked straight over to the suits and said over his shoulder, 'I reckon you're a thirty-eight regular.' He turned to a silver-haired assistant. 'What do you think, Mr Martin?' Mr Martin looked me up and down. 'A thirty-eight for sure, Mr Barrie.'

Barrie pulled a grey jacket off a hanger and held it for me. I was so nervous, I struggled to get my arm into the sleeve, but eventually it was on. He patted the shoulders, stood back and said, 'What do you think, Mr Martin?' Mr Martin put his finger to his chin and tilted his head sideways. 'It sits well, Mr Barrie. But a little drab?'

Barrie helped me take it off and laid it on a nearby chair. 'Oh, that was just for size'; he pulled another jacket off a hanger. 'I thought this might look good on him.' They were now talking about me as if I wasn't there, but this was Wonderland and I was well down a rabbit hole, so who cared? Barrie draped the jacket across his arms. 'This has just come in. What do you think?' It was sand-coloured and had intricate stitching along the edges of the lapels. I thought it was amazing. I gulped. 'It looks great.'

Barrie held it up for me and expert as I now was, my arms slid in easily. Mr Martin beamed. 'Delightful,' he said. Barrie took the trousers off the hanger, handed them to me and said, 'The fitting room is just behind the stairs. Slip these on and then we'll have a look at the whole thing.'

I locked the fitting-room door and began to change. When I had walked into the shop, I had felt pretty smart, but now my old clothes hanging over the back of a chair looked shabby. I put the new creation on and looked in the mirror. I couldn't believe it was me in this shop and in this suit. The strange thing was, I didn't feel like an imposter. That was just as well. A couple of years later, when I joined John's law practice as a clerk, Dianne and I didn't have much money and Barrie used to give me his old suits. I have never been more grateful to be the same size as somebody.

I eased back the bolt on the fitting-room door and walked out. Barrie and Mr Martin looked at me and clapped. Barrie said, 'Do you like it?' I said, 'I love it, but—'

Barrie said, 'Let's sort the accessories.'

He walked to a bank of oblong boxes, ran his finger along them, and picked out one with a peach-coloured shirt in it. He held it against my chest. 'Perfect. Now I've got to make a quick call. Mr Martin, will you help Rob select a tie?'

*   *   *

As I was carrying my bags along the street towards my house, I was still trying to work out how much all this would have cost. Barrie had given it to me: all of it.

When I got home, I put the whole lot on to show my parents. My father said, 'Very nice, too,' but my mother was ecstatic. 'You look like Roger Moore.'

And it was as I stood in my resplendent glory in front of the fire in the living room that the problem seemed to occur to both my mother and me at the same time. We both looked down and, as one, whispered: 'Shoes.' I had on my only pair – and they were black. I couldn't afford to buy new ones. My shoulders slumped; the whole thing was ruined. And it was then that my father came into his own – as if all his life he had been waiting for this moment of destiny. He put down his paper, blew out a puff of smoke, and said two words that may well have changed my life: 'Shoe paint.'

I had never heard of shoe paint, but my mother said, 'Dad's right. They sell it in the market in town. Auntie Hilda used it for Dorothy's wedding.'

Two days later, while my father was on night shift, my mother and I painted my black shoes brown. I had to wait an hour for them to dry, but the second they did, I put on all my new clobber – suit, shirt, tie and . . . brown shoes. Perfect. But if Barrie's aim was to take my mind off Dianne, he had failed: a plan was already rolling around in my mind and I couldn't wait for the next day to try it out.

Dianne was still working for the Sun Alliance Insurance Company and still walked up City Road on her way home from work. She left the office at 5 p.m. and it took her about fifteen minutes to reach the corner of her street. I decided I would hide in a shop doorway just after five, and when I saw her coming, I would accidentally bump into her, dressed in my new suit.

No battle plan of Napoleon Bonaparte was ever considered so carefully. I was to be dressed up like a dog's dinner at five in the evening, and yet somehow have to make a meeting with Dianne seem a quirk of chance. But it worked. As if fate itself was on my side, a group of schoolkids came out of a shop just in front of her as she reached the corner and I was able to mix in with them; I practically knocked her over as our bodies clashed.

That event occurred over fifty years ago, but I can still remember what she said: 'Wow – you look good!' I resisted saying, 'And so I should. I've got about three hundred quid's worth of gear on my upper body and the best part of a tin of shoe paint on my feet.' I said, 'Oh – just off to meet someone.'

One would have thought that by now I should be able to give a better explanation for what happened next. But the truth is I can't. Perhaps it is simply that absence really does make the heart grow fonder. Dianne said, 'Next week I'm going on holiday with my parents to Cornwall for a fortnight. Roger, my brother-in-law, is coming down to bring my sister home at the end of the first week. Why don't you join us then? He'll give you a lift down and you can come back with us.' By now I was beginning to believe that my new suit had magical powers, but even I was surprised they had worked that fast. I said, 'What about Phillip Bowden?'

She said, 'Oh, I'll sort Phillip Bowden out.'

* * *

The rain was pounding on the roof of the car and the wipers were struggling to keep up. Roger and I were five miles from the Bay Caravan Park in Cornwall when I asked him if we could stop at a garage with a toilet. We pulled into an Esso station and I grabbed my suitcase and ran in. It took me just five minutes to climb into my new outfit. When I came out, Roger's mouth dropped. He said, 'You might be a bit overdressed for a caravan park.'

I didn't care if I was. I had a plan, and my new suit was part of it.

We parked the car, but we had to cross a field to get to the caravan. The rain had stopped, but it was soggy and muddy underfoot. Roger knocked on the caravan door. Dianne opened it and he went in. I stayed outside. She smiled and said, 'You look smart. Are you coming in?'

I said, 'Can we go for a walk first?'

She put her hand out of the doorway to test if it was raining and said, 'Sure. I'll just get my coat.' She shouted to her parents. 'Rob's here. Just nipping out. We won't be a minute.'

As Dianne got out of the caravan, I grabbed her hand. She didn't seem to mind, and we walked in silence for a minute or two. When we got the edge of the field, I stopped, turned towards her and said, 'Will you marry me?'

She went to reply but just before she started speaking, she looked down. I followed her gaze towards the ground; the paint was coming off my shoes. Large chunks of black were showing through.

She hesitated, looked up, smiled, and kissed me long and hard.

*   *   *

Almost a year to the day that I applied the wonder potion to my black brogues, Dianne and I were married. It was

21 August 1971 at 12 p.m. Clive Jones, my best man, had slept the previous night at our house – the first time anybody from outside our family had stayed over. When we woke, the sun was shining but there was still a chill in the air as we washed in the sink in the kitchen. I was too excited to care. Soon it would be time to get all dressed up.

In an effort to adapt to my new role in the legal world and the society with which I would be mixing, I had decided that groom, best man, ushers and close male family members should wear morning suits, but the scheme had not gone entirely as planned. When I had broken the news to my father that I was getting married, he took it pretty well, but what he did not take well was the idea that he would have to hire a special outfit.

'Why would I want to hire a suit when I've already got one?' My father did indeed have a suit. He had bought it for his own wedding in 1934 and for almost all that time, save for the occasional christening, wedding or funeral, it had hung untroubled in his wardrobe. I honestly don't know whether he was being deliberately obtuse or simply bloody-minded. But bloody-minded or not, there was no persuading him. 'Nobody is going to make me spend money so I can wear somebody else's suit when I've got one of my own.'

Neither my mother's entreaties nor Dianne's protestations that 'the photographs will look ridiculous' would shift him. My father knew his place and that place was not trying to be in a higher station in life than that to which he was born. If I thought that by the time the big day drew close he would relent, I was wrong. Our wedding album bears witness to the fact that he did not waver in his resolve. In the middle of a row of smiling men decked out like penguins, my father stands in exalted dissonance. Perhaps he thought he was stepping into the shoes of his hero, Winston Churchill; he had fought them on the beaches and won.

My father may not have been taken with the morning-suit idea, but it certainly seemed to impress the small clutch of neighbours who had gathered outside my house to watch me make the short walk to the church. I smiled, waved briefly, and with smugness dripping from my black tails, walked fifty yards and into a new life.

Dianne and I were married by a grey-haired gentleman called Alf Harker, the same man who, years before, had called at a care home in Cardiff to collect a small boy and bring him to Sunday school.

Trying to look the part.

Chapter 9

A Murder Trial

When we got back from church, all the talk over lunch was about Ronnie's new job. As she carved the chicken, Dianne looked across at him. 'You've done so well, Ronnie. We are both so proud of you.'

He gave her a huge smile. 'Not bad.'

'When do you start?'

'Next Sunday. James said I had to be there at ten o'clock.'

Dianne laughed, 'No, not your putting-out-the-chairs job. When do you start as a waste operative?'

Ronnie shrugged. 'I don't know. Rob did all of that.'

'He starts on Tuesday,' I said. 'Seven-thirty a.m. sharp.'

'Well,' said Dianne, 'I think we're all going on a little shopping trip for some new clothes tomorrow.'

Ronnie shook his head. 'I've got clothes.'

'Not clothes for a new job, you haven't,' she said firmly. 'And anyway, you'll need a nice warm coat for that kind of work.'

Ronnie's face screwed up as if he might cry. 'I haven't got money for clothes.'

I put my hand on his shoulder. 'We'll lend you the money, Ronnie. You can pay us back when you get your first paycheque.'

He wagged his finger at us. 'And I'm not just going to pay you back. I'm going to take you both out for a meal. And no arguing.'

Dianne squeezed his arm. 'What a gentleman you are. Rob could learn a few tricks from you.'

'Rob's great.'

Dianne sighed.

*   *   *

After work the next day, the three of us set off for a retail outlet on the edge of town. As we walked into the first shop, Ronnie's face shone. Without any hesitation, he wandered from rack to rack. Dianne stayed by his side. 'When did you last buy clothes?'

'I haven't bought any. In the homes they gave you clothes.'

'What about after you left?'

'I had some to take with me.'

'That was a long time ago.'

'I know. But they lasted.'

Dianne turned her head away and I took over.

'Right. First task – a warm coat. What size are you?'

Ronnie looked down. It was just another question in life that he couldn't answer.

Dianne looked him over and said, 'I think you're a medium, Ronnie.' She pulled a black quilted coat from the rack. 'This one might do?'

I took it off Dianne and held it up for him. 'Try this one on for size, sir.'

Taking off his old coat and laying it on the floor, he slipped his arms into the new one. Dianne took a pace back, looked at him and clapped. 'Perfect. I'm a style genius. You look amazing. Have a look in the mirror.'

Ronnie did up the buttons on the coat, smoothed the front with his hands and looked into the full-length mirror. He was in his new coat, flanked by two people gazing on like proud parents who were buying their child's first school uniform. It struck me that it was a reflection he had never seen before.

An hour later, Ronnie's basket was full: three shirts, two sweaters, two pairs of trousers, a pack of socks, a pair of trainers and the black coat. As Ronnie lifted each item to examine it, I whispered to Dianne, 'He's got a job as a dustman. We've kitted him out as if he's the banqueting manager at the Dorchester.'

Dianne smiled as she watched him. 'He needs new clothes for all kinds of things.'

As we joined the queue to pay, Dianne leant into me and asked, 'What about underwear?'

I turned to Ronnie and whispered, 'Have you got enough underpants?'

Ronnie didn't hesitate. 'I don't wear any.'

I mouthed to Dianne, 'He doesn't wear any.'

Her face darkened and she hissed, 'What! A grown man with no knickers? I'll keep our place in the queue. Go with him now.'

Like lambs, Ronnie and I went in search of boxers and Y-fronts; in fact, anything at all that would get us both off the hook with Dianne.

*   *   *

Back home, Dianne said, 'I'm going to put some pasta on. Will you two lay the table?'

Ronnie looked uncomfortable. 'I'll help, but I don't want anything to eat, thanks.'

Dianne looked concerned. 'Are you all right, Ronnie?'

'I'm fine. Just a bit tired. I think I'll have an early night.'

As Dianne got the meal ready, Ronnie and I cleared some books and magazines off the table and began to lay out the cutlery.

'Are you sure you're all right?' I asked.

'I'm fine. Just a bit tired that's all. Nothing wrong.'

*   *   *

I was woken on Tuesday morning by Dianne shaking me. 'Time to stir. Big day today. There's a cup of tea on your side table.'

I peered over the top of the sheet, 'What time is it?'

'Ten past six.'

I turned over and slid back under the covers, but she wasn't going to let me off. Shaking my foot as she walked past the bottom of the bed, she said, 'Come on, Rob. We said we'd help him.'

I sat up slowly in bed, reached for my tea and took a sip. 'Why ever did we do that?'

She sat next to me. 'He's been up ages and I've been fighting the shower battle. I asked him if he'd had one and he said yes, yesterday. He's in there now, but I don't think he's very happy with me.'

'I'm not very happy with you.'

'I think you should give him a lift to work. It'll make sure he gets there on time. Actually, perhaps for the first week. He can get the bus after that. You can go straight to the office, can't you?'

'I suppose so.' I took another sip. 'What's wrong with this tea?'

'It's Earl Grey – some of the stuff from that hamper we were given. I couldn't find the normal tea. Ronnie's been tidying.'

Dianne got off the bed and prodded me. 'Come on, lazybones.'

I groaned and threw back the duvet. 'Up at six, in the office an hour early, and tea like dishwater. Welcome to Tuesday. What could possibly lift my spirits? Any chance of a quickie?'

Dianne laughed as she went through the door. 'As opposed to what?'

*   *   *

When I got downstairs, Dianne and Ronnie were sat at the kitchen table. He was in his new clothes, including his overcoat. I was going to make a quip about his being a little overdressed for breakfast, but seeing how sombre he looked, thought better of it.

We ate breakfast in silence and then he said, 'I'm not going to work today.'

We both looked up from our cereal.

'Why?' Dianne asked.

He shook his head but said nothing.

I said, 'Ronnie?'

He looked lost. 'I'm just not going to, that's all.'

I was about to yell, but Dianne got in first. 'I'm sad about that, Ronnie.'

Ronnie took a quick intake of breath and his shoulders fell, his face to the table. When he spoke, his voice was flat. 'I'll go.'

The hard work done, I jumped in. 'You'll be a brilliant waste operative, Ronnie.'

'A what?'

'You'll be a brilliant dustman. You're amazing at tidying things.'

'Not bad.'

'And Rob's going to take you to work all this week,' Dianne said.

Ronnie got up from the table. 'I'm going to my room for a bit.'

'See you down here in ten minutes?' I said.

'Fine.'

When he had closed the kitchen door, Dianne whispered, 'This is really hard.'

I took a piece of toast off her plate and bit into it. 'It's not surprising. He feels as if he's failed at everything he's ever done. Why should this be an exception?'

'Because he's got us now,' Dianne said.

'But he doesn't really know that does he? So many people have let him down.'

'Well, we won't.'

I got up and put my arms around her. 'You're attractive when you're feisty. Are you absolutely sure we haven't got time for—'

Dianne grabbed her toast back. 'Absolutely sure.'

*   *   *

Ronnie was back downstairs before the ten minutes was up. 'Leave the dishes. I'll do them when I get home tonight.'

Dianne left the table and walked towards him. She put her hands on his shoulders, straightened his overcoat and patted it. 'No, I'll do them after you and Rob are gone. You'll be tired when you get in.'

'Not me. I'm strong, I am.'

Dianne went to the worktop and picked up a small plastic box. 'I've done you a couple of sandwiches for your lunch, and there's a chocolate bar and a banana in there.'

He took the box. 'Thank you.' He turned and walked out of the kitchen, his shoulders hunched as he made his way along the hall to the front door.

Dianne ran after him. 'Hey – tell me all about it when you come home?'

He smiled knowingly. 'I'll be fine.'

It was still dark as Ronnie and I walked to the car together. I pulled the collar of my coat up against the wind and glanced at my watch: 06:55. It was only a three-mile journey to the depot and at this time of the morning there'd be almost no traffic; we were going to be early.

Ronnie didn't speak for the whole of the ten-minute trip, just sat staring straight out of the windscreen, his face pale. I pulled into a lay-by just short of the entrance.

'OK, Ronnie. We'll see you tonight. All the best. You'll be brilliant.' As he opened the door to get out, I asked, 'Can you remember the name of the man you have to ask for?'

His forehead wrinkled as he leant his head to one side. 'Mr Clarke?'

'No, Ronnie, it's Mr Clark*son*.'

'I'll be fine,' he said, getting out and closing the door.

I pulled forward so I could watch him walk up the path into the yard. He made his way towards some low, flat-roofed buildings where a group of men stood talking and laughing. As he went towards them, dragging his feet, he looked out of place – isolated. The phrase 'dead man walking' came to mind. I suddenly opened the car door and ran after him.

'Hey, Ronnie!' Both Ronnie and the men turned at the sound of my voice. 'I forgot to give you this.' I pressed a key into his hand. 'This is the key to your house. We'll see you tonight.'

I went back to my car, got in and started the engine. As I drove away, I started to cry.

* * *

I had just qualified as a solicitor and had been with John Loosemore for five years. I was a full hour early getting to the office, but John's car was already in his parking bay. He had begun his legal practice in a room in his parents' house, and had moved to this city-centre block shortly after that. I parked my car next to his and unlocked the outer door that led to the hallway. His office was on the first floor, and I could hear him on the phone as I climbed the stairs. I was making my way towards the kitchen, when I thought that I might as well get some credit for turning up so early and turned towards John's room.

As I did so, he came bursting out of the door. 'We've got a murder. I'm going to the police station. Come on. I'll tell you about it in the car.'

*   *   *

From the day when I was twenty-one and watched open-mouthed as John roared up the street and parked outside the Gospel Hall in a brand-new Alfa Romeo, he had never disappointed when it came to cars. His current one was a red Jaguar XJ6. To say it was fuel-greedy would be to state the obvious, but to feed that greed, it had two huge fuel tanks on either side at the back. He once asked me to fill it up with petrol for him. The man behind me in the queue at the pumps was already impatient with the amount of fuel I was putting in the one tank, but when that was full and I made my way around the boot to start on the other one, he had rolled down his window, leant out and shouted, 'What have you got there, son – a jumbo jet?'

John had the engine started even before my backside had hit the passenger seat. Over the years I have travelled in his car many times and, despite my hands often gripping my thighs as he weaved, he was never involved in an accident. He drove fast, swerving between lanes if he saw the slightest advantage in a line of cars alongside him.

I spoke as he reluctantly braked at a red light. 'What's happening?'

He didn't take his eyes off the traffic signals. 'I'm duty solicitor and I got a call from the station about thirty minutes ago. A woman has stabbed her husband. He died in the ambulance on the way to hospital.'

'Wow!' I puffed under my breath. I stared out of the window as we sped along the high street, watching people going about their everyday lives. I actually pinched myself.

John swerved to avoid a cyclist and turned to me. 'You're quiet.'

'I was just thinking that an hour ago I was eating cornflakes and now I'm on my way to meet a murderer.'

'No, you're not,' said John.

'I'm not what?'

'You're not on your way to meet a murderer.'

'But you said that she had stabbed—'

'She did, but that doesn't make her guilty of murder. She's going to have enough people trying to get her banged up for twenty years without her defence lawyers prejudging her.'

I felt foolish. 'You're right.' And then, as if to strike back a little, 'Why are you driving so fast?'

'Because, as of now, this woman is our client. But it won't be long before someone at the police station rings a mate of theirs in one of the big firms and there'll be some shark down there within minutes, trying to steal her off us by persuading her that we've never done any criminal work in our lives; that the only thing we know about is conveyancing.'

Even as he spoke, he threw the car through the gates of the police-station yard and into the last space available – the one marked 'Chief Superintendent'.

We walked into the building, John showed his business card to the desk sergeant and introduced me as his assistant. He said, 'I've come to interview Sheila Gladstone – I'm her solicitor.'

The sergeant smirked, 'Good luck with that one. She knifed her old man good and proper.'

John didn't answer the taunt. 'Can we see her now, please?'

The sergeant gestured towards a bench. 'Take a seat. A constable will be along shortly to take you down to her cell.'

John sat next to me and whispered, 'It's either a bit of a power play or he's stalling, waiting for his mate to arrive from another firm.'

Eventually, a young PC appeared and we followed him down a flight of stone steps. As the constable opened a huge steel door at the bottom, we could hear shouting from the long line of cells either side of the corridor. In the distance, somebody was singing a drunken version of 'My Way'.

'She's in here,' the PC said as he put his key in the lock.

When we first walked in, I thought the cell was empty, and then I saw her crumpled up in a blanket on the floor in the corner. The door slammed behind us. John walked across to her and put his hand on her arm. 'Hello, Sheila. I'm John Loosemore. This is Rob Parsons. We're your solicitors and we're here to help you.'

The woman looked up at him. Her face was streaked with mascara runs and across her cheek was a red weal an inch wide, as if somebody had struck her hard with a belt. John pulled a chair towards him and said, 'Come on, Sheila – sit on the edge of the bed and tell us what happened.'

She looked up. Her eyes flitted from John to me and back again. Finally, she heaved herself off the floor and onto the bed.

'Good,' said John. 'Rob will take some notes.' He nodded to the other chair. I sat and took a blue counsel's notebook out of my briefcase. He said, 'Is that OK, Sheila?'

She looked more than tired. It was as if any life still in her was fighting for the right to leave. She shook her head slowly as she spoke. 'I stabbed him. That's all. I killed him.'

'Why did you do that, Sheila?' John said.

She hesitated. 'Well, he had me by the hair and he was pulling me around the living room. I was on all fours and he was punching me in the face as he did it. There was a bread knife on the table and I grabbed it. When he saw me take it, he laughed and said, "Go on, do it," and then he hit me again.' She started crying, her shoulders heaving with the sobs.

John gave her a handkerchief and said, 'Go on – what happened then?'

Sheila blew her nose and said, 'So I did. I shoved the knife up into his chest. At first, he just looked surprised, but then I saw blood coming out of his mouth and I knew he was done for. He fell on top of me. I called an ambulance, but it was too late.'

John said, 'I am so sorry, Sheila. Now I am going to ask you something that is very important, OK?'

She sniffed.

'Has he ever hit you before?'

And then Sheila laughed. But not a kind of laugh I have ever heard before. It was something in between a laugh and a wail. And then she rolled up both her sleeves and her trouser legs.

We were both silent for a while and then John got up from his chair and put his arm around her. 'We're going to fight for you, Sheila.'

As we drove out of the police station, John said, 'I'm going to get a top pathologist on this case. And I want you to run it with me.'

Later that day, John, myself and one of the most eminent pathologists in the United Kingdom met at the Cardiff Royal Infirmary and I attended my first post-mortem. The pathologist showed John and I where the point of the knife had punctured the edge of Sheila's husband's heart. He said, 'The skin is the hardest thing to penetrate, but once the knife had gone through that, it wouldn't have taken much more to do the damage she did. She was unlucky that the blade touched his heart. It doesn't look to me like a blow that was intended to kill him – more as if she was trying to defend herself.' That was enough for John. When the case eventually came to trial, our barrister was worried that Sheila had used excessive force in defending herself. So as to avoid the risk of being found guilty of murder, he had suggested she plead guilty to the lesser charge of manslaughter. John was having none of it.

'No way. I believe the jury will have enormous sympathy with her. I'm going to try to persuade her to plead not guilty.' Our legal counsel wasn't happy, but that didn't bother John.

*   *   *

When we got out of the post-mortem, I went straight home and found Dianne and Ronnie already back from work. Dianne looked tired, but Ronnie, still in his new overcoat, seemed energised. I kissed Dianne and said to Ronnie, 'Well, how did it go?'

He launched into a blow-by-blow account of his day. At the end of a long catalogue of bin types, street names, and a brief description of a poster on the wall of the mess room – 'You know . . . a rude one . . . with her . . .' – he paused and cupped his hands at his chest – '. . . out. And Mr Clarkson said I'm perfect as a bin man.'

Dianne smiled. 'We're really proud of you. You've been so brave today.'

Ronnie held something up in the air. 'And I used this today.'

'Ah, your key,' I said.

'Do you want it back now?'

'No. You hang on to that.'

He put his hand deep into his overcoat to find a pocket. 'I'm keeping this safe. This is special.'

Dianne flicked his hair. 'You're special too, Ronnie.'

I put the kettle on. 'You'll never guess what I've been doing today.'

Dianne looked flustered. 'Actually Rob, tell me later. I need you to help me move something in our bedroom.' She glared at me.

I tapped the end of my nose. 'Roger Wilco.'

'Don't be funny. We won't be long, Ronnie. Perhaps you could lay the table.'

Ronnie took off his overcoat. 'Fine.'

*   *   *

I followed Dianne up the stairs and into our bedroom. 'If MI5 ever offer you a job, you might need to work a little on your spy-craft.'

She sat on the end of the bed. 'Tell me about your day.'

'I've been involved in a murder case.'

'Wow!'

'When I got into the office, John was about to rush off to the police cells to see a woman who has been charged with stabbing her husband. He wants me to help him run the case. I've actually been in a post-mortem this afternoon.'

Dianne screwed up her face. 'What was that like?'

'Strange. It was hard to believe that it was a real person they were cutting up.'

Dianne caught hold of my hand. 'Well, I've got some news as well.'

'Promotion come through?'

'No.'

'Give me a clue.'

'Well, you know we said that seeing Ronnie off to work was like seeing a child off to their first day of school?'

Perhaps because it had been such a long and unusual day, I was slower than normal. It took me a while to speak. 'Are you being serious?'

She winked at me. 'What do you think?'

*   *   *

When we went downstairs, the table was laid but the kitchen was empty. Ronnie was in the living room with the television off. He sat in a chair, smiling.

'You look happy,' Dianne said.

'I've been waiting for you to come down. There's something I forgot to tell you.'

'Come on, mystery man,' I said. 'Spill the beans.'

He spoke slowly, as if savouring every word. 'When Rob dropped me off at the yard this morning, one of the men said, "Who's that who brought you to work in the car?"' He stopped, a smile continuing to play in his eyes.

Dianne said, 'Go on. What did you say?'

'I said, "That's my solicitor."'

*   *   *

Three months later, on a wet Tuesday afternoon, John and I waited in the lawyers' room at Cardiff Crown Court. The jury had already been deliberating for six hours. During the trial they had heard the catalogue of violence over many years that the husband had inflicted on his wife; nevertheless, her stance of self-defence was a huge risk. After all, she had deliberately stabbed him. As we sat waiting, I looked across at John; he looked paler than usual.

It was almost 7 p.m. when an usher came into our room and said, 'The jury is coming back in.'

I sat in the court and watched as the jury filed into their seats. Their faces were inscrutable, apart from one elderly lady, who smiled at Sheila.

The giving of a verdict by a jury is always a moment of high drama. Everybody in the court – judge, prosecuting and defence lawyers, family in the gallery, and press – knows that a destiny hangs on whether, when it comes to the vital part, the foreman will speak two words or just one.

The jury were now seated and the court clerk announced, 'All stand!' as the red-robed and wigged judge took his seat. He turned to the jury. 'Have you reached a verdict on which you are all agreed?'

The foreman replied, 'We have.'

The judge leant forward. 'And what is your verdict?'

Sheila was standing, but on hearing the foreman speak,

sank into her seat, supported by two prison officers. She was still sobbing uncontrollably as her son led her down the steps into the foyer, and finally outside the court and into the noise of the street. John and I were at her side. She tried to speak to us but all she managed was a continuous, 'Thank you.'

Ten minutes later we had said our goodbyes, and her son was helping her into his car when she suddenly turned, ran back towards us and hugged John. As she was disentangling herself, John said, 'Rob did a great job for you as well.' She turned, hugged me briefly and was gone. But I didn't care. John's stardust was all over my shoulders and I wasn't going to brush it off anytime soon.

*   *   *

Not long ago, a friend asked me, 'Why did John Loosemore choose you to join his legal practice? Sure, he might have seen potential, but even so, there must have been others with that.' I thought a lot about that question; in fact, I wondered why, in all the years I'd known John, I'd never asked him. I still see him occasionally at a church we attend. He is now in his mid-eighties, with a mind as sharp as ever. I decided to ask him. At the end of the service the seat next to him became vacant and so I wandered across the aisle and sat by him. After a few pleasantries, I said, 'Why did you choose me all those years ago?' He smiled but he didn't say anything; then he pointed a finger upwards.

And all along I had thought it was my brilliance.

'I'm good with babies, I am.'

Chapter 10

The New Car

Ronnie had been in his job for almost four weeks. It was a Saturday; Dianne and I had slept in late and were having coffee in the kitchen. She said, 'I think we need to make some decisions about Ronnie.'

'I know.'

'I've been thinking.'

'I thought I heard something rattling.'

She poked me in the ribs. 'I was just thinking that it would be good for him to be with us for a bit longer. He's really changed and I really am very fond of him, but I think we need to have some boundaries.'

'Boundaries?'

'Yes. He's been with us since Christmas and since then we haven't had a minute to ourselves. And that's not good for us. It's probably not good for him either.'

'What's the plan?'

'Let's make his room a bit more comfortable, get him a

television and make it more homely – a place that feels like his own. Then we'll get the living room back.'

I was silent. Dianne nudged me. 'So what do you think?'

I spoke slowly. 'I think it's a good idea, but how the heck are we going to break the news to him? He's spent his whole life with people telling him he isn't wanted.'

'I know. I've been worried about that too. It's just that I think we'll be able to have him stay for longer if we can have a break from each other occasionally.'

'He doesn't know about the baby yet; perhaps we can say that you need a bit of space . . .'

Dianne glowered at me. 'Don't blame it on me.'

'I'm not blaming it on you – just saying that I think it might be a good way to break the news, that's all. Anyway, your idea is inspired. Let me know how you get on with telling him.'

For the second time that morning my ribs were assaulted.

*   *   *

I went downstairs, still in my pyjamas, and into the living room. 'Morning, Ronnie.'

He was engrossed in *Tarzan, Lord of the Jungle*. 'Hi, Rob.' Ronnie seemed absorbed by the long-haired figure swinging his way through the trees, but then he suddenly sprang from his chair and beckoned me to follow him. 'I've got a surprise for you.'

I had been the recipient of the same surprise at least three mornings a week ever since Ronnie had moved in. I followed him into the kitchen and waited for the words that would kick off the ritual.

'Guess, Rob.'

The second time we had played the game I had guessed right, but Ronnie had looked forlorn. I'd learnt my lesson.

I glanced around the kitchen. 'You've cleared off the worktops?'

He shook his head at my foolishness. 'No.'

I scoured the kitchen for clues. 'You've emptied the waste bin?'

'No.'

'You're too good for me, Ronnie.'

'Go on. Have another guess – you might get it.'

I spoke with confidence. 'I know what it is.' Ronnie's forehead wrinkled with worry, but his concern was unnecessary. 'You've brushed the floor?'

He shook his head with a smile. 'You never get it, do you?' He walked to the dishwasher and opened it with a flourish. It was as devoid of crockery as when we'd played the game on Monday . . . and Wednesday.

My shoulders slumped. 'You've emptied it.'

He shrieked with laughter and wagged his forefinger at me. 'I always get you, don't I?'

'You certainly do, Ronnie.'

He spoke as he closed the door on the dishwasher. 'Big day for me next Friday.'

'Why's that?'

'My first paycheque.'

'Wow – that's amazing, Ronnie! Well done. Have they said anything about keeping you on permanently?'

'Mr Clarkson said he's going to.'

'Well, that's a reason to celebrate tonight.'

'Only one thing, though.'

'What's that?'

'I've got to have a bank account they can pay my money into.'

I was suddenly annoyed. 'How long have you known that?'

'A couple of weeks.'

I just about managed to stifle the scream of 'Why didn't you tell me sooner?' that had got as far as the back of my throat. After a moment's thought I said, 'We'll go down to the Principality Building Society this morning and open you an account.'

'Thanks, Rob.'

'It's fine.'

He brightened. 'And I'm paying you back the money I owe you for the clothes, and taking you and Di out for a meal, mind.'

'You don't need to take us for a meal, Ronnie.'

'I want to.'

'That's really kind – thanks. By the way, I've got two bits of news for you too.'

'Oh?'

'Di and I are going to have a baby.'

I waited for the big reaction, but Ronnie wasn't strong on appropriate emotional reactions.

He said, 'That's good. What's the other bit?'

'Ronnie! Sound a bit more excited.'

He shifted from foot to foot. 'Sorry. What's the second one?'

'We'd like you to stay with us a bit longer – until you're able to see how the job is going. So we're going to make your room a bit nicer; get you a comfortable armchair and a television of your own.'

'My room is fine and I watch telly with you.'

'I know, Ronnie, but especially with a baby on the way, Di and I will sometimes need a bit of time on our own. We'll still see loads of you. But it will be good for you to have your own space as well.'

He looked as though he was about to protest, but instead simply turned and made his way towards the door. 'Fine.'

I had wounded him and for the time being, there was no changing it.

* * *

When I got home late on the following Friday, Dianne and Ronnie were watching *Coronation Street*. There were fresh flowers on the table.

'Hi, both.' I kissed Dianne and sank into an armchair. 'Sorry I'm late. John and I were talking about opening another office.' I lay back and closed my eyes.

'You can't doze off now,' Dianne said. 'Ronnie and I are bursting with curiosity. Aren't we, Ronnie?'

Ronnie didn't respond.

I opened my eyes and kicked my shoes off. 'Well, there's a building come up for sale right on the high street. Most law firms are tucked away on the upper floors of buildings. If we get this, people will be calling in while they're doing their shopping.'

Dianne exclaimed, 'You hear that, Ronnie? Rob's taking over Marks & Spencer.'

'And there's another bit of news.'

Dianne raised an eyebrow. 'I'm not sure I can take much more excitement.'

'OK, then I won't—'

'Oh, come on, don't sulk.'

'John wants me to become a partner in the legal practice.'

Dianne clapped her hands together. 'That's brilliant! Will you have your name on the notepaper?'

'Yes, but even better than that.'

'What?'

I leant forward and smiled. 'Drumroll, please.'

Dianne performed a half-hearted roll.

'Not loud enough.'

Dianne gave a slightly louder rendering. 'Come on.'

I said, 'The firm are giving me a new car.'

Her eyes widened. 'What? Brand new?'

'Brand new. A Cortina.'

'Wow! When do you get it?'

'Drumroll.'

'Don't be pathetic. When does it come?'

'I've got to go to the dealership . . .' I paused for effect, '. . . next week!'

'Rob, that's amazing. Did you hear that, Ronnie? You're going to have a new car to take you to work?'

Ronnie was obviously finding Albert Tatlock's conversation with Ena Sharples a lot more interesting than my new Ford.

'Ronnie – you look a bit glum. All OK?' I asked.

He turned away from the screen. 'I'm fine.'

'Hey, I just remembered. You got your first paycheque today.'

He nodded, bit his lip and turned back to the television. Eventually he spoke without taking his eyes off the screen. 'I'm going to pay you back the money I owe you next month and take you for a meal then.'

'That's fine, Ronnie. But why not this month?'

He continued to stare at the action in the Rovers Return. 'It'll just be better then, that's all.' He stood up and made for the door. 'I think I'll have an early night.'

'I've got some chilli on, Ronnie,' Dianne said. 'Would you like some before you go to bed?'

'No, thanks. I'm not hungry. Goodnight.'

When he'd gone, I said, 'What's up with him?'

'I don't know. He was here when I got in from work and he's been quiet all evening.'

'I'm just going upstairs to have a bit of a chat with him. I won't be long.'

I knocked on his door. Nothing. I knocked again. He shouted, 'Come in.'

He was sat in a chair looking out of the window. I went in and perched on the end of his bed. 'What's wrong, Ronnie?'

He frowned. 'Nothing. I'm fine.'

'Did you get paid today?'

'Yes.'

'Did the money go into your building-society account?'

'Yes.'

'And did you go into the building society and ask them to make your book up?'

His shoulders slumped. 'Yes.'

'Can I see your book?'

He pursed his lips and shook his head.

'Why not?'

'There's nothing to see, that's all. Everything's fine.'

'Show me the book, Ronnie.'

He repeated himself. 'There's nothing to see. Everything's fine.'

'I'd like to see the book, please.'

He got up and, still shaking his head, dragged his feet to the wardrobe. He fiddled with his overcoat, trying to find the inside pocket, and produced the red passbook in its plastic cover. He handed it to me then sat back down; he had his head in his hands.

Inside were only two entries. The first was a deposit from Cardiff City Council and the second a cash withdrawal.

I got off the bed and went to him. 'What's this one, Ronnie?' I asked, pointing to the first entry.

He seemed glad to have a question he could answer easily. 'It's my wages.' He went to take the book from me.

I put my finger next to the second one. 'And this?'

His hand froze mid-air. 'It's nothing.'

'What do you mean, "*It's nothing*"?'

'It's just nothing, that's all. Everything's fine.' He looked as though he might cry.

'What did you do with all that cash?'

'Just bought a few things, that's all.'

'What did you buy?'

He screwed up his eyes and tilted his head to one side. 'Some flowers for Di.' He paused and thought again. 'Some Cokes.'

'How many Cokes did you buy?'

'Four. There's two in the fridge for you.'

I turned the passbook over and over in my hands. 'Ronnie, there's forty-five pounds in cash gone. What did you do with it?'

'I didn't do anything – just bought a few things, that's all,' he snapped.

'Ronnie, it's OK. Just tell me what happened to the money.'

Suddenly it was as if the bones had left his body, and what was left sagged. Any fight left in him was gone. He looked distraught and I felt guilty for doing it to him.

'You won't be in trouble, Ronnie. I just want to know.'

The words came out slowly, as if he resented using every one of them. 'I've done a bad thing.'

* * *

When I got back downstairs, Dianne was in the kitchen testing the chilli. She put the spoon down. 'Well?'

'He's blown almost fifty pounds on one-armed bandits.'

She looked troubled. 'Is he all right?'

'He seems devastated. Honestly, I'm not sure if I've done the right thing or not. At times I don't know whether he's my mate or my son. It's exhausting. I told him I want to look at his building-society book every week.'

Dianne walked across the kitchen and put her arms around me. 'You're a tough cookie. I feel sorry for our little girl when she's a teenager.'

I kissed the end of her nose. 'Our little boy, you mean.'

* * *

Thirty minutes later, we were eating our chilli in front of *Z Cars* when there was a knock on the living-room door. On the screen, a policeman was closing in on a cat burglar on the roof of a factory. Over the years I discovered that Ronnie had a knack of coordinating his knocks with crucial points in a TV drama.

I turned the television down. 'Come in.'

He didn't – just poked his head around the door and said, 'Can I see you for a moment, Rob? Can we go into the kitchen?'

The cat burglar had been caught and was in handcuffs. I got up. 'Sure.'

As we sat at the table, Ronnie said, 'I know I've done a bad thing. It won't happen again.'

'How long you have been using those gambling machines?'

He twisted his hands. 'Not long. It won't happen again. It's all in the past now.'

'It's all in the past now,' was a phrase I was to hear many times from Ronnie when he felt he had let us or himself down. He would almost always say sorry, but then he would want to quickly push the incident back into the mists of time, as if allowing it to linger in the present was simply too painful.

I looked across the table at him. I knew he had tried to lie to me. I knew he had wasted his money, and I think I probably knew that he would do it again. But I was sure that his grief at letting us down could not have been deeper. And no matter how frustrated he could make me, and even though he'd lived with us for such a short time, I cared about him; I wanted to protect him. 'Yes, Ronnie. It's all in the past now. But I'm still going to look at that book every week.'

'It won't happen again.'

'Good. But I'm still looking.'

He sat quietly then went to speak but hesitated. Finally, he spoke. 'Can I ask you something?'

'Of course.'

'Can we have a quiz?'

The quiz ritual had begun when Ronnie had been with us just a couple of days. He had got a question right as we watched *Mastermind* together. He was so pleased with himself that he had asked me to quiz him with questions of my own. If the dishwasher routine was the most regular of our routines over the past month, then the quiz wasn't far behind.

I hesitated. It was getting late; I was tired and just wanted to escape to the living room and watch some rubbish television with Dianne before bed. But I relented. 'A quick one.'

The gambling misdemeanour now firmly in the past, Ronnie settled himself in his chair, put both hands on the kitchen table and settled himself as I began the familiar spiel.

'This is the Parsons' House *Mastermind* challenge and in the chair is Ronnie Lockwood. Ronnie is a waste operative from Cardiff.'

He shuffled.

I waited for a minute before starting. The tension was palpable.

'Question one: name any two first-division football clubs.'

He looked at me as if I had insulted him. 'Man United and Spurs.'

I considered my mock answer sheet and paused. 'Correct.'

'Number two: what do you call somebody who gives a player a yellow card?'

'A referee.'

Occasionally, I threw in a harder one that sometimes needed a little help. 'What is the name of the highest mountain in the world?'

Ronnie screwed up his eyes and tilted his head to the side. He was stumped. I said, 'It begins with E . . . Ever . . . Everes . . .'

'Everest!' he yelled.

We made our way through the questions and, as always, he had the first nine right. But could he sweep the board?

'Question ten.'

Ronnie shifted in his seat as I paused before going on. This bothered him. 'Get a move on, Rob.'

I said, 'What is the name of the main cowboy in the film *True Grit*?'

Ronnie gave a huge sigh of relief and laughed out loud. By luck, the quizmaster had landed on his specialist subject. He shouted out, 'John Wayne.'

'Ten out of ten!'

Ronnie fought hard to control the smile that was bubbling just underneath his lips. He knew what was coming next. I put on my most sombre voice. 'Ronnie Lockwood: in the Parsons' House *Mastermind* you have scored ten points – with no passes.'

I did my best to replicate the furious clapping of the studio audience.

I said, 'Well, what do you think of that, Ronnie?'

The success was too great. His modesty was shot to pieces. The smile exploded. 'I'm brainy, I am.'

* * *

Ronnie started to help in the kitchen at the homeless shelter the following weekend and he was there when his new television was delivered to our house. All in all, it proved to be quite a day for Ronnie's bedroom. His armchair had arrived an hour earlier, courtesy of some friends who had just taken delivery of a new three-piece suite, Dianne had bought a throw for his bed, and we had taken one of the lamps from the living room to put on his bedside table.

I was keen to focus on getting the TV working, but that wasn't Dianne's priority – hers was soft furnishings. She put the new bedcover on, placed the lamp on the table and looked around the room. 'Can you go up to the loft and find the blue rug we put there?' She was on a roll and I knew there was no point protesting. Half an hour later I was sent back up for a picture of a horse in a field. I'm not much of a DIY virtuoso; an hour later it was fixed to the wall and I was nursing a bruised thumb.

With the transformation complete, we turned on the television and, to the background of *George and Mildred*, surveyed the scene. Dianne walked to the side of Ronnie's bed and turned on the table lamp. 'Turn the main light off.' And suddenly the harshness was gone and the room was bathed in a warm glow. 'It looks good, doesn't it?'

'He'll love it,' I said.

At the sound of his key in the door we turned the television off, did a final check, and hurried downstairs. We had got to the hall just as Ronnie was coming through the door. When he saw us, he made a beeline for Dianne, rummaged in a Tesco's bag and handed her a large bar of chocolate. Then he plunged into the bag again and produced two cans of lager.

I pursed my lips. 'I thought we were off the beer, Ronnie?'

He hunched his shoulders. 'They're not for me. You have them.'

'Thanks, Ronnie.' I put the cans on the table in the hall. 'We've got something to show you.'

He started to take off his coat. 'Oh?'

Dianne beckoned him to follow as she climbed the stairs. 'Come and have a look.'

Outside his bedroom door, Dianne stopped and said, 'Close your eyes.' Ronnie looked dubious, but she was determined. 'Oh, come on, Ronnie. We're not going to eat you.' He complied and, taking his arm, Dianne opened the door and led him in. 'Open them now!'

He looked around, his face expressionless. We were silent. Eventually he said, 'What is it?'

Dianne was crestfallen. 'Don't you like the new bedcover and the lamp?'

He nodded. 'Very nice.'

'And you've got your own television,' I said. I crossed the room and turned it on. I have never seen Ronnie look at a programme with less interest.

He said, 'I don't need a television. I watch television with you and Di.'

'Do you like the rug?' Dianne asked.

He nodded again. 'Very nice.'

I was determined to keep going. 'Try your new armchair.'

He walked slowly towards the chair, gripped the arms and lowered himself into it as though it had electric wires attached. Dianne and I tried to prompt a response, but the chair got exactly the same verdict as the rug and the lamp. The vibes in the room were not good. Dianne was upset and I was angry. 'Well, we'll leave you to it, Ronnie,' I said, and added, 'Come on, Dianne.'

*   *   *

I made some tea and we sat in the kitchen drinking it, my thumb still aching. 'Well, that went well,' I said. 'If we'd suggested he be circumcised, I don't think we could have got a more muted response.'

She was hurt but looked more thoughtful than upset. 'He was stubborn, Rob – even rude, but the truth is he doesn't want a room of his own. He wants to be with us. We're cross with him, but I'm not sure making us feel good is a gift he can give at the moment.'

As we spoke, Ronnie came into the kitchen. 'Can I chat with you, Rob?'

'Sure.'

'No, you know. In private.'

I got up from the table. 'Let's go upstairs.'

We made our way to Ronnie's room. Ronnie sat on the edge of his bed. I said, 'Why don't you sit in your new armchair?'

'I'm fine.'

'What is it, Ronnie?'

He spoke slowly. 'Is it because I did a bad thing?'

'What do you mean?'

'You know – with the machines and the money?'

My tone was harsher than intended. 'I don't know what you mean.'

'You know – the room and all that. Is it because I did a bad thing?'

I was taken aback. 'Let me call Dianne up.' I went out and yelled over the banister. 'Di, come up for a minute.'

As we waited, neither of us spoke.

Dianne came in and sat next to Ronnie.

'Ronnie thinks we want him to have a room of his own because he spent his wages on the one-armed bandits,' I said.

Dianne put her hand on his arm. 'Oh, Ronnie, that's not true at all. Rob and I love having you living with us. We just want you and us to have some space sometimes. One day you'll have a place of your own, but we want you to stay with us while you get settled in your new job and for this room to feel like yours.'

He kept his head bowed. 'I know I do bad things sometimes.'

Dianne spoke slowly. 'It's not because you've done a bad thing, Ronnie. It's because you've done lots of good things since you've been with us.'

He looked distant, went to speak, but hesitated. He got up from the bed, turned the television off and said, 'I like the rug.'

*   *   *

It was a Wednesday night, almost six months later – and I was late home from work; Dianne was already in bed. I made two cups of tea and went upstairs. As I reached the landing, the light shone from under the bedroom door and I sensed there might be trouble brewing. I took a deep breath and walked into the room trying to sound as jaunty as possible. 'Fancy a tea? It's decaf.'

Dianne's eyes were puffy and red. 'You're late.'

'Yes, sorry. There's so much going on at the moment and then I had a trustees meeting. I went straight from work.'

'You could've told me.'

'I thought it would be really quick, but it just went on and on. Anyway, are you OK?'

'No, I'm not OK. I've got a full-time job like you and am also a sister and social worker to Ronnie. I've had a tour of the Cardiff rubbish runs and know which streets have the heaviest bins, which houses give Christmas tips and how fast you have to go to be able to knock off early. And I'm pregnant. I'm pleased that you're saving the world, but don't forget you've got a family home here.'

'I've brought the new car home.'

Dianne turned over. 'Well, go and sleep in it.'

I sat on the end of the bed. 'Are you sure you don't want the tea?'

*   *   *

Breakfast was strained, but I broke the silence. 'Who wants to see the new car?' To say there wasn't a rush for tickets would be an understatement, but finally Dianne spoke, 'Come on, then. Let's take a look.'

'I'll have a look on the way to work,' Ronnie said. 'I'm going up to my room.'

As soon as we were in the hall, she turned to me. 'I don't like us being like this, Rob. But I can't do this on my own.'

I kissed her. 'I know. You're brilliant with Ronnie.'

'It's not Ronnie I'm worried about.'

It was cold outside, but Dianne did a reasonable job of looking impressed. Nevertheless, when Ronnie and I set off for work, I felt deflated. I had been like a kid driving home the night before: the new-car smell, an untouched driver's manual in the glove compartment, and the kind of modern functionality none of my old cars had ever had. I glanced at Ronnie; he was looking out of the side window. It was worth a try.

'Hey, Ronnie. Have you ever seen anything like this before?' When he turned to face me, I put my forefinger on the steering wheel and rotated it with ease. 'It's called power-assisted steering.'

He smiled. 'I know, Rob. We have it on the dust carts.'

*   *   *

It turned out that Dianne was a better prophet than me. It was a girl, whom we brought home from the hospital on a sunny Sunday morning in September 1977. It had not been a straightforward birth. When Dianne was ten days overdue, the consultant had taken us aside and said, 'Your baby's heartbeat is up – it's getting distressed. I think we'd better go in and get this little one out.' He made it sound like a hostage rescue by the SAS. Dianne said the look on my face was a study; as the doctor glanced down at his notes, she mouthed, 'Caesarean,' to me as though I'd never heard of the procedure.

Within an hour a registrar came back to the bed and said, 'We're going to take you down now, Dianne.' He was from

Melbourne on placement in the UK for a year; tall, blonde and impossibly good-looking. It is true that by now, Dianne was drugged, but even so, she gazed up at him as though she was quite prepared for him to take her anywhere at all that he fancied. As she lay on her trolley, being pushed along the corridor by a porter, the rugged doctor walked on one side and I, trying to keep up in more ways than one, on the other. When we reached the doors that led to the operating theatre, he said, 'Well this is it, Dianne – would you like a quick kiss before we go in?' She smiled up at him, 'Yes please.' He laughed out loud and said in his broad accent, 'No, you fool. I mean from your husband.'

* * *

Ronnie must have put the church chairs away that morning in double-fast time: he was already home and, as I opened the front door, I could hear the clatter of crockery from the kitchen. Dianne had Katie in her arms. I put my finger to my lips. I whispered, 'Let's surprise him. Wait here until I call you.' As I walked into the kitchen, Ronnie was checking that a line of mugs on a shelf next to the sink were equidistant. He turned as soon as he heard me. 'Hi Rob.'

'Hi Ronnie, how was church?'

'Good. I put away two hundred chairs.'

'You're the best, Ronnie.'

He smiled, 'Not bad.'

I said, 'I've got somebody I'd like you to meet.'

'I know who this is going to be.'

I shouted to Dianne to come into the kitchen.

She came in and walked up to Ronnie. She pulled the shawl back that was covering part of Katie's face. 'This is the new member of our family, Ronnie. Her name is Katie.'

Ronnie looked at Katie briefly and said, 'Very nice.' And then he looked towards the dishwasher and said, 'I've got a surprise for you.'

Dianne managed not to look disappointed; she carefully lifted Katie out of her blankets and said, 'Would you like to hold her, Ronnie?'

He said, 'I don't think that's a good idea.'

Dianne held Katie out towards him. 'You'll be fine.' She pointed to a chair. 'Take a seat for a moment and I'll pass her down to you.'

Ronnie rubbed his hands on his trousers and sat at the kitchen table.

She said, 'Hold your arms out.'

Ronnie extended his arms wide enough to catch a small elephant. 'No, pull them in a bit and closer to your chest.'

He obeyed and Dianne lowered Katie into his hands.

He pulled Katie close to him and looked down at her; a silence – almost a holy silence – hung in the air. Katie, as if she knew she had to do her part in this little drama, looked as though she'd have been happy to have stayed in his arms for ever.

I said, 'You're a natural, Ronnie.'

He looked up at us. 'I've never held a baby before.'

'Well – you'll be doing a lot of it from now on, so get used to it.'

Dianne reached out to take Katie back, but Ronnie looked reluctant to give her up. Finally, he passed the little bundle to Dianne as though he was holding a most precious and fragile treasure; as she took Katie from him, he laughed, perhaps out of relief that he had passed the test. 'I'm good with babies, I am.'

Victory for Ronnie as football manager.

Chapter 11

The Creaking Stair

Alan Bennett's *Lady in the Van* tells the remarkable story of his allowing Miss Shepherd to live in a broken-down van on his driveway for fifteen years. During that time, he cared for her in remarkable ways, but after her death he wrote, 'I am filled with remorse for my harsh conduct towards her, though I know at the time it was not harsh.'

We sometimes describe death as 'a visitor', but in reality, it is a burglar. Visitors do not leave brokenness and devastation behind them. Death is an interloper; it is impatient and demands that it be satisfied *now*. And death deceives us; we never believed that it would come so soon. It had always whispered to us: 'You have plenty of time to say your "I love yous", time for your embraces, time for your "sorrys".'

But perhaps its cruellest trick is the one to which Alan Bennett refers. After we lose somebody we care about, it causes us to rewind our relationship and re-examine every interaction. We revisit every cross word, each impatient moment, the small hurts we caused. And death taunts us: 'See how badly you treated the one you loved. If only . . .'

But it can only play that trick because our hearts and minds are befuddled with grief. A moment of clarity would be enough to assure us that the cross words, the impatience, the hurts, are so often just the stuff of life, the very essence of real relationships. And death's easiest targets are not those who have treated their loved ones appallingly, but the ones who have loved as best they could.

Jack Nicholson got an Oscar for his portrayal of Melvin Udall, a bigoted, obsessive-compulsive novelist who has daily rituals that imprison him; he never steps on the cracks in the pavement, never uses a bar of soap more than once and always eats breakfast at the same restaurant. And it is there that he meets Carol Connelly, played by Helen Hunt, a single parent and the only server who will tolerate his bizarre behaviour. Melvin falls in love with Carol and one evening as they are eating dinner together, he tells her that he has a compliment for her. He explains that his doctor has told him that taking a pill may help his ailment. As he talks, Carol is looking more and more confused. He goes on to say that he hasn't been using the pills because he hates taking stuff like that. Carol looks as though she might walk out at any moment, but he presses on. He tells her that since meeting her he has started to take the pills again. She's unsure why that is a compliment to her. But then he says, 'You make me want to be a better man.' She thinks that may be the best compliment of her life.

Somebody once told me that there is a part of us that we know and allow others to see, and a part that we know but don't allow others to see. But he said, there is also a part of us that we don't know ourselves. I'm not sure I ever want to know that last part; the bits of myself that I do know are enough for me to turn Melvin Udall's words into what has practically become a daily prayer: *Help me to be a better man.* And that has certainly been true in our life with Ronnie. I sometimes catch myself asking, *Could I have been kinder? Could I have loved him more unconditionally? Could I have done better?* Often the answer that comes to me is yes: if we could rewind the film and do it all again, there are so many things I'm sure both Dianne and I would change. But then at other times I think that even if we could roll back the years and have another run at it, we would probably simply make different mistakes. Even now, it is easy to remember only our short-temperedness, impatience and the frustrations that were part of our life with him, and so often that was born from trivial incidents – like the saga of the creaking stair.

It was a Sunday in 1980, late October, 7 a.m. Katie, our 3-year-old daughter, was asleep in the bedroom next to ours and our son Lloyd, just weeks old, was lying in a cot at the side of our bed. We were just a month into our new home. It was a large, red-brick, detached house. Our neighbours were a knighted CEO of a major company and a High Court judge. We had two inside toilets.

It had been a long night. Unlike his sister, who quickly

slept through the night, Lloyd resented every second in his cot. He was always hungry, believed that a new nappy should be filled the minute it was put on, and demanded to be fed on the hour. However, until thirty seconds before, he had been fast asleep, and for the first time in at least three hours, so were we.

The stairs in our new house had a board that creaked as if it was auditioning for a *Hammer House of Horror* movie. Ronnie, who was always up at least an hour before us, had inadvertently developed the knack of stepping on it at exactly the right angle to achieve maximum noise. Just days before, following morning after morning of being awoken by Ronnie, Dianne smothered her head in a pillow and mumbled, 'I might kill him.' So later that day, I'd spent ten minutes with him practising how, with a little dexterity, it was possible to circumnavigate the offensive stair. It may have been his damaged knees or a more fundamental issue with the biomechanics of his body, but the successes were few, and on one attempt he nearly killed himself. Not only did he miss the miscreant stair but several others as well, landing heavily at the bottom.

I have no doubt that he tried his hardest, but even when he did manage it, he often forgot to take care the next time. And this is exactly what happened at seven that morning. A screeching creak filled the air. Lloyd woke and joined in the chorus of noise.

Perhaps it was the effect of sleep deprivation, the sheer frustration that caring for Ronnie sometimes brought, or simply the sight of Dianne reaching for the pillow again, but whatever the reason, I lost all sense of perspective and rushed onto the landing as if the house was on fire. Bare from the waist up, with one leg in a pair of trousers and one out, the sight of my almost naked, crazed figure caused Ronnie to freeze on the stairs.

He looked up at me and began the familiar phrase, 'I know I've done a—' But he didn't get a chance to finish.

'Yes, you have. A very bad thing!' I yelled, and hopped back to the bedroom, slamming the door behind me.

When I went downstairs an hour later, Ronnie was sat in an armchair in the living room and Katie was on the settee opposite working her way through a bowl of Coco Pops. They were both watching *Play School*. Ronnie turned as I walked in. 'Sorry, Rob.'

'No. It's me who should apologise. That was over the top. I'm sorry. Di and I didn't sleep too well last night.'

'Don't worry about it. By the way, Katie was crying, so I brought her down.'

'That's fine, Ronnie. Thank you.'

'Anyway, come into the kitchen – I've got a surprise for you.'

* * *

One surprise later, I went back up to the bedroom. Dianne was asleep, but Lloyd was still screaming. I picked him up and carried him downstairs, grabbing an envelope from the hall table on my way to the living room. I sank into an armchair and rocked him until he fell asleep.

As soon as he settled, I opened the envelope and began looking at the draft designs for our new office notepaper. The new logo was in gold leaf and next to it our headquarters' address: a prestigious city-centre office block. At the top of the notepaper were the names of the firm's sixteen partners: John was at the top and I was next. At the bottom of the page was a list of our eleven UK offices and eight agent offices around the world. The practice had grown faster than anybody could have imagined. I looked down at Lloyd, still fast asleep, and stretched out my legs, then, putting my head back in the chair, closed my eyes.

Three months before, John had called me into his office and, as I sat in front of his huge desk, he said he had been asked by a major legal publisher to present a series of seminars for lawyers to talk about how our practice had grown so quickly.

I smiled at him. 'That's great, John. You'll be brilliant.'

He folded his hands on the desk and looked across at me. 'I'd like you to do it with me.'

When I'd first joined the practice as an articled clerk, I'd assisted at seminars in getting the room ready, managing the delegate list, and making sure there was enough coffee. 'I'll help in any way I can.'

'Great,' said John. 'There are four talks throughout the day. I'd like you to do two of them.'

I didn't actually wet myself, but I felt as if I might. I could hardly believe I'd managed to qualify as a lawyer, let alone have the gall to stand on a podium advising other lawyers how to run their practices. I stuttered my reply. 'I can't do that, John. I'm not experienced enough.'

John possessed two attributes which have never deserted him. The first was an absolute confidence in his ability to do anything to which he turned his hand, and the second was an inability to take no for an answer. 'You'll be brilliant. You're a great communicator.'

'Thanks, but what will I communicate?'

'You're fantastic at getting and keeping clients. Tell them how you do it.'

'Honestly John—'

'Don't underestimate what we've done in the practice – or your part in it; that's why we've come to the attention of the publishers. They're not looking for an academic lecture; they want ideas – and we've got them. Draft a couple of talks and we'll look at them together.'

If I had said no in that instant and meant it, I might have had a chance of escape, but I wavered. 'All right,' I said. 'I'll show you some possible bullet points.'

'Great,' said John. 'You'll be a star.'

* * *

Nine weeks later, I found myself getting out of a taxi outside the London Hilton Hotel on Park Lane. As John strode through the hotel's revolving door, he was animated. I felt I might be sick on the pavement.

The London Hilton is the cuckoo on Park Lane. Its snootier rivals, the Dorchester and the Grosvenor House, seem to look down on the bling of their younger rival. But bling or not, the Hilton is impressive. As we entered the massive foyer, there was a gigantic display of fresh flowers in the centre, brilliantly lit from below. Above the display a huge, crystal chandelier threw shards of light in every direction. Reception staff in black jackets, and bellboys and porters in blue all hovered or scurried around to meet every need of the guests that had flown in from each corner of the globe.

Our hurriedly formed seminar company was called Lawyers Planning Services, a title that was decided only marginally faster than the name for the Blue Jets. At one end of the hotel's reception area was a sweeping staircase, at the foot of which was a placard:

John Loosemore and Robert Parsons of Lawyers Planning Services welcome you to the London Hilton on Park Lane. 'How to Expand Your Practice'. The Ballroom – first floor.

As we walked up the stairs, my nausea grew. John leant into me and laughed. 'Isn't this fun?'

My mother was no academic but she was wise, and when I was in my mid-teens she gave me a piece of advice that has proved useful in many situations: 'If you can't fight, wear a big hat.' As I climbed the stairs towards my fate that day, I had on a brand-new three-piece suit, shoes that shone so brightly it could have been my father who had polished them, and a file of papers under my arm so large that it practically yelled, 'Do not mess with the person carrying this. He is clever.' And all of that might have looked impressive, except that as I got to the top step I tripped, the file fell out of my hand and my notes scattered across the carpet.

I hastily picked up my talk and walked with John towards the ballroom. Outside the main area was a foyer that was crammed with people drinking coffee. My first thought was that we were in the wrong place, until John whispered, 'Looks like we've got a crowd.' We made our way through the throng towards the doors of the ballroom, and as we did, people nudged each other and pointed at us. The back of my neck burned as I heard a man say to a colleague, 'That's them.'

It seemed that some delegates had registered at the last minute and so, by the time John walked to the podium to welcome the audience, the staff were still bringing in chairs at the back. I sat next to him on the stage and did a quick head count: 235.

John gave his talk first. I have no idea what he spoke about; I was too busy concentrating on the notes resting on my lap, checking and rechecking my flies, and trying to look confident. Finally, I heard him wind up his talk and say, 'It's been my privilege to work with Robert Parsons over the past ten years. Robert is one of the most dynamic entrepreneurs in the legal profession today.' My mother had warned me never to try to be something that you can't spell, but it was too late for that now. He went on, 'Ladies and gentlemen, please welcome Rob to the podium.' The audience clapped. I took a sip of water and stepped up to the microphone.

I heard myself say, 'Every legal practice in the world wants new business. But new business is secondary. The first aim, above every other, should be to keep and develop our existing clients. In the next hour I will share with you ten strategies we have used to do exactly that.'

The hour passed and at the end of my talk people clapped enthusiastically. I tried not to show my relief and surprise, and took my seat. As the crowd continued to applaud, I glanced at John. He winked at me. We were off.

*   *   *

Lloyd stirred in my arms. Opening my eyes, I put the notepaper designs to one side and glanced across the room at Ronnie. Katie was still glued to *Play School*, but he was writing on a large pad, his tongue out and hanging to one side of his mouth in concentration.

'What are you doing?' I asked.

He was about to answer when the doorbell rang.

I got up slowly and, with Lloyd still in my arms, went to the front door. Standing in the porch was a woman in her early sixties carrying a small bunch of flowers. She had a blue rinse and a smile that looked as if it had been painted on recently. She looked at me for a while, seemingly unsure what to say, then, with a glance over my shoulder as if hoping somebody more impressive might appear, said, 'I'm Susan Haines, the chair of the Neighbourhood Watch group. Is this your house?'

I gave a half-smile. 'Yes, we moved in just a couple of weeks ago.'

She thrust the flowers at me. 'You're much younger than I thought you'd be. Most residents in this road are old fogies like me.'

I took the flowers from her. 'You're very kind. Will you come in?'

'No, thanks – can't stop. Just wanted to welcome you and make you feel one of us.'

I took a sniff of the flowers. 'That's very considerate. Thanks.'

'And how is your wife?'

'Dianne. Oh, she's fine, thank you. She's resting in bed. Our second child has just been born.' I pulled the blanket back. 'This is Lloyd.'

She looked at him briefly and the smile wavered. 'Not the best of times to have chosen to move house.'

I smiled. 'That's exactly what Dianne said to me.'

'Well, we're entertaining tonight and I have to get the meal started.' She turned to leave. 'You must come across for a drink when your wife is up and about.'

'That would be lovely,' I said.

She started to walk away, then stopped and turned back. She seemed to be chewing her words silently, as if deciding whether or not to let them out of her mouth. Eventually she spoke, slowly, as if every word was carefully chosen. 'Forgive me, but I've noticed that about four o'clock each day a dustbin lorry stops just outside and a man walks up your drive.'

'Yes. That's Ronnie. He lives with us.'

'Does he work for the council?'

'Yes. He's a dustman, or a waste operative, to give him his full title.'

'So he lives with you permanently?'

'Well, we're not exactly sure how long he'll be with us. But yes, this is Ronnie's home.'

To her credit, the painted smile slipped only for a millisecond. 'How sweet. Well, enjoy the flowers.'

'We will. Thank you again.'

She turned and walked briskly down the drive.

I watched her until she had disappeared from view, then pulled the blanket back again and whispered to Lloyd's sleeping face: 'Cruella de Vil.'

* * *

I put the flowers in a vase in the kitchen and went back into the living room. Ronnie was still writing. I looked over his shoulder at a long list of names.

'What's this, Ronnie? The work rota for the bin-round?'

He laughed. 'No – I'm picking the team for Boxing Day.'

Ronnie had made his foray into football management on a rainy Boxing Day two years earlier. For over forty years the church had held an annual soccer match between the youth-club kids and a team made up of a ragbag of older men who gathered on a Thursday night for a class called Men's Keep Fit. The title for this group was singularly inappropriate, not least because it gave the impression that the members had a reasonable level of fitness which they were engaged in 'keeping'. The reality is that most of them were out of shape to such an extent that the greatest threat to their wellbeing was actually attendance at the class.

The match was refereed by an ageing civil servant who, because of the physical difficulty he found keeping up with the play, based most of his decisions on guesswork. Even so, he was not to be trifled with. In one tenaciously fought and somewhat bad-tempered match, he had sent off a full-back in his sixties who, in a moment of passion (caused by the referee awarding a more than dubious penalty to the youth team), had cast doubts on his lineage. Dozens of people turned out on Boxing Day to watch this spectacle and to contribute to the whip-round in aid of the homeless centre.

It was late November and Ronnie was in his second year with us when somebody from the Men's Keep Fit group asked him if he'd like to join their team. Rather surprisingly for a man who showed great reticence in almost every area of his life, he agreed instantly. When asked: 'What position do you play?' he didn't need time to think about it: 'Striker.'

Ronnie was by far the youngest member of the squad and the prospect of having this new talent in their team filled the Men's Keep Fit members with optimism: this could be the year when five successive losses would be forgotten.

In spite of the slight drizzle, there were almost forty people gathered to watch as the teams trotted out of the changing room. Actually, one of the players was not trotting like the others. It seemed that Ronnie's knees had lost all ability to hinge. Straight-legged, he goose-stepped his way onto the pitch. And within five minutes of the game starting, it became apparent to all, not least his team-mates, that even if Ronnie had once possessed the basic skills required of a striker, they had long since deserted him.

It wasn't that he didn't run. In fact, he ran in almost every direction and whether or not the ball was in that vicinity. It was simply that even when he and the ball briefly came within each other's ambit, he could not connect with it. The crowd was split in its reaction. The older members began shouting encouragements for the slightest display of skill, while the younger ones were merciless in their yelled advice to the opposing team. 'Give it to Pelé!' being one of the most polite.

As the game progressed, it was apparent that Ronnie was becoming more and more agitated, so at half-time the two captains devised a plan to help him score. But this noble endeavour was not easy to achieve.

Getting the ball and Ronnie close to each other was a challenge, and on the single occasion it happened, he was unable to guide it even remotely in the direction of the goal. Various attempts were made by the opposing team to make scoring easy for him: they made passes that went straight to him, they fell over at his feet, they took throw-ins and guided the ball straight to him. It soon became obvious that the aim of increasing Ronnie's self-esteem at football was not going to be achieved quickly. Finally, as most of the players looked on, stamping their feet against the cold, the opposing team's goalie came out towards him, stumbled around a bit and managed to kick the ball so that it bounced off Ronnie's leg and into the net.

Ronnie went wild. He ran around the pitch with his hands in the air, team-mates hugged him, and the crowd, largely out of relief, exploded into cheering.

The game raged on for another painful twenty minutes. The Men's Keep Fit won by a single goal. And it is here that the youth-club kids came into their own. They rushed towards Ronnie and in a magnanimous gesture of sportsmanship did what their ageing opponents could not: they lifted Ronnie onto their shoulders and marched him around the perimeter of the pitch yelling, 'Pelé. Pelé. Pelé.' Ronnie waved at the crowd as if he was the Duke of Edinburgh.

And that's when he became a football manager. Pleased as everybody was that Ronnie had experienced such triumph, it was obvious that the game had turned into a charity match in more ways than one. Nobody had the enthusiasm for an annual repeat. And then somebody suggested asking him to hang up his boots so he could manage the Men's Keep Fit team. Ronnie looked as though he'd bagged a coaching spot with Barcelona. The gesture was spontaneous and good-natured, but nobody had any idea how seriously he would take the challenge. Every year after donning that mantle, he began the selection process in early October, choosing the ageing characters he hoped would bring him victory.

I'm hopeless at football, but it had one advantage: it made teasing Ronnie easy. As I settled back into my armchair I asked, 'Am I in the team?'

He shook his head.

I protested. 'Well, that's poor, Ronnie. We're friends.'

He didn't look up at me. 'I can't pick you just because we're friends. You've got to be good.'

'Are you saying I'm not good?'

Ronnie became flustered. 'I'm not saying anything. You can be sub.'

I got up from my chair. 'I'm going back upstairs to Di. I'm too hurt to stay down here.'

He looked at me, his forehead creasing. 'I know you're joking.' The fear in his eyes showed he was not completely sure.

I laughed out loud. 'Of course, I'm joking.'

His relief was palpable, a huge smile filling his face. 'I know you are.' He wagged his finger at me. 'You're a wind-up merchant, you are, Rob Parsons.'

*   *   *

Somebody once told me that although we often describe life as a series of exhilarating mountain-top experiences and dark valleys, the reality is more like a railway line with twin tracks. On one track life is going well – good things are happening. But at exactly the same time, on the other track, life is hard; we are experiencing things we never thought would be part of our lot.

This was a wonderful period of our lives. We were in a lovely new house, we had a 3-year-old daughter and a newborn son, and my career in law was flourishing. This was the fulfilment of the dream that had seeded in my mind as I broke the news to my parents of John's offer to pay for me to go through law school. Life was good.

But in the air was the sound of something coming down that second track.

"One of the most successful seminars ever held"

WHAT THEY DIDN'T TEACH YOU AT LAW SCHOOL

John Loosemore and Robert Parsons have acted as consultants to the legal profession for the last ten years. They have advised hundreds of firms and lectured to thousands of solicitors in various jurisdictions. They believe that the profession can face the future with optimism if it takes realistic steps now to meet the challenge of competition.

Venue: The Hilton on Park Lane, London
Choice of dates: 14 February & 15 March

LAW SOCIETY'S CONTINUING EDUCATION SCHEME – 8 POINTS

One of the seminars that I ran with John Loosemore
at the London Hilton.

Chapter 12

Hard Times

I sometimes wonder when it was that Dianne and I began to struggle in our marriage. I can't put a date on it, or point to an incident that began the process. It is best described by the phrase 'a creeping separateness'. But I can remember with stunning clarity the day I knew for certain that we were in trouble.

It was dark and cold as I pulled into the drive. There were no lights on at the front of the house, but I could see the outline of somebody in the kitchen window at the side. I'd left my house key behind that morning, so I rang the bell. I heard Dianne shout something, and a few moments later Ronnie answered the door. His lips were pursed.

'What's wrong?' I said.

He wagged his finger at me. 'You're in trouble, you are.'

I walked past him towards the sound of *The Archers* theme tune coming from the kitchen radio. I decided to try the upbeat approach. Ronnie was behind me as I opened the kitchen door and popped my head around it. 'How are my favourite son and two girls?'

Lloyd was in a carrycot on the floor, but as I stepped into the room Katie ran towards me. I lifted her high in the air. Dianne was standing next to the sink with her back to the door. I put Katie down, walked up behind Dianne and put my arms around her waist. 'Sorry I'm a bit late.'

She turned. 'You're not a bit late, Rob – you're very late. And you're not sorry either. Because if you were, you'd stop doing it. You're always late. I think you care more about the office than you do about us.'

'Hang on a minute. I've only just come through the door.'

She threw a tea towel onto the worktop with venom. Ronnie immediately walked across the kitchen, picked it up and started to fold it. Her face darkened. 'Just leave it, will you please, Ronnie.'

He shrugged his shoulders and put the towel down. 'I think I'll have an early night,' he said as he walked out.

Dianne sat at the table and looked up at me. 'So, what's it this time? Urgent completion? Vital meeting? Bank manager called?'

I sat next to her. 'Actually, we've got some hassle with one of the associates who wants to leave to join another practice. If he walks out, half his clients will go with him.'

Dianne straightened the knives and forks on the table. 'And what was it last night and on Monday night? And what was it last week that meant we were an hour late to go for dinner at Mark and Jess's?'

I put my head down. I didn't need this. 'I'm doing this for us, you know.' I gestured at Katie and Lloyd. 'And them.'

Dianne was angry, upset and incisive. I've seen easier cross-examinations in a courtroom. 'And can you tell me what exactly you are doing for us that means we never see you?'

I waved my arms around. 'This: the house, the holidays – all of it. I want our kids to have more than we had.'

She looked at me, went to speak and then stopped.

I said, 'Go on – say it.'

She spoke slowly. 'The problem is, Rob, you're so busy trying to give them what you didn't have that you can't give them what you *did* have.'

'What's that supposed to mean?'

'Time.'

Dianne started to cry. Katie's face buckled, then she burst into tears as well. Lloyd joined in, as if for the sake of the stereo effect. Dianne sobbed furiously. I got up and put my arms around her. 'I'm really sorry, Di.'

She spoke between sniffs. 'I'm sorry as well. I know you're trying to give us all a good life. But I'm worried.'

'What are you worried about?'

Her sigh was deep and heartfelt. She brushed the tears from her cheeks as if they had no right to be there and walked to the door. Just as she was about to leave the kitchen, she turned to face me. 'I'm worried that you and I are not going to make it.'

I pulled Katie to me and, when she stopped crying, lifted Lloyd out of his carrycot. I sat in the kitchen rocking him and with Katie hanging on to my knee. I'm not sure how long I'd been there when Ronnie came in. 'Everything all right, Rob?'

'Not really, Ronnie. Di and I have had a bit of a row and she's upset. Can you take Katie in the other room and put something on the television, and I'll get Lloyd ready for bed?'

'Have I done a bad thing?'

'What do you mean?'

'You know – with the towel and that. I hope I didn't offend you.'

'No, Ronnie. You haven't done a bad thing. Can you sit with Katie for a bit?'

'Fine.'

*　*　*

I carried Lloyd upstairs and settled him into his cot. Dianne was sat on the bed with her back to me. 'Are you OK?'

She spoke without turning to look at me. 'Yes, I'm OK.'

When I went back downstairs and into the living room, Ronnie and Katie were glued to *George and Mildred*. I picked Katie up from the settee. 'Was it nice watching telly with Ronnie?'

She said, 'I love Ronnie. He's kind.'

I tweaked her nose. 'He certainly is. Time for bed now. Thanks for looking after her, Ronnie.'

He was glued to the television but made himself turn around briefly. 'It's fine.'

I put Katie into bed and tucked the sheets around her. She looked up at me. 'Can we have a story?'

I reached for the dog-eared copy of *The Princess and the Pea* which lay on her bedside table. 'This one?'

She replied as she snuggled further under the bedclothes. 'Yes.'

I began: 'Once upon a time there was a prince who wanted to marry a princess . . .'

She giggled, reached up and pulled my nose. 'But she would have to be a *real* princess.'

I smiled at her. 'You don't need me to read this story – you know it word for word.'

'I like it when you read it.'

'So, he travelled the whole world to find one . . .'

We had reached the part of the story where the queen's idea of the pea is about to be tested when I heard the phone ringing in the hall downstairs. I looked towards the door.

Katie said, 'Don't go, Daddy.'

I laid the book on the bed. 'I'll only be a minute.'

'Please, Daddy—' But I was already taking the stairs two at a time.

It was Steve, a fellow trustee of a charity we were involved in. 'Hi, Rob. Sorry to interrupt your evening. We've got to sign a new mandate for the bank. I wondered if I could pop around and get a quick signature?'

'Sure – I'm in all evening.'

'Great – I'll slip round now.'

'See you later. Bye.'

I hung up and had my foot on the first stair when the phone rang again. I went back and picked it up. It wasn't a quick call, and it was only just coming to an end when I realised that I'd left a princess perched precariously on a mountain of mattresses. I said, 'Must go – got to sort the kids out for bed.'

As I ran back to Katie's room, light shone underneath her door. I pushed it open. 'Sorry Katie . . .' But she was asleep, the book still open at the page I had left it. I put it on the bedside table, leant over and kissed her.

I closed her door softly and went into our bedroom. Lloyd was asleep in his cot but Dianne wasn't there. I hurried along the landing, past Ronnie's room and the sound of his TV, and downstairs to the kitchen. She wasn't there either. In the living room, the television was still on but there was nobody watching. I had a sick feeling in my stomach.

I went into the kitchen and sat at the table. After thirty minutes or so, I heard the front door opening. I rushed into the hall. 'I wondered where you were.'

Dianne took off her coat and laid her scarf on the hall table. 'I've just been walking.'

'Di – I'm really sorry.'

'I'm sorry too. But something's got to give, Rob. We can't go on like this.'

'I—' The doorbell cut me off. 'It's only Steve with something for me to sign. I won't be a minute.'

Dianne didn't react, her face pale and vacant. 'I'm going to bed. I feel exhausted.'

Steve left two hours later. I turned the lights off and went upstairs. Dianne was asleep. I walked around the bed and, just before turning off her bedside light, looked down at her. I felt an overwhelming sense of grief, but I wasn't sure why.

*   *   *

Six weeks later, I was sat in seat 9A as our British Airways 747 broke through the clouds above London on its approach to Heathrow from New York. I peered through the porthole next to me; below us the fields were covered in Christmas-card snow. The flight back had been perfect; a strong tail wind meant we were almost thirty minutes ahead of schedule, which was a big relief, as today was Katie's birthday and I'd assured Dianne I'd be home in time for the party at 5 p.m.

It had been quite a week. John Loosemore and I had been speaking at an American Bar Association conference. Not that it was all work. We'd climbed the Empire State Building, explored Radio City, eaten pastrami at what may well be the best sandwich shop in Manhattan, and would have seen *Cats* on Broadway if John hadn't left the tickets in the hotel. But dwarfing all of that was the journey there. John, unknowingly adopting my mother's advice on fighting and wearing big hats, had decided that we could at least arrive in New York in style. We got there in just under three hours, having broken the sound barrier over the Atlantic: we were on Concorde.

As I looked out of the window, I smiled to myself, my mind going back to the extra bit of excitement we had had as we came in to land in the USA. John was talking to the passenger on the other side of him. The bits of conversation

I picked up sounded interesting, and I practically had a cricked neck trying to listen in. As we were landing, I heard her say, 'Where are you heading in New York?'

John said, 'The Hilton in Manhattan.'

I caught her reply. 'Well, you're in luck. I've got a car meeting me. We pass the front door of the Hilton. We'll drop you off. My name's Shirley, by the way.'

As the three of us walked out of Arrivals into the morning sun, her car was indeed waiting. It was a block long, with a uniformed driver who looked like an all-in wrestler. He came towards our new friend. 'Welcome home, ma'am.'

She smiled. 'Good to see you, Dexter. We're going to drop these gents off at the Hilton in Manhattan.'

He took the trolley laden with cases from me. 'That would be a pleasure.' Dexter parked the trolley near the boot and then opened the rear door. John and I got in behind Shirley. I sat down and began to look around. I've seen bungalows with smaller interiors. Shirley sat on a bench seat opposite John and I, and as the car pulled into the airport traffic, she pressed a button in her arm rest. A shelf lowered, revealing a small cocktail cabinet. 'It may be a little early, but can I interest you guys in a drink?'

My mother had warned me about accepting lifts and drinks from strangers, but I was having too much fun to care. As I took the glass of champagne from her, I glanced over her shoulder. To her left was a small television screen with share prices on it. I was a kid from Cardiff whose childhood ambition was to have an inside toilet – and I was impressed.

By the time we were crossing the Brooklyn Bridge, both John and I had stopped trying to look cool; we *were* cool. We sipped our second drink as if this was a typical Tuesday afternoon.

John eventually posed the question that I'd been dying to ask since we got in the car. 'Do you mind my asking what you do for a living?'

'I'm a sculptor.'

John nodded his head vigorously, as if that explained everything. He was quiet for a moment and then, noticing a wedding ring on her finger and apparently not caring if his rudeness got us both ejected on the bridge, blurted out, 'What does your husband do?'

Shirley was unfazed. 'He plays in a band.'

John couldn't stop now if he'd wanted to. 'Wow! What's the band's name?'

She replied with not a hint of drama. 'Oh. It's called the Rolling Stones. I'm married to Charlie Watts.'

I almost swallowed my glass, but John didn't miss a beat. 'Robert used to play in a band.'

But Shirley had never heard of the Blue Jets.

*   *   *

If only our trip back was as smooth as John. As I watched the same London landmarks disappear and reappear beneath us, the pilot's voice cut into the cabin. 'Good morning, ladies and gentlemen. I'm sure you've noticed that we've been circling for quite a while. The bad weather has caused severe delays at Heathrow and I am very sorry to tell you that we have been diverted to Gatwick.'

By the time I got home, it was late and the house was in darkness. As I turned on the kitchen light, discarded paper plates, party hats and half a cake littered the table. Four used candles lay on their sides next to it. I felt leaden and went upstairs. Dianne's bedside light was on, but she was asleep. I turned it off and slipped into bed next to her.

She stirred. 'Welcome home.'

'It was a nightmare getting back. I'm so sorry I missed . . .' I whispered, but she was asleep again.

*   *   *

I woke early the next morning. It was dark as I tiptoed across the room, pulled back the curtains and looked out. Snow danced in the beams of the lamppost opposite and it looked as if it was settling. I knew that later that day the jetlag would kick in, but just now I felt wide awake. The house was silent, and as I stayed by the window watching the falling snow, Dianne breathed softly in her sleep. I couldn't remember the last time I'd been this still for so long. It felt good.

With a sudden jolt, I caught myself swaying, as if I had been asleep on my feet. I made my way across the bedroom and got back into bed. Dianne was awake. She reached across and took my hand. 'I've missed you. Sorry you had such a bad journey home.'

I kissed her gently. 'Missed you too. I'm really sorry I didn't make the party.'

'It wasn't your fault. She had a brilliant time.'

I squeezed her hand. 'I love you.'

And then Dianne started to cry; huge sobs filled the room as I pulled her close to me. 'Whatever's wrong?'

She spoke between great gulps of air. 'I don't know what's happening to me. I feel as if I'm walking around in a fog. I haven't done it in front of the kids, but I can't stop crying. I know you're shattered, but can you take Katie to nursery today?'

Before I could reply, there was an almighty creak on the stairs. Dianne closed her eyes. When she opened them, she said seven words that ushered in what was to become the darkest period of our lives together.

'I don't think I can cope anymore.'

* * *

I got home early that evening, but as I entered the hall, the house was eerily quiet. The kitchen and living room were empty. I went upstairs and knocked on Ronnie's door. I needn't have bothered. I couldn't hear his television and that was akin to not hearing his breathing. It was unusual, though; it was gone five and Ronnie was normally back from his shift by four-thirty. I went into our bedroom. The curtains were closed and it was in darkness. Dianne was asleep, but the kids were nowhere to be seen. I shook her gently. 'Di? Is everything OK? Where are the kids?'

She woke, scrunched up her eyes, blinked and looked around as if she wasn't sure where she was. She spoke slowly.

'I felt really unwell after you'd gone to work. I didn't want to bother you in the office, so I rang my sister. The kids have been with her for the day. She said to pick them up about six.' Her eyes closed.

For a moment I just watched her lying there. I felt as if the tectonic plates were shifting beneath me. What was happening to us? And where had my funny, competent wife – the one who was always there for everybody – gone? I spoke to her closed face. 'I'll go and get them now.'

When I got downstairs, Ronnie was in the kitchen.

I said, 'You got in late today.'

He looked worried. He had acquired many survival skills from the kind of life he had lived. He was strong, could defend himself and had learnt how to keep his head down when trouble was around. But whatever other skills he had, bluffing wasn't one of them. He spoke without taking breaths between his words. 'There's nothing wrong. Everything is fine. I'm going upstairs to watch some telly.' He may as well have had *I've been gambling again* tattooed on his forehead.

'Can I have a look at your building-society book?'

He looked terrified and shook his head. 'There's no need. Everything is fine.'

'I'd like to look at it, Ronnie.'

Now he looked cross. 'Everything is fine, I'm telling you.'

'Please get the book, Ronnie.'

He stood shaking his head. Eventually he said, 'You know I've done a bad thing, don't you?'

'Yes, Ronnie, I do. I just want to know *how* bad.'

'It won't happen again.'

'Ronnie, get the book.'

He went to his room and quickly returned, handing me the red book in its plastic cover. As I opened it and scanned the pages, he sat at the foot of the stairs with his head bowed.

I closed it and gave it back. 'Over the past week, you've taken out thirty pounds a day in cash. What's happened to all that money?'

He lifted his head and reached out his hand for the book, but tentatively, as if he didn't want to touch it. 'I just bought a few things, that's all.'

'Like what?'

He screwed up his eyes and tilted his head to one side, as if trying to remember. Finally, he said, 'Some Cokes.'

This was one of the worst days of my life, but even so, I only just stopped myself laughing. 'How many did you buy with two hundred quid?'

His head went down again. 'You know what I've done, don't you?'

'Ronnie, I'm mad with you. This is your money, but making somebody rich by shoving it in their slot machines is crazy.' I took a deep intake of breath. 'Well, if you've got money to spare, you can chip in a bit more towards the running expenses of the house.'

He looked panicked. 'I know you're joking, Rob.'

'You just watch me, Ronnie. I'll work some figures out tonight and let you know.'

He turned and began to make his way up the stairs. Halfway up he turned. 'Where's Di?'

*   *   *

When I got home with the kids, Ronnie was at the kitchen table. As I came in, he said, 'I'm sorry, Rob. It won't happen again.'

'It had better not.'

'It won't. It's all in the past now.'

'Good.'

Lloyd was crying; Katie was pulling my trouser leg and asking, 'Where's Mummy?' My head ached.

'Rob?'

'Yes?' I snapped.

'Are we still going to do that thing?'

'What thing?'

'You know – the thing with me paying more money.'

I slammed my fist on the table so hard he jumped. 'Yes, Ronnie. We are going to do *that* thing.'

Ronnie and I holding the fort.

Chapter 13

The Long Winter

It was Easter, six months later, the night before Good Friday. The winter had been long. There had been many days over those dark months when Dianne hardly got out of bed. Barbara, her sister, kept up her help with the kids, and the legal practice let me leave work early to pick them up at the end of the day. Friends were kind, but the big surprise was Ronnie: I leant on him. He made up bottles for the baby, kept an eye on the kids while I was looking after Dianne, helped clean the house, made endless cups of tea and numerous offerings of what we came to call 'Ronnie's signature dish'.

That ritual started one evening when Dianne was asleep and the kids were in bed. 'Shall I teach you how to cook a French dish, Ronnie?' I asked him.

He looked at me suspiciously. 'What's it called?'

I put on my best French accent. 'It is called *haricots sur des toasts*.'

He didn't look convinced. 'I think it might be a bit hard for me.'

'No, Ronnie. You'll be great at it. First, get two slices of bread out of the bread bin.'

He wandered across to the pantry, shaking his head. He waved the bread in the air. 'Got them.'

'Now get a can of baked beans.'

He laughed. 'You're winding me up.'

'I'm not, Ronnie. I promise you: this is *haricots sur des toasts*.'

He came back with the tin.

I said, 'Now take the lid off the tin tenderly with the opener, then turn the tin upside down and gently slide the beans into a bowl.'

He opened the tin slowly, with his tongue in his cheek to aid concentration.

'Now put the beans in the microwave for two minutes.'

'This is just beans on toast.'

'Ronnie – this is French. Now, place the bread in the toaster, push the button down and look into it until the bread is golden brown.'

He depressed the button and began peering into the red glow of the appliance. After three minutes, with smoke beginning to appear, he said, 'It's golden.'

'Take it out and lay it on a plate.'

He laid two pieces of completely burnt bread on a dinner plate.

I put on my French accent again. 'Now, Monsieur Lockwood, this is the moment of truth that separates great chefs from the rest. Pour the haricots onto the bread.'

'What are haricots?'

I handed him the bowl from the microwave. 'English people call them beans, but really they are haricots.'

He tipped the beans onto the bread.

I picked up a knife and fork. It was time for the accent again. 'And now is the tasting time, Monsieur Lockwood. Will you be awarded a Michelin Star for your *haricots sur des toasts*?'

'What's a Michelin Star?'

'Monsieur Lockwood, it is the greatest honour a chef can have. It is awarded only to the world's finest.' And with that, I cut off a piece of the beans on toast and put it in my mouth. I moved it around with my tongue slowly. Ronnie was watching me in anticipation, as if he was in the final of *MasterChef*. Finally, I swallowed and put a finger in the air. '*Magnifique*! Perhaps the finest *haricots sur des toasts* I have ever tasted.'

His face lit up.

I made myself eat the whole thing. 'From now on, Ronnie, we are going to call this your signature dish.'

'My signature dish,' repeated Ronnie to himself.

*   *   *

There were many evenings after that when he would say to me, 'Shall I cook that thing, Rob?'

'What thing, Ronnie?'

'You know the haricot thing.'

'That would be wonderful.'

I have often tried to unpick the puzzle; he must have known that at least part of this little ritual was in fun and yet he still loved the praise. It never came close to pride; I have never met a more humble man, but every positive comment lit up his face as if it was oxygen to lungs that craved for breath. And as we consistently practised praise wherever we could, we noticed that over the years he began, very slowly, to look at his own life differently. One evening he came home after playing in a church cricket match. Ronnie was dreadful at all sport and Dianne held out no great hopes when she asked him, 'How did you get on in the match, Ronnie?' A huge smile creased his face. 'Pretty good: two runs and almost a catch.' Imagine learning to harvest every possible crumb of success – so that 'almost a catch' can count. But it wasn't all just nice words; the signature dish ruse seemed to produce actual results, and in fairness, his cooking improved over time; he even tried different dishes. Nevertheless, his signature dish remained his favourite and often, as I tucked into yet another offering of *haricots sur des toasts*, he would say, 'I'm a good cook, I am.'

'Not just a good cook, Ronnie, a Michelin Star.'

We got close during that long winter. Before this, I had been a combination of ad hoc social worker and surrogate father, but suddenly he became a friend – and perhaps the brother I never had. He was a rock. The sun came up every morning and hard on its heels was Ronnie.

* * *

All kinds of explanations were offered for Dianne's illness. But whatever it was, Dianne's body had seemed to have crashed. That shouldn't have been such a surprise: she had just had her gallbladder out, we had moved house, and within weeks she was giving birth to Lloyd. But there was no shortage of opinions; one friend suggested postnatal depression. I could understand only two of those words. 'Natal' was easy; the seven-month-old boy for whom I would already have given my life was evidence of that. 'Depression' I could grasp; that soulless, guilt-ridden emptiness that had somehow burgled its way into my vibrant wife's brain and bloodstream. But 'post'? What did that mean? Is it a month? A year? A lifetime?

Perhaps I found the experience of Di's illness harder than I should have, but I struggled terribly. I think there were several reasons for that. One was that although our close friends were supportive, from others in our church there was an underlying, and at times obvious, suspicion of the reality of Di's sickness. If she had broken a leg, they'd have brought a lasagne around, but anything from the neck up was much harder for them to come to terms with. One woman took me aside and said, 'My husband and I will always be there for you, Rob, but we can't abide laziness.'

But it wasn't just the fickleness of some, or the foolish shame of emotional illness; there was a struggle going on in me that was much harder to handle. Up until now, I felt I was in control of my life. Finances were good; as I sat behind my desk in the legal practice, I could ask for a cup of coffee and it would arrive within moments; bankers, estate agents and accountants all wanted to take me to lunch. But I discovered during that winter that actually, for all of us, being in control is an illusion. A momentary lapse in concentration on a busy road on a dark, rainy night, the first feeling of a lump on our body, a silly fumbling kiss at an office party and, in a millisecond, everything can change. Life can be brutal in the ease with which it disabuses us of the idea that we are actually in charge of very much at all.

Somebody once described Ronnie's young life to me as 'powerless'. There were many times over this period when I felt exactly that. I recall one February night about 10 p.m. when Lloyd simply wouldn't settle. I woke Ronnie and asked him to babysit Katie while I pushed Lloyd around the block, trying to get him off to sleep. It had snowed that afternoon and I had to shove the pram hard to get traction. My head was down as I trudged along. I was tired, cold, and he was still yelling. I stopped pushing to catch my breath. *This is not how I thought life would be.*

Perhaps the most difficult question for people of faith to answer is, 'Why does God allow suffering?' It seems this question is not a surprise to him; it is the cry of Job – the oldest book in the Bible. And it is a question I asked on that winter's day. I think up until Dianne's illness, I believed I had a secret deal with God; it went something like this: 'I will believe in you and in exchange you will bless me. I know I may have to bear occasional inconveniences – minor illnesses, perhaps a failed examination or two – but no big stuff: no cancers that don't heal, no crying by graves that hold people who are too young and too good to die, and no woman that I love lying in bed trapped in a body that has stopped working, with a mind that seems to have lost the will to fight.'

On that Easter evening, Dianne was fast asleep upstairs. Ronnie had helped me get the kids to bed and was now in his room watching a western. The house was quiet. I turned off the living-room lights and sat in the darkness, my brain empty, and sick in my gut. *Perhaps I am depressed too.*

Then the doorbell rang.

It was Norman, one of the leaders from the church. He is quite simply one of the most caring people I know. During that difficult time, he took it upon himself to watch out for me. As I opened the door, he smiled. 'Can I borrow a cup of sugar?' I smiled back and waved him in. The room was still in darkness, and I didn't feel like changing that.

We sat in the gloom, hardly saying a word for almost five minutes, then he said, 'Shall I make us a cup of tea?'

And then I started to cry. He got up, crossed the room and wrapped his arms around me. He held me as I sobbed.

I eventually sniffed my way back to composure. 'Will you pray for Di and me? I need help to get through this.'

'I'll do it now. Let's pray together.'

I slid out of my chair and knelt on the floor. I thought, *I'm supposed to be a hot-shot lawyer. People come to me with their problems and I fix them. But I can't fix this.* He prayed out loud, but I can't remember what he said. When he went out to make the tea, I stayed on my knees.

Norman took a long time making that drink.

*   *   *

I'm not sure exactly what happened to me as I knelt by myself in the darkness that night. At first, I felt a crushing loneliness, an isolation and blackness that was cloying. But then, after a while, something happened. I can't call it a presence, but there was *something*. And suddenly, in the very depths of my being, I understood that not being able to fix everything was all right. I knew in that moment I wasn't bright enough, wealthy enough, or powerful enough to make Dianne well. But as I knelt in the dark with my face wet with tears, I understood something that at first seemed to be very bad news but was actually liberating: *There is no deal.* If I am going to go on believing in God, then I had better come to grips with the words of one of the most ancient poems in the world – written by an old prophet and tucked away at the heart of the Hebrew Tanakh. Thousands of people have recited this poem, who were not just going through the kind of stuff that was affecting our family but in some of the most horrific circumstances known to man: they recited the poem in Auschwitz, in Dachau and in Birkenau.

> Though the fig tree does not bud
> And there are no grapes on the vines,
> Though the olive crop fails
> And the fields produce no food,
> Though there are no sheep in the pen

And no cattle in the stalls,
Yet I will rejoice in the Lord . . .
(Habakkuk 3:17-18, NIV)

I think that in some ways, I grew up in the darkness as I cried that night. I think before then I was confident in my place in the world, and perhaps a little more hard-hearted than I am now. I cry more easily these days; sometimes I think I cry more as a man than I did as a child. None of us wants to cry, but we are hardwired for it – it is the first thing we do as human beings. Writer Frederick Buechner said, 'Pay attention to your tears, for they often lead to your destiny.'

But on that Maundy Thursday night, there was something else – the seed of a disturbance in my very being that made me feel as if I had been wakened from a deep sleep by a noise so distant it was almost too quiet to hear.

But it was about to get louder.

*   *   *

The 'post' in 'postnatal' turned out to be long – very long, and eventually Dianne was diagnosed with ME – myalgic encephalomyelitis, also known as chronic fatigue syndrome: both a blessing – at least a nametag on which to hang an illness – and the curse of a controversial disease. Some who had doubted Dianne all along were not to be pacified by a couple of dodgy letters. 'Really? Is that an actual, medical, verifiable illness?'

Well, actual or not, life began to change from that Easter

Thursday evening. Firstly, I stopped caring quite as much what people said or thought. My task was to begin to rebuild our marriage, look after our kids, and help Dianne and I get through this together. And little by little over many months, Dianne improved. And as she got stronger, we spent long evenings talking to each other. And as we talked, I realised that those of us who live life at a hurricane speed often seem to do pretty well for a time, but sometimes the people to whom we are closest pick up the cost. And one night it dawned on me that although there was so much that I couldn't change, there was one thing I could: *me*.

Nobody in the legal practice was forcing me to work long hours, and I was going to stop doing that. I loved the various voluntary roles I had, and I wasn't going to ditch them all, but I was going to stop saying yes to the whole world and no to those for whom I had primary responsibility. I decided that I was going to call a halt to trying to prove to everybody that my old form teacher was wrong about me. I was unlikely to run into him anyway. But I vowed that if I did, I would tell him the very rude thing that my friend Alan Jones told me the 'BA' after his name stood for.

But even with those insights, and slowly but surely putting my resolutions into practice as best I could, it still wasn't enough: the noise was still there.

*   *   *

What do we do to kids in care? We feed them, keep them warm, educate them, and take them to the doctor when they are ill. But if they are so well 'cared' for, then why do a quarter of them end up homeless and a similar proportion of the men do time in prison? Why do half of under-20-year-olds who are in touch with the criminal justice system have a background in care?

Granted, many of these children are traumatised before they go into care, but even so, why are the outcomes so uniformly bad? The Independent Review of Children's Social Care, which was published in May 2022, believed it discovered at least part of the answer: 'The system too often tries to replace organic bonds and relationships with professionals and services.'

Over the years that Ronnie was part of our family, he experienced something of the 'organic bonds and relationships' that the review spoke of, and there is no doubt that he changed in remarkable ways. But I have often asked myself whether there was one thing in particular that contributed to that change; was there a silver bullet? I believe there was, but it was many years before I recognised it.

In Kirsty Capes' novel *Careless,* which she based on her experiences of growing up in care, one of the main characters, Bess, says, 'I could be happy and functional, if only I had people who belonged to me, and I belonged to them.'

This concept of *belonging* really struck me, and even more so when I read Lemn Sissay's *My Name Is Why.* Like Ronnie, Sissay was placed into care as a child and, again like Ronnie, shunted from one care home to another. He talks of that experience as being 'moved from pillar to post'.

Sissay's account echoes that of many people I have spoken with who have come through the care system. It was of a life with no roots, where one never felt secure: a misdemeanour – even an innocent one – could mean a move to a different home.

Ronnie rarely spoke of being taken from his parents and put into care, but whenever he did, the constant theme was that it was his fault. And he was tormented by the possibility that he might do something that could affect his relationship with us. He often asked the same question: 'Have I done a bad thing?' It's not hard to understand why he was so terrified: a sense of belonging did not come easily to him.

It was Dianne's illness that transformed things. It was during those dark days that Ronnie changed from being somebody on whom we poured our charity to becoming a member of our family. He became the one who helped me make up the baby's bottles, and the one who sat with Katie watching *Ivor the Engine* while I walked the streets pushing Lloyd in his pram, trying to get him to sleep. It was he who helped clear up the vomit – or worse – from one of the kids' accidents, and it was he who, for the umpteenth time, warmed up the beans for his signature offering. It was during those years that something changed in our relationship with him. Ronnie became one of us: privy to and part of the tears, the laughter and the pain that goes on behind every front door. He and I were in this together. Somebody we loved was ill, and we were trying to get her through it. He came to believe that he was needed, and because of that he experienced something that had eluded him all his life: *Ronnie belonged.*

*   *   *

It would be satisfying for Dianne and I to think that Ronnie's sense of belonging came solely from his interactions with our family, but it wasn't just inside the walls of our home that he began to feel different about himself. It may have even begun to happen on that first Christmas Eve when we all went to the carol service together and he hid Mike Shaw's car keys: Ronnie discovered social capital.

Robert D. Putnam, the author of *Bowling Alone,* noticed an interesting phenomenon in American life: although we live in an age of growing ability to communicate with each other, people are becoming increasingly disconnected from family, friends, neighbours and social structures; they are less likely to join political parties, faith communities or, as in the title of his book, bowling clubs. He suggests that the lack of interaction with other people poses a serious threat to both civic and personal health. Our bank account of relationships is empty; as human beings we are running out of social capital.

Almost as soon as he came to live with us, Ronnie had an increasing exposure to a wider community, mainly through the homeless centre and the church, and he came to believe that he belonged there as well.

The fascinating thing about him was that although one

would have expected him to be retiring and shy when faced with people he had never met, the opposite was true. It was as if he had been starved of relationships all his life and was now ravenous for them. Ronnie devoured every opportunity for social interaction. That connection could be as simple as putting somebody in a headlock, as annoying as a hiding of keys, or simply grasping every opportunity to help in any way he could.

Ronnie as a football manager was quite a surprise, but in truth it was only one of several areas into which he diversified in the time he was with us. In addition to his day job as a dustman, he became the equivalent of the CEO of the church chair programme. In all the years that he took responsibility for putting out the chairs on a Sunday morning and stacking them away afterwards, he might have missed an odd day, but if that is the case, nobody can remember it. In an endeavour in which the helpers were often transient (students), fickle ('Sorry – can't make it this week because . . .'), or simply lacking in the basic requirement of strength and agility (two elderly ladies from the Friendship sewing class), Ronnie was a giant in both consistency and execution.

And he brought his special skills to the job. Just as in our kitchen he introduced an order – and, some would say, regimentation – to the storage of cereal packets, cutlery and crockery, so, under his command, each chair was placed at exactly the same distance from its neighbour. And as in the case of his kitchen expertise, this was not without challenges; there was more than one visitor to the church who was told gently but firmly by Ronnie not to mess with his layout. But if his commitment and skill in the matter of the chairs was a shock, it was nothing like the surprise of his excursion into the world of finance.

Each Sunday morning just after the second hymn, little red bags with wooden handles were passed around the congregation so the faithful could contribute to the running of the church. The bags were deep. This feature was not designed so they could accommodate vast quantities of money, but more that in the spirit of 'when you give, do not let your right hand know what your left hand is doing'. A hand could be plunged deep into the bag without one's neighbour knowing whether one had slipped in a £10 note or silently put in a ten-pence piece. Of course, not all of us are quite so pure of heart as we might be, and several members of the congregation had developed the skill of putting in twenty pence but, while their hand was in the bag, ruffling somebody else's tenner so that the sound of paper could be heard.

Six members of the church had the responsibility of taking the bags around. They would walk down the aisle, passing them to the first person in the row and then collecting the bags as they came back up the line of chairs, and so on down the church. One Sunday, one of the bag carriers was ill and Ronnie offered to step in. John Loosemore used to say that in regard to businesses, 'There are no such things as amalgamations – only takeovers,' and so it proved on that Sunday. Perhaps the man who had been sick was pleased to come to the end of his stint, but whatever the reason, he never regained his position. Ronnie was on the collection team and there was no changing it.

The fact that he loved to play tricks on others made him a target for all kinds of practical jokes, and his taking the bags around provided a rich vein for these. The first was basic: he would often lay his bag at his feet on the floor in readiness for the collection, and I would simply reach under his chair, slide it towards me and hide it. Of course, when he realised it was gone, it was me to whom he would always turn first, but I had developed the knack of having my eyes closed as if in prayer, and he would quickly move his accusations of theft to people around us. Until I handed it back, chaos would ensue.

But the second was much more fun. As part of his financial round, Ronnie would walk to the front of the church and oversee the bag as it was handed from person to person. I would make sure I was sat on the end of my row and when he passed it to me, I would say, 'What's this for?' He would reply with something like, 'It's for the money,' whereupon I would insert my hand, grab a note and say, 'Great! Thanks, Ronnie!'

'No – you have to put money *in*,' he would yell as he snatched the note from me. And then, after he had passed my row, he would often look back, smile and shout one of his favourite phrases: 'You're a wind-up merchant, you are, Rob Parsons.' He seemed to enjoy the teasing, as if even that told him he was valued.

And as well as all of that, Ronnie helped every week in the kitchen of the homeless centre. He rarely engaged in conversation with those who came week by week for a meal or to select donated clothes or bedding; he would simply stand at the sink and wash dishes. In all the time I knew him, he hardly missed a night. One evening when he came back from his shift, I looked down at the scruffy trainers he was wearing and said, 'Where are your new shoes?' He shrugged his shoulders. I think he wasn't sure whether I would be cross or proud of him. He said, 'I gave them to a man who needed them.'

A homeless man walking around in Ronnie's shoes. Now that's an irony worth thinking about.

Arthur and Margaret Tovey.

Chapter 14

Time for Ronnie to Leave

September 1987. In two days' time it would be Katie's 10th birthday and tonight she was at a sleepover at a friend's house. Lloyd was curled up on the sofa with his head in Dianne's lap. For the last ten minutes his eyelids had been flicking up and down as he tried his best to fight off sleep and get to the end of yet another episode of *The A-Team*. The sound of Ronnie's television and his laughter seeped through his floorboards and the ceiling above us. He had been living with us for almost twelve years.

My eyes left B. A. Baracus flinging some poor soul through a window and settled on Dianne and Lloyd snuggled up together opposite me. She looked really well – so different from the dark years of her illness. She had never completely recovered from whatever it was that had attacked her body, but both she and I had learnt to live with the occasional setbacks, the disappointments of relapses, and the misunderstandings of those who thought that faith and illness could never live together. Dianne stroked Lloyd's hair and stared into the flames of the coal fire. As I watched them, *The A-Team* lost the battle and Lloyd's eyes closed. Not wanting to wake him, I waved to get Dianne's attention. 'I think it's time for B. A.'s little sidekick to go to bed.'

She smiled and started gently lifting Lloyd's head from her lap. I crossed the room and bent to pick him up. As she passed him up to me, she whispered, 'When you come down, there's something I want to talk to you about.'

When I got back downstairs, the television was off. Dianne had laid out cheese and biscuits on the coffee table in front of the sofa and a corkscrew lay next to a bottle of Rioja. 'I only want one glass and didn't know if it was worth opening it,' she said.

I reached for the corkscrew. 'I'll do my best.'

I poured the wine as Dianne peeled the wrapping from the cheeses. 'Well, come on, mystery woman – what is it?'

She sipped her wine. 'I've been thinking.' She took another sip.

I said, 'You've been thinking?'

She put her glass down and looked at me. 'This is a large house, but we only have one bathroom and Katie is becoming a young woman.' She took another sip of her drink. 'I was just wondering . . .' – another sip – '. . . I was just wondering if it was time for us to find Ronnie a little flat near us.'

I was silent for longer than I should have been. Dianne put her glass down hard. 'Well, say something.'

I didn't have words.

'Rob, say something – anything. This isn't fair. I'm not finding this easy either. Of course I don't want Ronnie to leave us. Well, I do sometimes, but I know that he's part of us. I just think it's time for him to have his own home.'

'I know you're right, but he's been abandoned by so many people, and he won't be able to see the logic of it. He'll just think he's being moved on again. And when you were ill, Ronnie was a lifeline. He helped with the kids, cleaned the place . . .' I attempted a smile. 'He even tried to cook. I feel as if I'm betraying him.'

She looked cross. 'I know all that. Don't make me feel worse. And we're not abandoning him. We're going to find him a flat near us. He'll be able to come around for meals and stuff. I just think it will give everybody a bit of space. Half the time I'm not sure if I'm his mother, his sister, his friend or his carer. And it changes so fast. One minute I think he's made incredible progress, the next I'm asking him if he's got deodorant on. It's exhausting. I'm not even sure that what we're doing is best for him. What would he do if anything ever happened to us?'

That thought had crossed my mind too, but I quickly pushed it aside. 'How would we tell him?'

Dianne picked up her glass again and spoke deliberately. 'I've been thinking about that. We'll say that he's done really well. He's been in his job for eleven years, he's really good at it, and with that and all the jobs he does at church and the homeless centre, he's proved that he is reliable and competent. He's earned the right to be independent; it's time for him to have a place of his own. He will still be part of our family – that will never change.'

'Do you honestly think he'll buy that? He doesn't want to be independent. He'll see it as a punishment, not a reward.'

Dianne looked frustrated. 'Well, perhaps that's not the best way to tell it, but we have to do something.'

'Di, you've been brilliant with Ronnie. I know that so much of it all falls on you.'

'We've both done our best. I'm just wondering if it's time for a change, especially with Katie growing up.'

I said, 'So, what shall we do?'

'We never really thought about any of this, did we, Rob? We just did it. First it was for a meal, then "stay one night", then another, and the years just went by.'

'Are you sorry we did it?'

'No, of course not. I'm glad of what we've been able to do for him. And the kids love him – in fact, I think they'll find it harder than us. I just think that it's time.'

'So, what do we do?'

'Let's talk about it over the next week. We're never going to think we've got it right, but let's at least try. But we do need to make a decision. Don't go all soft on me.'

*   *   *

It was a strange week. We were both quiet. There should have been hours of conversation, but perhaps it was just too painful. We had a couple of stabs at it, but it always came down to the same two things: it was probably right for him to move on, but both of us were struggling badly with what it would do to him – and perhaps even what it would do to us as a family; the kids had never known life without Ronnie.

And then one Saturday night we were meant to have the whole evening to discuss it but neither of us wanted to. Perhaps that was selfish or because we cared so much. Or maybe it was because there really was nothing else to say. On that night, we were in bed and about to go to sleep when I turned to Dianne. 'It's very hard, but it's the right decision.'

She kissed me briefly, turned away and sank her head in the pillow.

The next afternoon we were in the kitchen together. I said, 'I think I'll go and speak to Ronnie.'

Dianne picked up a tea towel and started drying plates that Ronnie had already done. 'Do you mind if I don't come?'

I took the towel off her and pulled her close to me. 'It'll be fine.'

She smiled weakly. 'You sound like him now.'

*   *   *

That evening, I knocked on his bedroom door. He shouted, 'Come in.'

I walked into his room. He looked around, said 'Hi Rob,' and turned back to the television. I don't know how long I stood there watching *Bullseye*, saying nothing. Finally, he turned around again. 'Everything all right, Rob?'

I went to speak, then stopped.

He looked worried. 'Have I done a bad thing?'

'No, Ronnie, you haven't done a bad thing . . . It's just that . . .'

I hadn't heard her on the stairs, but suddenly Dianne came in. She spoke breezily. 'Hi, Ronnie. Rob, I need you for a second. Sorry, Ronnie.' She turned and walked out. I followed her like a lamb. Halfway down the stairs she turned and whispered, 'Did you . . .?'

I shook my head.

When we got downstairs, we went into the living room. Dianne sank into an armchair and started crying. I walked across and put my arm around her. 'Come on, Di – we'll work it out.'

She pulled a tissue from her sleeve, blew her nose and said, 'We can't do it to him. This is not your fault. *I* can't do it to him.'

We sat there together saying nothing. After five minutes or so, we caught the sound of Ronnie's television as his door opened and heard him starting to come down the stairs. Dianne wiped her eyes and, looking across at me, mouthed, 'Three, two, one . . .' And then a stair creaked.

* * *

It had been a long day. My last appointment had just finished when the phone on my desk rang and the receptionist said, 'I've got a Margaret Tovey on line one for you – will you take it?' Neither Arthur nor Margaret had ever rung me in the office before. I said, 'Put her through.'

Margaret spoke in between sniffs. 'Rob, I'm so sorry

to bother you at work, but I thought you'd want to know. Arthur is in hospital.'

I breathed in hard. 'Oh, Margaret, I'm so sorry. What's wrong?'

She said, 'I'm not sure, but he's very ill. He collapsed in the garden. He tried to talk to me, but he couldn't. I called an ambulance. I've been at the hospital all day. I've just slipped out of his room to ring you.'

'But what is it? Has he had a heart attack? A stroke?'

'He's had a stroke before, but really I think it's the Alzheimer's and . . .' The line went quiet.

'Margaret – are you there?'

I could hear her crying. 'Rob, I don't think Arthur is going to make it. He seems to be slipping in and out of consciousness. Perhaps not even through the night.'

'I'm on my way. I'll see you at the hospital in thirty minutes.'

'I don't want to trouble you. I know how busy you are.'

'I'll be with you soon.'

'Thank you, Rob. It will mean so much to Arthur to see you.'

*   *   *

As I sat bumper to bumper in the evening rush hour, I felt both desperately sad and deeply ashamed of myself. He'd been an incredible mixture of mentor, friend and, in some ways, father. If Arthur hadn't come into my life, so many things would have never happened – meeting Dianne, learning to give talks, and John Loosemore hearing me. But above all, Arthur had made me feel special. There were things I should have said to him. I should have told him about my life now and how he'd affected it. I should have thanked him more. I should have visited him more often. I had always intended to, of course, but somehow life always got in the way. *Perhaps it isn't too late. It will still be all right.*

As I drove through the hospital gates, it was raining hard. This was a busy time anyway, but the weather didn't help, and the car park was crowded. I made several circuits of the multistorey before finding a space. Finally, I ran out of the car park across the road and into the concourse of the University Hospital of Wales. It was crowded. Visitors, patients in dressing gowns and slippers, enjoying a brief escape from their wards, and doctors – some in scrubs straight from theatre – all milled around or sat at the tables in front of the coffee shop. I wandered into WHSmith and picked up a copy of *Reader's Digest* and a bag of grapes. It was only as I was about to pay for them that I realised how stupid I was being. I apologised to the sales assistant and left them on the counter.

I made my way up the first flight of stairs and past a huge painting of Aneurin 'Nye' Bevan, the minister who had spearheaded the creation of the National Health Service. In the corridor, I glanced at a painting of the Queen, who had opened the hospital in 1971, the year that Dianne and I were married. Seeing that date made me think of how we had met in Arthur and Margaret's study group and of that Christmas Eve he had caught us kissing in the Prothero's front garden.

Arthur had believed in me. He saw something that my teachers were blind to. Just the year before, I had been invited by the Law Society of England and Wales to be a keynote speaker at the Law Society's National Conference in Vienna. The profession was in the middle of a great debate about its independence: there was a motion on the table that our rules should be changed to allow solicitors to enter into financial arrangements with other professions. John Loosemore and I had written extensively in the professional journals against the motion, believing it would compromise our duty of care to our clients. It was this that had prompted the vice president to call and ask me to be one of the main speakers.

Thirty minutes before the event was due to start, I'd phoned Arthur. He'd answered almost immediately. 'Rob – it's nice to hear from you. How are you and Dianne?'

'Arthur, I haven't got much time. I'm in Vienna – Austria.'

'Wow!'

'Yes. I'm speaking at the Law Society Conference. I'm about to go on stage in front of a thousand lawyers.'

'My word, that sounds scary.'

'It is.'

'Well, I'm sure you will do well. I'll be saying a little prayer for you.'

'Thank you.'

'You must come and see Margaret and me and tell us all about it.'

'Arthur?'

'Yes?'

'You taught me to do this.'

There was a long pause and then . . . 'Did I?'

Suddenly I found myself at ward B4. I was an hour too early for normal visiting times, but the second I mentioned Arthur's name at the front desk, an auxiliary nurse ushered me towards a side room. It was dark inside. He lay with his eyes closed; a heart monitor bleeped next to him. Margaret sat at his bedside, his hand in hers. She let go long enough to hug me. 'Thanks for coming, Rob. He's very sleepy.'

Margaret patted Arthur's hand. 'Arthur?' She raised her voice slightly. 'Arthur – look who's come to see you. It's Rob Parsons.'

He opened his eyes, looked up at me and smiled.

Margaret said, 'Well, what do you think of the boy who came to our Wednesday evenings?'

He whispered, 'I'm proud of him,' and reclosed his eyes.

I sat talking to Margaret, our voices lowered. Arthur didn't respond to anything we said or open his eyes again. Margaret said, 'I think he can hear us. But he's very tired.'

We sat just watching him and the rise and fall of the sheets. Finally, I said, 'I'll leave you alone with him now. Please ring us if there's any change or if we can do anything.'

'I will. Thank you for coming. It will mean a lot to him.'

I stood and looked down at the bed, biting my lip against the ache in my throat. 'Bye, Margaret.' I walked to the door, then stopped, turned and went back to his bed. I bent low over him and put my mouth close to his ear. 'Arthur, thank you for everything. You changed my life.' I kissed his cheek. He died three days later.

*   *   *

It was two weeks after I had made the journey up the stairs to tell Ronnie it was time for him to leave us and descended the same stairs with that mission unaccomplished. The kids were in bed, Ronnie had turned his light off an hour ago, but Dianne and I were still up, sitting in front of the fire, reading. I looked across at her. 'I've been thinking about something that Ronnie told us when he first got his job as a dustman.'

Dianne turned her book over and laid it on her lap. 'Oh?'

'Do you remember that I once asked him what he was smiling at when he came in from work?'

'No.'

'Yes, you do. I used to take him to work in those days on my way to the practice.'

'And?'

'Well, one evening, he was sat in the chair giggling, and I asked him what was so funny. He said, "When you dropped me off at work, one of the men asked me, 'Who's that who brought you to work in the car?'"'

'What did he say to them?'

'He said, "That's my solicitor."'

Dianne laughed. 'I remember that now. What made you think about that?'

'It's just struck me that the reason wasn't so much that I was a lawyer, but maybe that he had never had a mother take him to school on his first day or a father say when he was eleven, "How did it go in the new big school, son?" And now, at last, somebody was at the gate.'

Dianne picked up her book and turned it over. 'I think you're right.'

'But that's not all.'

She lifted an eyebrow and turned her book face down again. 'Don't push it.'

'I've only just realised that he's probably never had anybody tell him that they love him.'

'That's really sad, isn't it?'

'I've decided to change that,' I said.

'How?'

'Well, you know he comes into the living room every night to say goodnight?'

'Yes?'

'Well, as he's leaving, I'm going to say, "Goodnight, Ronnie. I love you."'

Dianne blew her breath out slowly. 'It's a lovely idea, Rob, and I don't really know why, but I don't think I can do it. It feels strange.'

'I understand that. It does feel strange. I'm sure he knows we both love him, but I think he needs to actually hear it sometimes.'

I was fascinated to read some years later of Lemn Sissay's need to hear those words as he expressed it in *My Name Is Why*. He recalls the fact the workers in the children's home used to say, 'I do this job because I love children.' But in all the time he was there they never said, 'I'm in this job because I love *you*.'

The next evening, Dianne and I were watching *Morse*

when Ronnie popped his head in to say goodnight. As he was closing the door, I said, 'Goodnight, Ronnie. I love you.' He didn't reply, just closed the door. But moments later there was a knock. I shouted, 'Come in.' He walked in slowly and sat in an armchair opposite us. His forehead was creased, and he spoke tentatively. 'Don't be upset with me, will you?'

I said, 'It depends on what you've done, Ronnie.'

He said, 'I haven't done anything. I just want to ask you something, that's all.'

I said, 'Well, ask away.'

Neither Dianne nor I were prepared for his question. Afterwards, we wondered whether he had overheard one of our conversations and that as I had climbed the stairs on that Sunday, he already knew what I intended to say to him. Or perhaps it was a sixth sense that allowed somebody who had spent all his life being moved on to realise that something was in the air.

He hesitated, then spoke slowly. 'We three are firm friends, aren't we?'

Dianne said, 'Yes, Ronnie. Of course, we are.'

He swallowed hard, as if the words lingering at the back of his throat were afraid to come out. 'And we'll be together for ever, won't we?'

Neither Dianne nor I spoke. We just sat gazing at him, his question hanging in the air.

Finally, I turned and looked at Dianne. She brushed a hand across her eyes and made the tiniest of nods towards me.

I smiled at him. 'Yes, Ronnie, we'll be together for ever.'

*   *   *

In some ways the workhouses that prompted Charles Dickens to write *Oliver Twist* were the precursor of children's homes. By 1839 almost half the workhouse population were children. As I was writing this book, I discovered that my great-great-grandfather, George Parsons, lived and died in the Bridgewater Union Workhouse. I found this discovery profoundly moving; there was nobody to do for him what we were able to do for Ronnie. Oliver Twist is rescued from a life of poverty and crime by Mr Brownlow, and as I read the novel again, I realised that in saying to Ronnie, 'We'll be together for ever,' I was stepping into Mr Brownlow's shoes as he says to Oliver:

You say you are an orphan, without a friend in the world; all the inquiries I have been able to make, confirm the statement. Let me hear your story; where you come from; who brought you up; and how you got into the company in which I found you. Speak the truth, and you shall not be friendless while I live.

Rob Parsons, Director of CARE for the Family with his wife Dianne.

The launch of Care for the Family.

Chapter 15

A Key in the Door

When I was a child there was only one source of heat in our house: the coal fire in the living room. Sometimes, even as I woke, I would hear my mother downstairs, cleaning the grate or bringing in coal from the store in our garden, so it would be warm as we ate our breakfast. I loved that fire; I would sometimes sit and gaze into it. When it was unlit, the fire grate was a cold, sterile place, but the touch of a match could transform it into a wonderworld; the flames would dance for me and the reddened and half-burnt coals make themselves into a labyrinth of caves and tunnels that a small boy could easily get lost in. My older sisters used to call me 'the dreamer'. A little while ago I came across this quote.

Ships at a distance have every man's wish on board. For some they come in with the tide. For others they sail forever on the horizon, never out of sight, never landing until the watcher turns his eyes away in resignation, his dreams mocked to death by time. This is the life of men.

(Zora Neale Hurston, *Their Eyes Were Watching God*)

But my dreams had not been mocked to death by time; my ship had come in. Not only did I have a lovely wife and two great kids, but the boy who had come last in class was now a joint senior partner in a law practice and an international speaker.

Almost twenty years before, as I had walked down my street to break the news to my parents of John's job offer, I had dreamt. *Me a lawyer. Think of it. We're going to have an inside toilet and a bathroom.* My ship had not only come in, it had docked, practically sinking under the weight of my fulfilled dreams.

And yet somewhere deep inside me was a faint note of discord. It wasn't malignant, judgemental or condemnatory; it wasn't that I, or anybody else, was doing anything wrong. It wasn't born out of a dissatisfaction with what I was doing: I loved my job. It was more a *yearning* – a reaching out for something; perhaps even that I was being called to change the direction of my life. It may be that Dianne being unwell was part of it – jolting me into a different mode of thinking. And I know when I first felt it: it was as I cried in the darkness on my knees on that evening before Good Friday. Something shifted in my soul that night.

Dianne's illness and the difficulties in our marriage had shaken me deeply. But those weren't the only things that made me re-evaluate what I was doing. We had been involved for a number of years in supporting families on the housing estate where the church was located, but suddenly it was us in need of help. We were both pretty open about the struggles we were facing; even when Dianne was getting better, we told people that we were still on a journey, and it was long and hard. And then we began to notice something: people wanted to talk to us. First it was a couple going through a torrid time in their marriage, next a young mum experiencing postnatal depression, and then it was a young executive near to emotional breakdown with the pressure of keeping both his boss and family on side. It wasn't that we had any clever answers, but it didn't seem to be answers that people wanted. I think they thought we would understand, and they craved somebody to just *listen*.

So many came that one day Dianne said to me, 'I know we're still working through loads of things ourselves, but there is so much need out there. I'd like us to start a weekly group where people can meet and support each other – somewhere where we can all be honest and perhaps realise that we're not the only ones who feel rubbish at life.'

I said, 'It'll be a disaster. We'll just depress each other.'

Dianne said, 'You'll see. When people come to talk to me, the only two gifts I can give them are the dignity of listening and the knowledge that they are not alone – that others have walked this path and got through. Those two simple things change everything. And the fact that you and I have struggled ourselves is the key that will make it work.'

And so, the Strugglers' Group was born. Each Wednesday night for over three years, all kinds of people crammed into our home – civil servants, surgeons, unemployed people, teachers, homemakers, single, married, young and elderly. Those who were broken came for help, to us – the broken. And it was on one of those Wednesday evenings that the nagging feeling in my soul found its voice: *What would it take to start an organisation that helped families and had, at its heart, the value of vulnerability?* It was a vision of the Strugglers' Group writ large.

One night, as Dianne and I were washing the cups up after the group had finished, I said, 'That was an amazing evening. Can you—' I stopped myself going on.

Dianne flicked my head with the tea towel. 'Come on – you can't leave me hanging.'

I bit my lower lip before speaking. 'Can you imagine doing this all the time – helping people who are struggling like we are? Do you think we could start a charity or something like that?'

She folded up the towel carefully and laid it on the worktop. 'I'm not sure I've got the energy for more, Rob. I'm just hanging on myself.'

* * *

As the Strugglers' Group continued to grow, so did the yearning, and I began to think seriously about leaving the law practice. But alongside the yearning were doubts: *What if it was all a dreadful mistake?* I would not only be risking my own future, but Dianne's, the kids', and Ronnie's as well. And then one day, two friends who had extensive experience in the charity arena told me of an opportunity to help begin the kind of organisation I had been dreaming of. There was no salary, but their wisdom and support would mean I wasn't ploughing a lone furrow. The nudge had become a push.

But the final shove happened in a scrapyard.

*   *   *

It was a Saturday afternoon in July 1988. The schools had just broken up and the next week we were all off to Spain for a fortnight's holiday. The kids were at a friend's house, and Dianne and I were wandering around a reclamation yard. As I watched Dianne, she seemed animated – as if this experience was one of the greatest adventures of her life. She would pick up a small concrete statue, turn it over in her hand, then discard it and seize on a piece of stained glass that she suggested 'would look lovely just standing against the wall at the end of the garden'. She was like a kid in a toy shop, as old window frames, floor tiles and bits of driftwood were lifted for examination and set down again. But as Dianne's ambling got slower, I was getting more bored by the second, and then, just as I was about to suggest we call it a day, we turned a corner.

In front of us and stacked against a huge wall were dozens of front doors: doors of all colours – bold red ones, timid greens and a yellow that must have driven the neighbours crazy. There were doors from large houses and ones from cottages. There was even a huge door with massive iron hinges that looked as though it may once have protected the hall of a castle. One or two looked almost new, but most looked as if they had lost their battle with the elements. And then I saw the door that changed everything.

It was, in almost every sense, an unremarkable door with peeling blue paint and a tarnished letterbox. But in one respect it was different from the others that lay against the wall: it had a key in the lock. The door looked forlorn, and I wondered what stories it could relate of those who had once turned that key – the families who had lived their lives behind it. And I wondered too, what whispers the other doors languishing in the yard could have breathed about the families they had known. Once they had protected those who lived behind them. Those doors had heard it all: the laughter and crying, the commitment and betrayals.

I stood in front of the door and touched the key in the lock. Something was gnawing in my gut. I turned to Dianne and waved my hand towards the doors stacked against the wall.

'Look at them. Imagine we could ask them what went on behind them and they could tell us their stories.'

She said, 'You're very philosophical for a Saturday afternoon.' I scratched my face to buy a little time. She asked, 'What is it?'

'I've been thinking a lot lately about us.'

Dianne looked troubled. 'Are we OK?'

'Yes, of course – we're fine, but there's something I want to talk to you about. Can we grab a coffee somewhere?'

*   *   *

Penarth is a seaside town on the edge of Cardiff. As we drove along the front, with the water shimmering in the summer heat to our left and the string of coffee shops and restaurants to our right, it seemed that most of the population of Wales had decided to visit on that afternoon as well. We drove up and down looking for a parking place until Dianne pointed to a grey van pulling out into the road near the pier. As I reversed into the gap, I felt as if we'd won the lottery.

We headed for the Victorian pier that poked like a finger into the sea, bought a ticket at the turnstile and ambled along the long wooden walkway. Since it opened in 1898, the pier had been a magnet for fishing, romance and ice creams; today was no exception. Men sat by rods, their lines bobbing underneath in the Severn Estuary, lovers ambled hand in hand, and children, ignoring signs threatening all manner of sanctions, threw bread for the swooping seagulls. I bought the coffees and we sat on a wooden bench, just vacated by an elderly couple who tottered towards the end of the pier arm in arm.

Dianne nudged me. 'That'll be us one day.'

I kissed her. 'I'd settle for that.'

She squeezed my hand, sipped her coffee and waited.

Finally, I spoke. 'I've been thinking—'

'You already told me that.'

'Don't interrupt. This is serious.'

I shuffled on the bench. 'I've been thinking about how we're going to spend the rest of our lives. This may be a bit of a mid-life crisis, but I don't think so.'

Dianne raised an eyebrow. I went on. 'Something happened back there in the reclamation yard. When I saw that door with the key in it, it seemed so vulnerable, I wondered what had happened to the family who had lived behind it.'

Dianne looked puzzled.

'I know I'm not making a very good job of this, and I promise you I'm not going to do anything rash, but lately I've been thinking about the future; are we going to go on doing what we're doing now, or might there be something else out there for us?'

Dianne looked across the water. 'Is this that thing you mentioned before? You and I working with families?'

I shrugged my shoulders. 'I think so. I honestly don't know. But yes, perhaps it's exactly that.'

'Rob, you hardly have time to fit in the Strugglers' Group – I honestly can't see how we could do more.'

'No, that's not what I mean. I mean giving our lives to it.'

Dianne looked startled. 'You mean leaving the law?'

'Well, yes. Not the seminar company – I'll still do those with John – but yes, I'd resign as a partner from the legal practice. That's what takes most of my time.'

Dianne turned her eyes away from me and spoke as she looked across the bay. 'It's a bit of a thing to be hit with on a Saturday afternoon.'

'I know, and I love being a lawyer, but when I see how well we work with people who just want to talk with us about their lives . . . I've been thinking that perhaps we could start an organisation that helps families.'

She turned back to me. 'How would we manage for money?'

'Well, I can't imagine that I'd have a salary at first, but I'll still be doing the seminars and the consultancy work. We'll need to begin talking about it properly and talk it all through. I honestly didn't intend to mention what I was thinking yet. It's your fault for dragging me to that junk yard.'

Dianne had a hundred questions. 'Would we have to move house? And if so, what about Ronnie? Is it for ever or just a trial? Will you be able to go back to law if—'

'I don't know. I don't think we'll need to move house – we haven't got a big mortgage. But obviously there won't be as much money about.' I hesitated. 'I think we may be being called to do this.'

'You mean called by God, don't you?'

I hesitated. 'Di, better men than me have struggled to be sure of that. But yes.'

She looked across the estuary, then turned to face me. 'What about John? You've been together for almost twenty years.'

'That's the hardest part of all.'

Dianne smiled. 'Oh, thanks very much.'

'You know what I mean. John has been so good to me. I know I've been good for the practice as well, but I feel as if I owe him a real debt.'

Dianne said, 'He's bound to find it hard.'

I stood up. 'Let's walk a bit.'

We held hands as we walked in silence.

At the end of the pier, we looked out across the water until Dianne said, 'I need time to get my head around all this. Let's talk about it next week in Spain.'

I let go of her hand and put my arm around her shoulder. 'I know this is a big one, Di. I promise you we won't rush it.'

Coming towards us were the old couple. They shuffled in time with each other, but he seemed to be leaning more heavily on her than when we first saw them.

*   *   *

It was our third day in Spain. It had been a wonderful start to our time away, and on this occasion, Ronnie was with us. He didn't always join us for holidays, but when he did, he always seemed to find his forays into foreign climes exciting, if not a little challenging at times. As we had made our way to the beach that morning, we had stopped at a grocer's to pick up a few things. I was wandering around the shelves and had glanced across the shop to see Ronnie talking with an elderly lady standing behind the counter. She was gazing at a piece of paper he was showing her and shaking her head vigorously. I walked across to them. 'What's going on, Ronnie?'

He said, 'I haven't done a bad thing. Just asked her for a bread roll, but she couldn't understand me, so I wrote it down for her.'

We had been to this same small fishing village in southern Spain several times before. It was famous for three things: the Balcón de Europa – a wonderful structure that prods its way into the Mediterranean, its caves, and Ayo's paella. As we sat on the beach I said to Dianne, 'I'm going to wander up to the restaurant to see if the paella man is cooking today.'

Some say that Ayo has been making paella on the beach there for so long that no matter what age they are, not one of the black-dressed women who sit outside the doorways of their whitewashed houses in the cobbled streets leading down to the sea can remember a time when it was not so.

As I got near the top of the beach, I could see that my luck was in. It was midday and the August sun was hot – almost as hot as the fire made of sticks and brushwood that roared under the huge iron pan into which Ayo threw mussels, prawns and pieces of chicken with careless abandon. And as always, a small group of holidaymakers was watching, enthralled. Some of them scribbled on bits of paper, hoping to capture and then steal Ayo's recipe, but if he cared, he didn't show it. As a piece of fish, hauled from the sea that very morning, made the water in the pan splash, it was clear to any who were wise that even if one took down every ingredient and mixed it in exactly the same proportions as did Ayo himself, the paella would not taste like his. As the old woman who sat on a dining chair collecting odd coins from those who used the toilet used to say, '*Ayo – tiene magia en sus dedos.*' (Ayo – he has magic in his fingers.)

As I gazed at him through the smoke and sparks, he

seemed like a god in charge of his domain. He had long, grey, wispy hair pulled back from his face by a red bandana; he wore a sweat-soaked white T-shirt, and shorts that looked as though he had borrowed them from a man six inches taller. The bottom of them played at the edges of the shin guards that were made from pieces of cardboard and tied with string, protecting the only exposed parts of Ayo's legs from the heat of the fire. Nobody knew how old he was; locals would sometimes guess perhaps fifty or sixty, but more likely they gave a shrug that implied it was not a question one should ask. Ayo made paella on the beach so good that everybody knew – even the people who lived in the village of Frigiliana that hung precariously on the mountain above the town – it was the best in all of Spain. And that was all that mattered.

I continued watching for ten minutes or so then left Ayo to the tourists and ambled down the beach towards the sunbeds, where I had earlier left Dianne, Ronnie and the kids. As I walked, I thought how grateful I was that Dianne and I were able to have this time away together to consider one of the biggest decisions of our lives. On the previous two evenings, when the kids were in bed, with Ronnie often not far behind them, we had sat outside in the cool of the evening and talked. On the second night, Ronnie had come onto the balcony behind us without our knowing. He must have overheard something that troubled him, because over the following three days he asked us at least six times if we were moving house.

As I got near the sea, I saw that Dianne, Katie and Lloyd

had left the beds and were playing at the water's edge; but there was no sight of Ronnie. I sneaked up behind Katie and Lloyd and splashed them. Katie laughed, but Lloyd filled a bucket with water and drenched me. As I shook the water off, I said, 'Where's the man?'

Dianne laughed and pointed back towards the sunbeds. 'I think we may have overdone the warnings about sunburn. I've tried every day to get him to change into something cooler, but he won't be moved.'

I picked my way back up the beach, past dozens of people lounging in the sun. I was a good twenty feet from our sunbeds when I first caught sight of him. If I had been concentrating, I could probably have spotted him from a mile away. The beds all around him were filled with the usual variety of humanity found on beaches: bronzed, muscular young men dressed in the most frugal of swimwear, tanned women in tiny bikinis and white-chested men with beer bellies. But amid them all – in the heart of the Speedos and thongs – lay Ronnie on his bed. If there had been a competition for the person with the least flesh exposed on the beach that day, Ayo would have come second. Ronnie's white hat was large and floppy, his face bright red beneath it. Covering his chest was a long-sleeved shirt with the buttons done up at the cuff. His single concession to the temperature was a pair of shorts, but even this gesture was somewhat blunted by the full-length black socks that ended just below his knees. A pair of blue trainers completed the outfit. No ancient knight around Arthur's table had armour more impenetrable. Ronnie had heard the warnings, heeded them, and now dared ultraviolet light to do its worst.

But even though he was obviously uncomfortable, he was sitting bolt upright and focused on an event occurring over the sea. A brightly coloured parachute billowed behind a powerboat and underneath it hung a man. Ronnie was transfixed.

He looked up at me and pointed skywards. 'What's that, Rob?'

'It's called paragliding. A very fast boat pulls you on a parachute above the sea.' I pointed to a small area of the beach that had been cleared of sunbathers. 'People land there.' I looked up and shielded my eyes against the sun. 'That man up there will be coming in soon.'

Ronnie suddenly got up. 'I'm going to watch him.'

'OK, but you don't need that shirt on – or those socks. Di's put in a nice top for you – it's in the bag.'

'I'll be fine.'

I watched him as he wove past the hordes towards the area where the daredevils landed. He was gone for over an hour and when he came back, the four of us had started to eat lunch. He was carrying his shirt and socks. Dianne threw him a bottle of sunscreen and said, 'Get this on now, Ronnie. Rob will help you.'

He did as he was told and had just finished putting the lotion on his chest and arms when he retrieved a piece of paper from his shorts pocket and held it up so I could read it. 'What do you think of this?'

It was a receipt. I rubbed lotion into his back. 'What's that for?'

'Can't you work it out?'

We were all too hot for one of Ronnie's guessing games.

Dianne said, 'Come on, Ronnie – tell us.' The kids joined in with a chorus. 'Tell us, Ronnie. Tell us, Ronnie.'

When Ronnie told us, four jaws dropped in unison.

Dianne was the first to speak. 'Is that wise?' She stared at me, and while Ronnie momentarily looked away, mouthed, 'No.'

I cleared my throat. 'I'm sure you'd be very good at it, Ronnie, but it may be better to leave it until the end of our fortnight. It will give you a chance to watch some other people doing it a bit more.'

But Ronnie was in his we-shall-not-be-moved mode. 'I'll be fine. I've watched them. You just have to hold on.'

I turned to Dianne. 'We're always telling Ronnie to try new things. I'm sure he'll be OK.'

Dianne exhaled air and began buttering a bagel as though she was attacking it. 'What time are you doing it?'

I had finished his back and he handed me the ticket. 'You're a better reader than me, Rob.'

I glanced at it. 'Ronnie is airborne at three o'clock.'

Dianne glared at me. 'It's not funny, Rob.'

At ten to three I said, 'Well, Ronnie it's time for us to go.'

He looked a lot less confident than he had before lunch. 'Will you come with me, Rob?'

'Sure,' I said. 'We all will, but we won't be able to come up in the air with you.'

'Don't be funny, Rob.'

The five of us walked to the small kiosk that stood at the end of the landing strip. I went with him to speak with the woman who was sat inside smoking a small cheroot. 'Ronnie is paragliding at three p.m.'

She pushed a two-sided piece of paper towards Ronnie and said, 'Sign that, please.'

Ronnie passed it to me. 'You read it, Rob. You're brainier than me.' I glanced down at endless clauses. There were warnings of terrors so awful they belonged in a Hitchcock movie. And next to every one of them was a declaration that all liability was with the customer. Ronnie was gazing over my shoulder. 'What does it say, Rob?'

'It says you're going to hospital, Ronnie.'

He laughed – but nervously. 'You're a wind-up merchant, you are, Rob Parsons.'

I handed him the pen that was lying on the counter. I pointed to a signature strip at the bottom of the page. 'It says that if you get hurt, you won't be able to ask these people for any money.'

He scribbled a signature. 'I don't need any money. I've got money in my building-society passbook.'

The woman took the paper off Ronnie and helped him into a life jacket. He was looking more apprehensive by the second. 'What's this for?'

The woman looked at me and then back to Ronnie. 'It's to save you from drowning.'

Perhaps we should have stopped him. Yes, we definitely

should have stopped him. But life with Ronnie was often full of those should we/shouldn't we decisions. I can only say that as I saw him, sporting his red life jacket, walking into the sea towards the boat, I felt a deep affection for him.

The boat pulled out, Ronnie ascended, and at first it seemed that all would be well. Soon he was in the air and waving at us. I hadn't seen him look so proud since the opposing team had lofted him onto their shoulders in the Boxing Day match after he had scored. As I watched him flying free above the waves and going further out to sea, my mind went to my conversations with Dianne about leaving law and starting the charity. The belief that we should do it was getting stronger in my mind; people sometimes say they feel an urge or call to change direction in their lives. I have heard it described as the lure to 'march to the beat of a different drummer'. Was that happening to me? To answer that call would take some courage. But then I turned and looked at Dianne sat with Katie and Lloyd, and I thought, 'Perhaps it's not brave – just reckless; perhaps it's not a call at all, just a silly flight of fancy in my mind and it will end badly.'

But even as I was grappling with deep philosophical questions, I looked upwards; Ronnie seemed to be having the time of his life. The boat swerved and turned; it slowed so that Ronnie descended briefly until his feet touched the water and then sped up again before he could sink. Even at a distance we could hear his cries of excitement. It was only when he was nearing the end of his ride that the smallest clouds of potential tragedy appeared in an otherwise azure blue sky. Dianne turned to me in panic. 'He won't be able to land.'

I laughed. 'Of course, he will. Nothing surer.'

And it was then that she whispered two words that made me begin running towards the water's edge and the boat as it came in: 'His knees.'

As I reached the sea I looked up towards the fluttering chute. I could see a look of horror on Ronnie's face. It seemed that the problem had occurred to him at precisely the same time as Dianne. Unlike other paragliders, who had begun bending their knees as they came in to facilitate a soft landing, Ronnie's inability to do this meant that his legs were ramrod straight. And it was not only us who spotted the problem – several people on the beach had begun to sense tragedy and were pointing upwards. The only person involved who seemed totally oblivious to the difficulty was the boat driver.

By now I was up to my waist in water and screaming upwards. 'Bend your legs! Bend your legs!' But it was obvious that not just his legs but Ronnie's whole body was stiff with fear. As I looked back towards the beach, Dianne had her head in her hands.

When he first hit the sand, it seemed for a millisecond that all might be well; after all, both Ronnie and the parachute were now on terra firma. But then, in an effort to stop himself toppling forwards, he began to run. He quickly reached the end of the makeshift landing strip and, parachute flowing out behind him, carried on towards a section of the beach crowded with sunbathers. He hit the first umbrella with such force that it flew out of its holder, got taken by the wind and careered towards the water's edge. Various families fled from the dervish who had appeared out of the sky, and he eventually came to land on top of a large middle-aged man who was sleeping on his sunbed. The man woke with a tirade in German. But Ronnie did not seem perturbed. He put his arm around the unfortunate Teuton, looked up at me with a smile and said, 'I did it.'

*   *   *

That evening, Dianne and I sat alone on the balcony of the villa. The kids were in bed and Ronnie was sitting at the table inside, doing one of Lloyd's jigsaws. The sun was setting over the mountains in the distance and the smell of bougainvillea filled the air. We sipped Rioja in the semi-darkness, the silence occasionally punctuated by loud cries of delight from inside as Ronnie managed to slot in a particularly difficult piece. At one stage he yelled out, 'I'm good at this!'

We sat for almost half an hour saying nothing, then I said, 'I think we should do it, Di.'

Dianne hesitated for a moment and then said, 'So do I.'

I stood up and walked to the edge of the balcony and looked down the valley towards the sea. To the right, the sun was losing its battle to try to stay above the ridge of the mountains.

Dianne joined me and put her arm around me. 'In a strange way I'm excited. You know I've supported you in your law career and it has given us a wonderful life, but I think perhaps with this, it will be something we can do together.'

The sky was pink, the aroma of the flowers intoxicating. We had just taken a momentous decision. It was a magical moment. The wonder was suddenly broken by a loud laugh from the living room behind us, followed by, 'Got it! I'm brainy, I am.'

*   *   *

John Loosemore and I had lunch together the Monday after we got back from holiday. The Rummer Tavern was a restaurant we had used many times – fast but not fast food. Almost as soon as we sat down, he said, 'I've got some news.'

I took a sip of my Coke. 'Don't tell me. We're taking over Linklaters.'

He laughed. 'Not this Monday. No. But that bank I've been talking to wants to appoint us as consultants to advise them on expanding into the legal market.'

'That's fantastic. What's the deal?'

The waiter had brought our food and was hovering, looking unsure. John looked up at him. 'Mine's the chicken pie.'

The waiter put our meals down and John started eating. He spoke between mouthfuls. 'It's brilliant, Rob. A retainer deal for three years. We've got to iron out the details, but they are very keen.'

I swallowed some lasagne. 'How much time do they want?'

'That's the beauty of it: just regular phone conversations, occasional meetings in London. They essentially want to use us as a sounding board.'

'It sounds amazing, John.' I got up. 'Just nipping to the loo.'

As I walked towards the toilets, I tried to breathe deeply. I knew the first words to come out of my mouth were crucial. The problem was I wasn't sure what they should be.

I was gone a long time. When I got back to the table, John had almost finished his meal. He laughed. 'Touch of the squits?'

'Sort of.'

His face became serious. 'Sort of what?'

I took a deep breath. 'John, you've been brilliant to me. I couldn't have had a better boss, partner or friend.'

John had antennae that wouldn't have been out of place on the roof of NASA. 'Come on – out with it.'

I said, 'I'm not sure how to, John.'

'Just say it.'

I pushed the lasagne around on my plate. 'I think it's time for me to leave the practice.'

He looked angry at first and then he said, 'If you tell me you're going to join Jacobs and Jones, I'll kill you at this table now.'

I smiled weakly. 'I'd never leave you to join another practice. It's just that I feel I may be called to help start a charity to support families who are going through tough times – all kinds of hard times.' I hurried on before he could say anything. 'I won't need to stop doing the seminars with you or any of the consultancy work if you still want me to. It's just that I wouldn't be able to work nine to five at the practice any more.'

He was silent for a while and then he said, 'You really feel called to this, do you?'

I spoke slowly. 'Yes. I know I might be making a mistake, but yes, I suppose I do.'

'And we'll still do the seminars together?'

'For as long as I can, John.'

I brushed away the wet from my eyes. 'John, you have been so good to me. I could never betray you. I really feel this is something I must do, even if I fail at it.'

He hesitated, then put his hand on my arm. 'You won't fail. You must follow your heart. I'll support you in any way I can.'

*   *   *

Four months later I put the key into the door of the new office of Care for the Family. It was situated in a suburban road on the first floor above one of the law practice's branch offices. My room in the law firm had been large, with an enormous desk and windows that looked across the city. This one was cramped, my furniture was second-hand, and the view was of a bin store.

I sat behind my desk and looked around. The paint on the magnolia walls was peeling, one of the blinds at the windows was broken and hanging down as if pleading for help. There was a small damp patch in the shape of a lion's head on the ceiling, and one of the two visitor chairs had a leg that was leaning, Pisa-like, daring anybody to attempt to put weight on it. I sighed, rearranged the pens on my desk and rang Dianne. She answered immediately.

'How's it going?'

I said, 'I can't talk for long. I've got some major work to do. Firstly, I've got to find my kettle, walk to the toilet at the end of the corridor, fill it and make myself a cup of instant coffee.'

She burst out laughing. 'Great pioneers have faced worse; I don't think you're going to get in *Foxe's Book of Martyrs* for that.'

'Di, it's so quiet. I've got stuff to do, but it's dawning on me how different it's going to be.'

'Of course it is. It will be different for both of us. But we're going to give this our very best shot.'

I tried to sound more confident than I felt. 'Yes, we will. I'll see you tonight. I think it's fair to say I won't be late.'

'Yes – see you later. Bye.'

'Bye. Love you.'

'Love you too. And Rob?'

'Yes?'

'Enjoy the peace. It won't be quiet for long.'

My father.

Chapter 16

Moscow

The evening I reassured Ronnie with the words, 'Yes, we'll be together for ever,' was as significant for us as it was for him. From the first night he spent with us we had been talking about how long he would stay, but now we had articulated and promised what we had, perhaps, known in our hearts after the first few months: Ronnie was a part of our family and he was going nowhere.

And it wasn't all one-sided. Although he had really come into his own in terms of helping around the house when Dianne was ill, he did his part in many other ways. We often joked about his meticulous passion for tidying the kitchen, but nobody complained about that when the dishes were piled high. And just as in the church he had jobs that became his own, so around our home there were tasks that belonged to Ronnie alone. There were families living near us who had their own cleaners and gardeners, but nobody had their own dustman. He brought to the task of monitoring and disposing of our household rubbish the same fastidiousness that he gave to arranging the crockery. And there were other advantages to his being in residence: whereas our neighbours had to be very careful not to overfill their bins to avoid them being left unemptied, 'That's Ronnie's house,' gave us a special licence when the dust cart arrived: we could put any amount of junk outside and it would be taken away. But perhaps, above all, Ronnie gave our home a sense of security. He was always there. Ronnie, with us for ever.

*   *   *

I was in Moscow when I got the news that my father was dying. It was 1991. Katie was 14 and Lloyd had just started in high school. Dianne and I had been married for twenty years and Ronnie had been with us for sixteen of those.

The charity had grown quickly in the three years since it began, and I was often asked to speak about the issues we dealt with; those invitations were mostly in the UK but occasionally overseas, and one of them was to give a series of talks at Moscow University. It was an incredible time to be in Russia. *Perestroika* – the period of economic reform that began to open Russia to the West – was drawing to a close, but there was little evidence of its demise on the streets. There was an air of excitement everywhere, and an optimism about the future. The pace of change was breathtaking. Russian Army uniforms that had once commanded high respect and not a little fear were being bartered for American dollars within sight of Lenin's tomb.

It was 6 p.m., and I was in my hotel room preparing my next talk. It had been a fascinating day. I was in Moscow as a guest of the government and that day they had arranged for me to go to Star City – the hub of the Russian space-training programme. It was a surreal experience; six army officers in severe uniforms yet with smiling faces entertained me to lunch. I remember thinking that the warmth of their welcome seemed regimented, as if they were trying to convince both me and themselves that the Cold War was over. After we had eaten, a colonel showed me around the facility. At the end of the tour, he took me into a small room, where he pointed to an orange space suit. He said, 'That's the one Yuri Gagarin wore.' I tentatively reached out to touch it. My hand hovered in the air, just inches from the material, and I looked towards the colonel; he shrugged his shoulders. I pushed my hand forward quickly, in case he changed his mind. The boy my form teacher had put in a tiny box, touched the glove of the first man in the world to fly among the stars.

As I began reading over my talk, there was a knock at the door. I opened it and a porter handed me a message on a silver tray. 'Ring home immediately.' Within five hours, I was on a British Airways flight to Heathrow. I couldn't sleep on that journey. As the plane made its way through the darkness above Europe, my mind was going back over my life with my father. I turned my face away from the woman next to me as I began to cry. The truth had suddenly dawned on me: I didn't know him. The overriding image I had of him was the difficult, distant, on-the-edge-of-an-explosion person. But there must have been more to him. Did he ever feel joy? Did he ever know love born out of passion, not simply duty? I remembered his kindness and acceptance of Ronnie that first Christmas Day and wondered if, somewhere inside him, was a different man. *Perhaps I have been wrong about him?* I knew there were questions I must ask – things I needed to say to him.

The cabin lights were down and most passengers asleep; a man near to me was snoring softly. I tried to doze, but every time I closed my eyes my mind began to race with thoughts of my father. I remembered when I was a child, walking with him in our local park. Other kids were climbing trees, tormenting the ducks on the lake or playing tag among the trees, but I was walking sedately at his side. It was a position my mother had broken free of, at least in her heart, but the child had no such power. I walked slowly, making sure to stay off the grass. *But there must have been more to him.* I scoured my memory for any incident with my father that was at all fun; I drew a blank. But then, just as the cabin lights came on and the pilot announced that we were an hour away from London, I recalled two incidents that, in the years since, I have clung to like a drowning man to a piece of driftwood.

The first of these is, in many ways, at once both the simplest and most difficult to understand. We didn't have many presents as kids, but whatever we did have were bought, wrapped and given by our mother. In the whole of my childhood, I can only remember one deviation from that, and it was this incident that came back to me on my flight home from Russia.

It was a Christmas morning, and I was 10 years old. In those days, there was a Christmas-morning delivery of post, and by lunchtime my father was still not home. At almost 2 p.m. I heard the front door open. He didn't come into the living room but went straight upstairs. I heard his steps on the landing and his footfall as he moved around his bedroom and came back down the stairs. When he came into the room, he still had his heavy Post Office overcoat on, which was covered in a light dusting of snow. Underneath his arm was a large parcel wrapped in brown paper and tied with string. He didn't say hello to my mother or even take off his coat. He just handed the parcel to me and said, 'Merry Christmas.' I don't know who was more surprised, me or my mother, and I took it from him, forgetting to even thank him. It was one of the few times in my young life that I saw my mother come to his defence. She said, 'Say thank you to your father.' I thanked him even as I was ripping off the paper; it was a bagatelle board – a primitive pinball game – as large as a washboard, with small cups made of nails and a spring-fired trigger with a ball bearing. To me, it was a thing of wonder. It was the first and last Christmas present I ever received from him, and the incident has left me with a host of questions. 'When did he buy it?', 'How did he choose it?', 'Did my father wrap it himself?', 'Where in his bedroom had he hidden it?', but most of all, '*Why*?'. Was it simply a random act? Or could it be more? Was it a show of rebellion against my mother – was he asserting his right to be liked and perhaps even to be loved? As I thought back on that Christmas gift, I found myself wondering if, at least in part, he was saying, 'There is a side to your father that you neither know nor understand.'

A father and his son, and a bagatelle game. I wish I still had it.

The second incident that came to me on that plane journey occurred just a year after that Christmas morning. I was 11 years old, and as a reward for passing the Eleven Plus exam, my mother had bought me a bike. I say 'my mother' because my father didn't want me to have one and my mother had to get an extra cleaning job to get the money to buy it.

It had three gears, white pedals, and something that was to get me into a lot of trouble: butterfly handlebars; these things stuck out much further than normal ones. I was riding down a busy road with cars parked either side when a cat ran across my path; I braked, wobbled and then heard a sound; the brake attached to the handlebar on the left-hand side had put a long scratch down the side of a grey Vauxhall Cresta car parked next to me. I stopped my bike and examined the damage. As I did, a tall, distinguished-looking man in a pinstripe suit leapt out from in front of the car and grabbed me by the collar. He demanded my name and address: it was a burst of shock rather than honesty that made me give them to him. He said, 'Your parents will have to pay for this. I'll call at your house this evening between six and seven o'clock.'

I was terrified; scared of the man, but even more worried at what my father would say. When I got home, my mother was making our tea and my father was sat doing his football pools. As soon as I walked into the living room I started to cry. My mother came in from the kitchen, wiping her hands on her pinafore. 'Whatever's wrong, love?' she said. My father looked up from his chair. 'What's up with you?' I stumbled out what had happened, and worse, what was going to happen that very evening. My mother hugged me and said, 'Don't cry, love. It'll be all right.' My father said, 'We'll see if he comes,' and went back to his pools.

At just before 6 p.m. I went into our front room – the one that was kept special for the visitors we never had. From the left-hand window, I could see down our street as far as the main road. Only one family in our cul-de-sac owned a car, and Mr Sullivan, who lived opposite us, was already home from work and his Austin parked outside his house. I knew if another car came around the corner, I was done for. My life went by a minute at a time; by 6.15 p.m. there was no sight of the grey Cresta, nor at 6.30 p.m. and even at five to seven. I was beginning to breathe more easily. And then, like Tom Jones coming home to the Rhondda Valley in his Rolls-Royce, my nemesis came around the corner and drove down my street. I put my head in my hands and then I heard a banging on the door.

My father answered the knocking and invited the man in. The tall man got as far as the middle of our passage and then began a tirade about the damage I'd done. He was either a brilliant actor or truly cared more about the scratch on his car than life itself. He made it sound as if I'd committed mass murder. My father listened patiently. My dad didn't understand about car insurance, or he'd have told the man to get it fixed himself. He said, 'How much will it cost to repair it, sir?' The man looked my father up and down and quoted a figure. My dad turned to my mother and said, 'Mabel, have you got any money?' In our living room we had a piece of furniture we called 'the china cupboard' and on one of the shelves my mother kept three cups. A piece of paper with a single word was Sellotaped onto each of them: 'Food' 'Fuel' and 'Rent'. My father got paid on a Friday and this happened on a Thursday, so there wasn't much money in any of them. My mother emptied the contents of all three cups into my father's hand and my father gave it to the man. The man looked at the money, snorted in derision, turned on his heels and slammed our front door behind him. I waited for the explosion, but it didn't come. My father sat back in his armchair, lit a cigarette and turned on the wireless. He never mentioned it again.

As I sat in the darkness on that flight, I suddenly realised something: although my father found it hard to express emotion, and although at times we all walked on eggshells around him, on that day he had stood up for me – just as he had all those years ago with Mrs Coulter. Either because of his upbringing, his disposition or perhaps what he experienced in the war, there was a lot my father couldn't give me, but, rather like the bagatelle board on that Christmas morning, he had given what he could.

* * *

By the time I got my bags and cleared customs at Heathrow, it was gone midnight. My brother-in-law was waiting at Arrivals to drive me back to Cardiff. He hugged me briefly and took the luggage trolley off me. We loaded up the boot and made our way out of the car park. As we stopped to insert the ticket into the exit barrier, I said, 'How's my dad?'

He took a hand off the steering wheel and touched my arm. 'I'm so sorry, Rob. Your dad died a few hours ago.'

* * *

On my father's 62nd birthday we had eaten birthday cake and given our presents, then he sat smoking and doing his pools while I chatted with my mother. Suddenly, he lifted his head and said to me, 'When you get to my age, you will look back on your life and it will have gone by so quickly it will seem like a dream.'

It is December 2010. I am the age my father was when he warned me about the speed of change. Both my parents and *Perestroika* have died. Somebody warned me when the kids were young that 'the days are long, but the years are short'. They were right, and in our home now, it is just the three of us again. Katie is married to Paul, and Lloyd to Becky. Our first grandchild, Harry, is almost 1 year old. The house is quiet. As I walk past the rooms that once belonged to the kids, I look into Lloyd's and think how we used to nag him to tidy it up; now that it's immaculate, we long for the mess. And then I push open Katie's door and imagine a little girl struggling hard to keep her eyes open so we could get to the end of *The Princess and the Pea*.

Ronnie has lived with us for almost thirty-five years. At the age of sixty he retired from his job as a waste operative and got a job helping in the kitchen of a nursing home. He worked there for five years. The owner told me he was their most faithful employee, never missing a shift and often turning up an hour early for it. The only drawback with him was that when he had to take the food around to the residents, it would be cold by the time he reached those in rooms at the end of the corridor; he would always get talking to the old boy in room number one and forget about the rest. He has a local authority employment pension, a state pension and more disposable income than most of my friends. His gambling addiction is long behind him. In fact, the other day he actually insisted on showing me his building-society passbook. The last page records the fact that he has just under £25,000 in his savings – and that is after giving at least £2,000 a year to help homeless people. He is still in charge of the chairs at church, still takes the collection bag around, and never misses his dishwashing duties at the homeless centre on a Sunday evening. Every day at the same time, he walks the half a mile up the road to the local Co-op and buys the exact same things – a can of Stella and two cans of Diet Coke. (Ronnie is not overweight, but the second the diet version came out, he swapped his allegiance.) He stoops a little these days, and as he shuffles home in his green duffle coat with the hood up, Dianne says he looks like an escaped garden gnome.

* * *

In just two weeks' time it will be Christmas again. Dianne is out for the evening with a friend and I am in the living room preparing a talk for the next day. I have been invited to speak at the parliamentary carol service in the Speaker's House at the Houses of Parliament. There is a knock on the door and I answer, 'Come in.'

Ronnie walks in. 'Hi, Rob. Not long now.'

'What for?' I ask.

'Christmas. I've got the presents. You're going to like them.'

I have never known anyone who enjoys giving, far more than getting, as much as Ronnie. But for as long as any of us can remember, he has given each of us the same present each year, carefully, if not expertly, wrapped in Christmas paper: a Marks & Spencer voucher.

'I bet you can't guess what you've got this year.'

I look up from my notes. 'I bet I can't, Ronnie.'

'Go on – try.'

I lift my shoulders and then let them slump. 'Let me see. Socks?'

He shakes his head.

I try again. 'A pen?'

Ronnie is in control and loving it. 'No.'

I screw up my eyes. 'Let me see. A book?'

He laughs out loud. 'You'll never get it.'

'Come on then, tell me.'

'It's a secret.' He wags his finger at me. 'You'll just have to wait and see.'

'You're too good for me, Ronnie. Now let's talk about something else. Am I in the team for Boxing Day?'

He is suddenly on the defensive and begins to make his way out of the room. But I press on. 'Come on, Ronnie. You can't keep me in suspense. Am I in or not?'

He sighs. 'I'll bring you on as sub.'

'Can I be a striker?'

'You'll have to go where I put you.'

'Well, can I be captain?'

'No, you can't. Lindsay Dobson is captain.'

I look hurt. 'Is Lindsay Dobson better than me?'

He has his hand on the door handle. 'I'm not saying anything, Rob.'

'Well, can I take all the penalties?'

He is now through the door and speaking over his shoulder. 'You're a wind-up merchant, you are, Rob Parsons.'

When the door has closed, I stay looking at it for a while. I think how suddenly he has got to look old, how he seems frailer. I get up, open the door and shout upstairs. 'Perhaps I should be the manager.'

He is out of his room in milliseconds and shouting down the stairs. 'You'll never be that, Rob. That's my job.' He goes back into his room and then comes out again immediately and yells, 'And you're not good enough.'

*   *   *

Twenty-four hours later it is cold and dark with a slight drizzle in the air as I approach the policeman outside the Houses of Parliament. He looks briefly at the letter I produce and ushers me inside towards the Central Lobby.

I am a little early and my host isn't there, but I am glad. I sit on one of the benches and take in the atmosphere of the place. The lobby is a huge stone octagon, built as a meeting place for MPs to be able to connect with their constituents. All around it are high windows, the arches of which are decorated with statues of the kings and queens of England and Scotland from the time of Edward I. Aides, security officials and politicians scurry back and forth across the tiled floor. Every so often I see a face that I recognise from television.

Then suddenly I feel a hand on my shoulder. 'Rob – lovely to see you. How kind of you to help us.'

I shake my host's hand. 'It's a pleasure.'

He looks at his watch. 'We're in good time. Let's make our way over to the Speaker's House.'

The Speaker's Drawing Room is already full, with over a hundred members of the Commons and Lords gathered. There is a low drone of conversation and the occasional outburst of laughter. Waiters move between the various groups offering small mince pies and wine. My host whispers,

'Not to put you off, but we have a couple of ex-prime ministers with us tonight.'

I nod nervously and gaze around the room; it is magnificent. In the corner is a huge Christmas tree, but the room itself seems to be part of the festive season. The walls are covered in maroon flock wallpaper and large paintings surrounded by gold frames. A huge chandelier hangs from the panelled ceiling, and engraved into the oak-panelled walls are the coats of arms of previous Speakers, stretching back hundreds of years.

My host glances at his watch. 'I think we've got time for me to show you a few things.' He begins to weave his way through the crowd with me hanging on to his coat tails. He stops at an ornate door. 'This is the State Dining Room; it was built to impress.' The look of wonder on my face does not disappoint him. He smiles, leads me quickly to another room, and with a flourish says, 'And this is the Speaker's Bed Chamber.' It is full of people eating mince pies and drinking wine. He sees my surprise that dozens of people are allowed to tramp around the Speaker's bedroom and waves his hand dismissively. 'Oh, he doesn't use it. But let me show you something even more interesting.' He takes me to a window overlooking the Thames and points to some steps leading down to the river. 'In 1642 when Parliament was trying to establish itself, King Charles I burst into this place with his soldiers to arrest John Pym, the leader of the parliamentarians, but he escaped down those steps.' He slaps me on the back. 'Enough of the history lesson. We've got to get started.'

The host taps a glass with a spoon and the tinkling sound slowly brings everybody to order. 'Welcome to our carol service. It's a great pleasure to have Rob Parsons with us this evening and we'll hear from him shortly, but first let's have our opening carol.'

And so it is that in this place of power and privilege we sing, 'Once in Royal David's city, stood a lowly cattle shed, where a mother laid her baby, in a manger for his bed . . .' In the place where John Pym took a stand for democracy and had to run from a king determined to destroy him, I tell the old story of a child born in poverty who was soon, with his parents, fleeing as a refugee to Egypt in a frantic effort to escape another king.

At the end of the service I stay for a while chatting, and then make my way out of the Speaker's House, back across the Central Lobby and past the policeman into Millbank. The wind has picked up, and I pull the collar of my overcoat up as I turn left and begin walking along the Embankment, past the statue of William Wilberforce and towards my hotel.

The rain has stopped but it is bitterly cold, and I walk with my head down against the chill of the wind. And because of that, I only see the couple when they are practically on top of me. The man is elderly, tall, and has a large suitcase which he is half carrying, half dragging along the pavement. He is not in any sense smartly dressed, yet he stands in sharp contrast to the woman. She is dishevelled. Her long grey hair is flying wildly in the wind, and her face is lined, as though not just the elements but life itself has warred against it. She is wrapped in a long dark overcoat that is far too large for her and would have better fitted her companion.

As they pass me, the man speaks. 'Excuse me, sir, but could you tell us how to get to Charing Cross Station?'

I stop and nod. 'Yes, of course.' I point back towards Parliament. 'If you carry on along this road—'

'Actually, sir, we're trying to find St Martin-in-the-Fields. The last person we asked said it was very near the station.'

Suddenly I understand why this mismatched couple are dragging a suitcase along a London street late at night in the heart of winter: they are trying to get to the church just off Trafalgar Square that has helped thousands of homeless people over the years.

I begin to explain. 'Go along here, past the Houses of Parliament, and then you'll need to—' Just then, there is a vicious gust of freezing wind. I look into the woman's face; it is pinched with cold yet her eyes are vacant, almost as if she is past caring. I say, 'Hang on. Give me a minute.' I go to the edge of the road and look both ways. It is only seconds before I see the yellow light I have been hoping for. I flag the taxi down and say to the driver, 'These people need to get to St Martin-in-the-Fields.' I hold some money out. 'This will cover it.' I am not sure if he will take them, but he looks up at me, winks and pushes the note back into my hand. 'I'll look after them, guv. Merry Christmas!' The woman says nothing as she climbs into the back of the cab, but the man turns and mouths, 'Thank you.'

I watch the taxi as it goes down Millbank and turns left past St Margaret's Church, then I lose sight of it as it makes its way around the roundabout and towards Whitehall; a man and a woman looking for a bed at Christmas.

* * *

Two weeks later it was Christmas Day. Dianne and I were asleep when there was a knock on our bedroom door. Dianne stirred. 'Come in.' Ronnie appeared carrying a tray, which he laid on our bed. 'Merry Christmas!'

Dianne rubbed her eyes and dug me in the ribs. 'Merry Christmas, Ronnie! Rob – look what Ronnie has brought us.'

I sat up reluctantly. Through all the years Ronnie was with us he never managed to master the art of making a decent cup of tea. Perhaps it was the frugality of his early years, but the water always looked as if the tea bag had only entered it momentarily and been extracted before it could disgorge any of its Typhoo essence. Dianne used to call it 'Ronnie's gnat's pee'. However, on this special morning, he had attempted an addition to his normal offering – fifty per cent of his 'signature dish': toast. The battered and bruised slices on the plate looked as though they had been subjected to an onslaught of burning and scraping. A thin covering of butter had been added in an effort to disguise the horror that lay beneath it.

I peered down at the tray. 'This looks amazing.'

Ronnie beamed. 'Not long now and we'll be opening our presents.'

'Yes,' said Dianne. 'Everyone's coming for lunch, so we'll do it after that.'

Ronnie's face fell. He had obviously thought that his breakfast would kick-start festivities a little earlier than usual. I said, 'I can't wait to see what you've got us.'

Dianne kicked me under the sheets and Ronnie wagged a finger at me. 'I'm not telling.' As he turned to go, I noticed a red mark on his forehead. 'What have you done to your face?'

He seemed flustered. 'Oh that – nothing. Just tripped up in the street.'

'When did you do that?'

'Yesterday, on the way back from the Co-op. But it's fine now.'

I was about to ask another question when Dianne nudged me and said, 'Well, Ronnie, thank you very much for breakfast – you'd better let us eat it now.'

The great thing about Ronnie is that he was very difficult to offend. 'See you later,' he said.

Dianne waited until she heard Ronnie's bedroom door close, then she whispered, 'I forgot to tell you, but he fell down coming out of church last Sunday as well.'

I shrugged my shoulders, 'It's probably just coincidence.'

She nodded and then looked down at the tray. 'You go first. I ate yesterday.'

Just then there was a knock at the door. I shouted, 'Come in.'

He didn't – just popped his head around the door and said, 'It's snowing.'

As Ronnie closed the door, Dianne leapt out of bed and pulled back the curtains. 'Oh, look, Rob – come and see.' I stood next to her at the window. The snow had done what it always does – transformed the dirty and grimy into the lovely, and made the beautiful magical.

I put my arm around her. 'Snow on Christmas Day,' I said. And suddenly we were sixteen again, singing carols with Arthur Tovey in the Prothero's garden and there were snowflakes on Dianne's lips. 'Do you remember our first kiss?'

She looked puzzled. 'No, but I can remember my first one with Alan Timson.'

I tried to look crestfallen. She squeezed my arm. 'Of course, I remember it.'

I pulled her close to me. 'It's good to have you well, Di.'

She looked troubled and I knew why. Whatever had plagued her body had never really left and there were sometimes relapses. She was afraid to presume on wellness. Nevertheless, we had learnt to enjoy the good times and hang on in the harder ones. She smiled, 'Yes, it is.'

'And because you are well, and because it is Christmas, and especially because it is snowing – I am going to give you a gift.'

'That sounds exciting.'

'Close your eyes.' I tiptoed to the bed, lifted the tray quietly and laid it at her feet. 'Open them now!' The toast missed me because I ducked.

*   *   *

Christmas lunch that day was over quickly, mostly down to Ronnie pushing us all along in an effort to get to present-opening time. When the dirty dishes had been carried into the kitchen, we all trooped into the living room for the big occasion. The gifts were all stacked under a large Christmas tree except for those Ronnie was giving, which were by his side in a small pile.

In a tone that didn't invite discussion, Ronnie said, 'I'll go first,' and handed Dianne an envelope. She had played this game many times and knew the routine and her lines well. First, she held it up to the light. 'Mmm . . . difficult to work out.' Next she smelt it and said, 'I wonder what this could be?' And finally, she felt it all over, prodding, pressing and smoothing the small package. Ronnie was beside himself with excitement. 'Go on – open it.' Dianne knew that how she delivered the denouement was critical. She slowly tugged at the ribbon surrounding the parcel and gently undid the knot. She slid her fingers tentatively into the tissue paper and like a magician surprised to actually find a rabbit, yelled, 'A twenty-five-pound gift voucher! Thank you so much, Ronnie. That is so generous.'

Ronnie was eager to see his beneficence through to completion. 'Your turn now, Rob.' And so it was that five other people went through the gift-voucher routine. It is fair to say that none matched the drama that Dianne had managed to create, but then again, it was easier with the first. And when the job was done, Ronnie leant back in satisfaction, smiled, and said, 'I got you all, didn't I?'

But now it was our turn. As we began giving gifts to each other, Ronnie suddenly got up and went into the kitchen. He reappeared waving a black plastic bag. 'I'm in charge of the rubbish.' From that moment on, the second a piece of wrapping paper touched the floor, Ronnie was on it like an eagle on a mouse. Our generosity to each other was punctuated with Ronnie rushing from person to person and filling his bag as though he was on commission.

'And now,' said Katie, 'a special present for Ronnie from Lloyd and Becky, Paul, me and Harry.' She handed him a small rectangular package.

Ronnie showed no desire at all to prod, sniff or hold his gift up to the light. He began to tear off the wrapping as soon as it touched his hands. A small box. He carefully lifted off the lid and looked in. 'What is it?'

Lloyd said, 'It's a phone, Ronnie. You've got your own mobile phone.'

Ronnie picked it out of its case and gazed at it intently. Then he held it up for the crowd to admire. It was basic. Hardly a smartphone. In fact, so unsmart it was practically retro while it was still new. But nevertheless, a phone. And Ronnie loved it. Nobody present that day knew what trauma that gift would unleash on the twenty or so people who were unfortunate enough to be the sum total of Ronnie's contacts list. These tormented souls were destined to be rung at all hours and – on enquiring as to the reason for the call – receiving the answer: 'Just chatting.' They could not have guessed how often he would ask various people what he should do about the message icon, or how he should adjust the time now that the clocks had gone forward or back. And they could never have imagined how, now that he had given up gambling, the phone would provide the means to spend money and win every time. One of the delights of his life was to go into the Co-op and add credit to his account. He only stopped this pursuit when I discovered he had over £100 of Pay-As-You-Go to use and I told him if he didn't stop doing it, I'd put his rent up.

The rest of Christmas Day went pretty much as it always does – a combination of old films, tangerines, Brazil nuts and Baileys – and before you could say, 'Has anybody seen the tin of Quality Street?' it was 10 p.m. and somebody was musing, 'Isn't it amazing? You prepare for it for so long and suddenly it's over.' Almost as soon as our kids had left, Dianne said, 'Goodnight, guys, I'm shattered. We'll do the dishes tomorrow.' Ronnie beamed and beckoned us to follow him to the kitchen. 'I've got a surprise for you.'

We trooped behind Ronnie into a spotless kitchen and Dianne, with a look of shock worthy of a place at RADA, shouted, 'You've done the dishes!'

'You're amazing, Ronnie,' I said. 'Brilliant presents, tidying up the wrapping paper and doing all the dishes. There is no end to your skill.' He was beaming. I thought he might explode with joy. Perhaps that shouldn't have been a surprise: it was Christmas, he was in a family, basking in the praise of two people he knew loved him, and in addition to all of that, there nestled in his pocket a present so wondrous that from that day on it would be shown to everybody he met.

Dianne and I were just about drifting off to sleep when he knocked on the door. I shouted, 'Come in.'

He stood there and said, 'I like my phone, Rob.'

I smiled at him, 'Yes, Ronnie, it's a lovely phone.'

'I'm going to look after it.'

'Well done, Ronnie.'

'Rob?'

'Yes, Ronnie.'

'Is it too late to ring Andrew Davenport?'

'Yes, Ronnie, much too late.'

'Hope I didn't offend you?'

'No Ronnie, you didn't offend us.'

'Well, goodnight.'

'Goodnight, Ronnie.'

When he had gone, I turned to Dianne. 'I think Katie and Lloyd have started something with that phone that we'll all regret.'

They definitely had. But even so, a day was coming when we were very grateful that he had it.

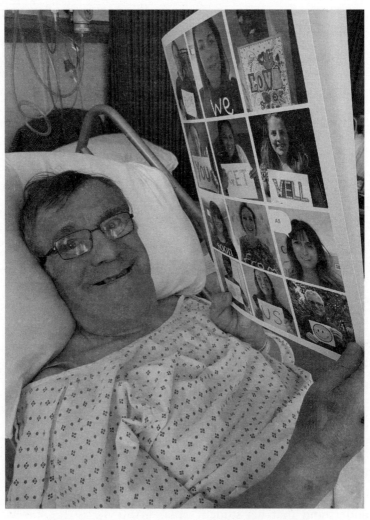

Ronnie in hospital with a card from friends at
the charity where he volunteered.

Chapter 17

Take Me Back

The post was late on that bitterly cold November day in 2019. The year was drawing to an end and the world had no idea of the traumas that 2020 had in store. The letter addressed to Dianne had arrived after two in the afternoon, while she was out shopping. That weekend we had the grandkids staying over, and as I looked out into the garden I could see Harry, Lily, Evie and Jackson playing hide and seek while Freddie, aged 6, was playing soccer with Ronnie. I laid the letter on the coffee table and ambled out to watch the action.

Freddie was trying to teach Ronnie how to do keep-ups with a football. Even as I walked towards them, I could tell that the lessons were not going well; Freddie did not understand that his student's inability to hinge his knees meant that anything above a score of one was a triumph. So, he persisted: 'Like this, Ronnie – keep your eye on the ball.' Ronnie did manage to keep contact with the ball with his eyes but unfortunately not with his foot, and finally he threw it away, shouting, 'I'm rubbish, I am.'

Having lost Ronnie as both a student and an audience, Freddie was about to turn his attention to me when Dianne walked into the garden. She looked upset. I shouted over my shoulder, 'Great managers don't have to do keep-ups, Ronnie,' and hurried towards Dianne. 'What's happened?' I asked.

'I've banged the car.'

I put my arm around her as we walked into the house. 'Are you OK? Is anybody hurt?'

'No – just my pride. It was silly. I was reversing out of a space and hit a car being driven by a young woman backing into the space next to me – both of us have dents.'

'Whose fault was it?'

'Who knows? The woman was lovely. We swapped names and addresses. I imagine it was six of one and half a dozen of the other.'

I said, 'Bumpers at dawn. Well, at least nobody is hurt; we'll let the insurance companies sort it out.' I sounded less fazed than I felt; I knew that the hassle of the phone calls, the paperwork and the drawing of silly diagrams showing two cars touching would probably end up on my shoulders. 'Go and sit down and I'll make some tea. There's some post on the coffee table for you.'

When I walked into the living room carrying two mugs of tea, Dianne was reading the letter. She took her drink from me, looked up and said, 'You remember I went for that mammogram? They want me back for another one.'

The mind has an incredible ability to quickly rearrange our worries in order of severity. And in those few seconds, the crashed car plunged down my hierarchy of concerns. I remember thinking, 'How can life change this fast?' Ten minutes ago, my biggest problem was finding Evie's shoe! I wanted to chase after the postman, push the letter back into his bag and say, 'This isn't meant for us.'

* * *

Dianne's repeat mammogram was a week before Christmas. We sat together in the waiting room smiling nervously at the half a dozen people also waiting. Dianne whispered, 'I have to go to the loo.'

I screwed up my forehead. 'What if they call you while you're gone?'

She tapped me on the arm. 'You'll have to be a very big boy and tell them your wife has gone to the toilet.' We both burst out laughing and looked away as a woman across the room glared at us. As soon as Dianne came back, her name was called. I got up to go with her, but she said, 'I think you'll have to wait here.'

And so I waited: waited for a result over which I had no influence, played no part, and yet had the power to change our lives for ever. I waited for a simple yes or no. *Please, God, let it be no.*

Dianne was gone for thirty minutes and then she popped her head around a door and beckoned to me. She was alone in a small consulting room wearing a hospital gown tied at the back. 'They've found something.'

I'd practised my response to this moment, but I breathed in faster and deeper than I intended. 'What happens now?'

'They've taken a biopsy – they'll send it off to check it.'

'How long will it take?'

A single tear ran down Dianne's face. 'We'll know in two weeks.'

*   *   *

The cancer was small and had been detected early. The prognosis was good. Dianne had a lumpectomy in mid-January at Llandough Hospital in Cardiff. Three months later, she had only just finished the last of her ten sessions of radiotherapy when, less than twelve miles away in Newport, Marita Edwards died. She was the first person in the UK to have caught Covid-19 in hospital. The nation was in lockdown.

I have never experienced the things my parents went through; never watched a flare drop in the garden of my home as my mother did one winter's night, knowing that thousands of feet above it a pilot was using its light to guide a bomb. But I know that Covid-19 was also effective in the terror it brought: silent, invisible and ruthless; in the United Kingdom it claimed five times as many lives as were lost in the Blitz of the Second World War. But perhaps Covid's real horror was the devastation it unleashed was so often brought not by enemies but by those who loved us dearly. A kiss, a hug, a touch that was meant to say 'I love you' could bring death to our doors.

The world was in shock. Television images of people fighting for breath in the streets because the hospitals were overflowing filled us with dread. Especially in parts of the world that were unused to natural disasters, where wealth and privilege protected us from the everyday hardships that face those in developing nations, we felt the virus had no right to be here. We demanded to know how it could happen to us. And so we attacked it. One expert said our efforts were like a cat chasing a laser beam – rushing from masks to social distancing, to extended handwashing, and eventually to lockdown. Our homes became the last bastion of defence – and our prisons.

Ronnie found lockdown very hard to cope with. As the restrictions increased, he became more and more agitated. It seemed that he was simply unable to understand why he couldn't play his usual tricks – whether it was hiding a pen or putting some poor soul in a headlock. I was especially concerned about social distancing because of Dianne's vulnerability after her cancer treatment, and I remember one day yelling at him like a man possessed because he rushed out of the house to help a Tesco delivery man unload his van.

It was an effort to get Ronnie to take even the most basic precautions. I told him that the government had said we must wash our hands for at least twenty seconds and said it had suggested that we judge the time by singing 'Happy Birthday' twice over. One day I caught him giving his hands a cursory wash at the kitchen sink. I said, 'No, Ronnie. Start again and keep your hands under the water for longer – and remember what I told you to sing.'

Later in the day, I saw him washing his hands again. He was mumbling, 'Happy birthday to me, Happy birthday to me . . .'

Three months later I was working in my study when my phone rang. It was Ronnie on his mobile. I was busy and ignored it. Five minutes passed. It rang again. I hit 'answer'. 'Yes, Ronnie?'

'Can you come up to my room?'

'What is it?'

'Can you just come up, please?'

I ran up the stairs. When I got into his room, he was sitting on the floor with his back leaning against an armchair. 'What's happened?' I asked.

He shrugged his shoulders. 'I fell over, but I can't get up.'

'Have you hurt yourself?'

He touched the top of his head and winced; when he lowered his hand there was blood on it. He examined it as though it might belong to somebody else. 'I think I banged my head a bit.'

'I'd better call an ambulance.'

'I'm not going to hospital.'

Dianne must have heard me rushing up the stairs. She burst into the room behind me and when I told her what had happened, she knelt next to Ronnie. 'I think it's best if somebody has a look at you, Ronnie.'

The ambulance arrived quickly. Dianne and I stepped

aside as two paramedics came into his room. We hovered like anxious parents.

Ronnie smiled at them. 'Sorry to bother you.'

'No bother, young man. Now let's have a look at you.'

A battery of tests was completed and one of the paramedics turned to us and said, 'I think he's fine. Just had a bit of a slip.'

Dianne's jaw was set. 'I don't think he's fine. He looks dreadful. Can you please take him in? He's been falling a lot lately.'

'Sure. It won't do any harm – they can give him a thorough check there.'

Ronnie started to say something, looked at Dianne and stopped. I said, 'Can we come with him?'

The paramedic said, 'Sorry – no. Covid and all that. No visitors are allowed. Give the assessment unit a ring in a couple of hours and they'll tell you if you can pick him up or not.'

I felt a deep sadness as I saw him go alone into the back of the ambulance. As he lay on the stretcher, he looked lost. I shouted, 'I love you, Ronnie.'

I heard his 'Love you, too', as the doors slammed shut.

* * *

After an hour we rang the hospital: Ronnie had gone for a brain scan, but there was no other news. We rang again later. The nurse said that the scan was back and the doctor wanted to talk to us but had been called to an emergency in another part of the hospital. She would ring us as soon as she came back on the ward.

I have never felt so helpless. In all the years Ronnie was with us he was never assessed formally with regard to his learning challenges, but we knew that in so many ways he thought and acted like a child. And he was alone.

Two hours later my mobile rang. I put the call on the loudspeaker and Dianne listened in. Ronnie had had a stroke and had lost most of the movement down his left-hand side. The doctor went on to tell us that the scan had shown several older, minor strokes. Suddenly the falls began to make sense. I asked if we could see him and was told it wasn't possible.

'But Ronnie has learning difficulties,' Dianne said. 'He won't be able to tell you how he's feeling. He was put into a children's home as a child, but he's lived with us for forty-five years; he'll think he's been abandoned again.' The call ended with the doctor promising to do all she could to reassure Ronnie.

We sat at the kitchen table together, for the most part silent. Then Dianne said, 'I can't bear it that he won't understand that we're not allowed to see him. He'll be terrified.'

'Let's try his phone,' I suggested – and then had a panic. 'Did he take his charger with him?'

Dianne ran upstairs to Ronnie's room. When she came down, she was smiling weakly. 'Well, his clothes are all still there, and his wallet, but there's no sign of his phone or his charger.'

'He'd have been more likely to have left his left leg behind.'

Over the next few hours, we rang constantly, but each time it went to voicemail. We had never known Ronnie fail to answer his phone and every time it happened, our feelings of powerlessness grew. At 10 p.m. we rang the ward and were told, 'Ronnie is comfortable,' and, 'Do ring in the morning.'

We went to bed, but neither of us could get to sleep. As we lay in the darkness, Dianne grasped my hand and said, 'I'd give anything to hear that stair creak.'

The next morning, we rang the ward as soon as we decently could. I spoke to the ward sister; she was amazing. I explained about Ronnie and how he would be feeling afraid. I said that his phone was a basic one and asked if we could get a smartphone for him so that he could Facetime us. She said that of course we could.

We tried so hard and so many times to speak to him on that smartphone, but he couldn't use it properly and it seemed to distress him. But in the brief time we saw his face, we shouted, 'We love you, Ronnie. Can't wait to have you home.'

In the end, I managed to have another conversation with the original doctor we had spoken with. 'I know how crazy it is for you all there at the moment, but is there anybody we can speak to about Ronnie so that you understand him and care for him in the best possible way?' She said that the hospital had a team of psychologists who helped patients cope with the anxiety and sometimes depression brought on by illness and hospitalisation. She promised to arrange for one of them to contact us.

Over the coming weeks, the psychologist assigned to Ronnie became a lifeline for him – and for us. Matthew spent hours talking with Ronnie and tried to get the hospital disability team involved, but as Ronnie had never had a formal declaration of a disability, they said they couldn't help.

Once, Matthew rang and told me that Ronnie wasn't cooperating with the physiotherapists. He asked if I had any suggestions. 'He responds to praise,' I said. 'Ask the physios to make some simple certificates and give him one whenever he makes an effort.' They tried their very best, crafted the reward with a border and lovely calligraphy, but by now, doubly incontinent and embarrassed to move, Ronnie was beyond certificates. The most successful relationship bonding with Ronnie occurred when Matthew discovered that he loved Diet Coke. He rang me and asked if we minded if he bought him some. I said, 'Yes, please; we'll pay you when we can come in.' He bought him a whole crate.

Matthew rang one day and said, 'I've arranged for you to see Ronnie. You still can't come inside the hospital, but I'm going to put him in a wheelchair and bring him just outside the main doors.'

When the day came, we were both nervous. We hadn't seen Ronnie face to face for over two months. It was sunny but cold, and we shivered a little as we waited on the benches outside the hospital café. But finally, we saw him being pushed towards us, covered in a large blanket and drinking a can of Diet Coke.

He smiled at us – a crooked 'this is the best I can do' smile. It was very hard not being able to hug him. He found it difficult to speak and it was an awkward, stilted conversation until I said, 'You know, Matthew, Ronnie is one of the finest football managers in Cardiff.'

His face lit up and he said, 'Not bad.' And suddenly the old Ronnie was back with us. I think if his body had allowed him, he would have put Matthew into a headlock just to prove to us that he was well.

The time went too quickly but with the wind picking up, Matthew needed to take Ronnie back inside. Dianne looked as though she was going to hug him, Covid or not, and then simply squeezed his arm, saying 'We love you, Ronnie.' Following her lead, I did the same and said, 'We can't wait to have you home.' Matthew pushed the wheelchair away and we watched them go towards the main doors. Just as they were about to disappear into the building, we saw Ronnie touch Matthew's arm and the wheelchair stopped. He looked back at us, gave us the crooked smile again, and said, 'I'm fine.'

*   *   *

Two weeks later the hospital rang to say he had had another stroke and we could go in to visit him. When we got to his ward there were curtains around his bed. We waited until a nurse said, 'You can see him now. I've just cleaned him up a bit.'

He lay, eyes closed, with tubes coming out of every part of his body. He was unshaven, his hair was matted, and a line of spittle was running down his face. Dianne and I were fighting hard to keep our composure.

'Ronnie, it's us – Di and Rob,' I said.

He opened his eyes and looked up at us. 'Take me back.'

His proudest possession – Ronnie's certificate for his voluntary work.

Chapter 18

Sat in Ronnie's Chair

Six days later, on a cold, rainy Saturday, Dianne was putting her make-up on in our bedroom, ready for an evening out with friends. I was in the kitchen emptying the dishwasher and, in the background, Radio 2's Liza Tarbuck was teeing up a Simon and Garfunkel song. The phone rang. For a moment I just looked at it; only cold callers and elderly relatives rang the landline. And although I knew that a landline phone has only one ringtone, this one was somehow different: urgent. As I answered it, I would have gladly welcomed a voice that told me that because I was such a loyal customer, I had qualified for a three-month free deal on repairs to my Sky television box.

As I walked into the bedroom, Dianne turned from the mirror towards me. 'Won't be a minute.'

I sat on the edge of the bed. 'The hospital has just rung. Ronnie is very ill. They think we should go in to see him as soon as possible.'

Dianne's mascara was running even as she got up and sat next to me. 'What did they say? Will he be all right?'

'I don't think he will, Di. He's comfortable just now, but the doctor said that he's very ill.'

Tears were now streaming down Dianne's face, and she was shaking her head, as if somehow that denial would change things. She spoke between sobs. 'He's not coming back, is he?'

I put my arm around her. 'No Di, I don't think Ronnie's coming home.'

We started making the calls as soon as we slipped out into the traffic. I rang our friends first and then Lloyd. His children were laughing in the background, and he shouted, 'Dial it down kids, would you!' When he came back on the line, I said, 'Mum and I are on the way to the hospital. I don't think Ronnie's got long.'

The line was quiet for a moment and then he said, 'I'll meet you there.' We couldn't get Katie but left a voicemail. With the phone calls over, I started to cry. 'He's had an amazing life and he knows how much we love him.'

Dianne took a tissue from her handbag and spoke as she blew her nose. 'I know, Rob, but I can't stop thinking about the times when I lost patience with him – and so often I don't think he could help it.'

'Di, he was part of our family; none of us were perfect – not the kids, not you and me, and not Ronnie. We loved each other, hurt each other, and tried to look out for each other. We lived together for forty-five years – and he loved you to bits.'

Dianne sniffed back more tears. 'He loved us all.'

It was raining heavily as we pulled into the car park at the University Hospital of Wales. Dianne grabbed a magazine from the back seat of the car and held it over her head as we made a dash for the covered walkway that led to the concourse. I remember thinking how strange it was that although Ronnie was dying, the hospital was the same as always. Patients in dressing gowns dragged on cigarettes outside the main door under the 'No Smoking' sign, nurses in uniform going off duty passed by, and consultants in their suits strode out quickly with confident steps. Inside the concourse, Starbucks was just closing up, Books Plus already had its shutters down and in WHSmith there was a last-minute smattering of people buying cards and flowers.

Everybody was in masks except us. We saw a box of disposable ones underneath the jar of sanitiser near the main doors, and took one each, putting them on as we walked across the foyer towards the stairs that led to the wards. My mobile rang. It was Katie. She was crying and barely able to speak. 'It's all right, darling,' I said. 'Mum and I have just had a good cry in the car on the way.'

'Dad, I don't think I can come in. I don't want my last memory of Ronnie to be seeing him like that.'

'I really understand that. They said he's unconscious. I honestly don't think he'll know if we're there or not. We'll ring you later. Love you.'

'Love you, Dad. Bye.'

By sheer accident, we had arrived during visiting time,

but there was a large notice on the door of the ward: 'Due to Covid restrictions, only one visitor per patient is allowed.' We pushed open the doors and walked up to the nursing station. We knew that Ronnie had been moved to a side room and asked the nursing auxiliary at the desk where that was. She didn't answer – just said, 'Only one visitor per bed.'

Dianne was polite but firm. 'We really appreciate all that you are doing under such difficult circumstances, but Mr Lockwood lived with us for forty-five years. We are all he has, and we are both going to be with him as he dies.'

To her credit, the woman didn't argue; she said, 'He's in the second room on the right. I'll take you there.'

We opened his door gently, as if there was the remotest possibility of waking him. The blinds were closed, and it took a while for our eyes to adjust to the darkness. He was in a hospital gown, white with small blue diamonds. The tubes that had been there on our last visit were all gone apart from a single oxygen line beneath his nose. His breathing rasped its rhythm.

We went to the side of his bed. I pulled up a chair for Dianne and as she sat, she reached out and took his hand in hers. He seemed to stir briefly, and his breathing caught a little, but then went back to its regular rhythm. I went to the window and looked out. A path skirted the building and people hurried along it. In the far distance I could see cars on the motorway. I turned and looked at Ronnie lying in the bed. I suddenly had a deep desire to do something. Lemn Sissay wrote, 'If the adults don't care to hug a child, why should he feel huggable?' I walked over to his bed, put my arms around him and held him close. I had not done that in all the years he was with us and I wished with all my heart I could turn back the clock. As I clutched his almost lifeless body, and with tears running down my face, I whispered, 'I love you, Ronnie.'

We sat in the darkness for a while and then the door opened. It was Lloyd. He walked straight to the bed and kissed Ronnie on the cheek. He stood for a while looking down at him, then said, 'We had some fine snooker battles, my friend.'

And then we all started crying again. I wonder if we were grieving not just for Ronnie's dying but for words we wish we had spoken, times we could have been kinder, frustrations that could have been brushed aside if only we had known that time was so short. And yet I think we also knew that was foolish. How could any of us live under that kind of pressure in the normality and stresses of family life? But of this we were sure: we had loved him. Perhaps if there had been no regrets, there would have been no love.

Just after Lloyd left, a nurse brought us tea and biscuits; it was just gone 9 p.m. We simply sat and listened to Ronnie's breathing. One would have thought the hours would have dragged, but they didn't. Although he never spoke, we cherished every minute that he was still with us. At almost midnight, his breathing changed – the gaps between exhalation and inhalation became longer, shallower. Dianne squeezed his hand, and he moved slightly. Suddenly she got up from her chair and laid her head on the pillow next to his. She began singing a children's song from our Sunday-school days – one that Ronnie himself would have sung: 'Jesus Loves Me, This I Know'. She sang it over and over again. His breathing was very laboured now. I put my ear close to his mouth, like a new mother checking that her baby is still breathing.

In and out, in and out, in and out . . . As I listened, and watched the rise and fall of his chest, Dianne was still singing the old song softly: 'Little ones to him belong; they are weak, but he is strong.'

In and out. And then . . . nothing: as if somewhere inside of him he said, 'I have struggled long enough.'

I said, 'I think he's gone.'

Dianne sat up, gazed at him and stroked his face.

I walked around the bed and put my arm around her. 'Nobody could have loved him more.'

And then a young nurse came in and ignoring all the Covid rules, wrapped her arms around us both and cried with us. I have wondered since whether we were crying also for some grief of hers unknown to us. The nurse wiped her eyes and tucked a loose strand of hair behind her ear. 'I'll make us all some tea.'

Dianne said, 'I'll come with you.'

*　*　*

Ronnie and I are alone together. And suddenly the years roll back. I am a young husband again, answering a knock on our door on a Christmas night. A homeless man is standing in the darkness. We speak for a while and then I say, 'Would you like to come in?'

Ronnie Lockwood says, 'Fine.'

* * *

Dianne and I hardly spoke on the journey home from the hospital. I felt a sadness so deep it seemed to engulf my soul. He had begun his life in an institution and ended it in one. When he was a child, he was abandoned, and I couldn't help but wonder if that was how he felt as he lay dying. I was sure he couldn't have understood why we were unable to visit him. Even now, among all the memories I have of conversations with him, three words stand out above all others – the last three words I heard him speak: 'Take me back.'

When we pulled into our drive it was almost 1 a.m. We walked into the kitchen together, still barely saying a word. I said, 'Would you like some tea? Shall I do you a decaf?'

Dianne didn't answer, she just came towards me and threw her arms around my neck. She began sobbing. I held her close, as if I could somehow squeeze the grief from her body. I don't know how long she was in my arms that night, but her crying went on and on as if she was wailing out the pain of the years. Finally, as her sobbing came to an end, she said, 'I'm going to bed. I'm so tired I can hardly stand.'

I said, 'I'll be up in a minute.' But I knew there was somewhere I would go first.

As I opened Ronnie's door, I willed him to be there, turn around and acknowledge me briefly before going straight back to the television and a gunfight outside a saloon. His chair was empty – of course, it was – but now there was an emptiness about the whole room. It was as if the walls themselves were resigned to the fact that he was not coming back. He had lived with us for almost half a century and now, suddenly, he was gone; death should be more incremental.

Perhaps it was harder to accept because we had not gone through a period of nursing him: there was no day-by-day acclimatisation to the knowledge that he was slipping away from us. And because of Covid, we were robbed even of the daily visits that would have, at least, allowed us to gradually come to terms with the fact that he was never coming home. We were part of the generation who were forced to wave at elderly mothers through the windows of nursing homes and blow kisses to dying children from behind masks; it had fallen to us to be socially distant even in our grief.

I walked across the room and sat in his chair. I remembered how we had furnished this room for him and how he had hated it at first, believing it was robbing him of time with us. The blue rug, the picture of the horse in a field, and the table lamp borrowed from our living room were all still there. I turned on the television. It was tuned to the last channel he was watching and on came an old quiz show he loved. And then I started crying again. I wanted him back. I wanted to hear him say, 'I'm brainy, I am,' or, 'You're a wind-up merchant, you are, Rob Parsons.' And I wanted him to beckon me towards the kitchen and say, 'I've got a surprise for you.'

And then suddenly I was assaulted by a hundred 'what ifs . . .?' What if I had answered his phone when he first rang me as I worked in my study? What if we had paid more attention to his couple of falls and got him checked out earlier? What if I had been stronger with the hospital – screamed and shouted louder that we must be allowed to visit him more and told them that even though there was no formal record of his disability in his medical notes, anybody with an ounce of sense could see it?

As the 'what ifs?' came, one after the other, it was as though my form teacher had written his assessment of my care of Ronnie and scrawled in my report card: 'Not good enough.'

I turned off the television and closed my eyes. When I opened them again, the early-morning sun was flooding into the room. I got up, stretched and wandered across to the small chest of drawers at the side of his bed. I opened the top drawer, feeling as if I was trespassing on holy ground. There were some letters, a leather wallet and, next to it, some old building-society passbooks bound by a rubber band. I picked them up and crossed the room to sit again in his chair. I slid the oldest one from underneath the rubber band and flicked through the pages to the first entry: February 1976, just over a month after he first knocked on our door. Next to the date was written, 'Deposit, Cardiff City Council.' And then my eye went to the second entry – a cash withdrawal. I remembered the time he had put his head in his hands at his despair that he had let me down over his gambling and, as I turned another page of the book, an inner voice whispered, 'You were too harsh. Too lacking in understanding. You could have been kinder.' I was to hear that voice many times over the coming years; even now, as I write, it still sometimes speaks to me.

I wrapped the band around the books and returned to the drawer. At the very back lay a small bundle covered in cloth. I picked it up and pulled back the fabric: five cards, all with the same inscription. I wondered where Carol was now. Was she still alive? And had she any idea of the deep impact that her simple act of kindness had had on a young boy? Her birthday cards had become icons.

I pulled at the second drawer, but at first it wouldn't open; something was jamming it. I slid my hand in and pulled at the piece of cardboard that had caught and stopped it opening. The drawer was bursting with cards from Dianne and I and the kids, and so many other people – birthdays, Christmases, wedding and party invitations, and more than twenty that read, 'Congratulations! You are the volunteer of the month!' A life crammed into a drawer. I put the cards inside, glanced around his room and closed the door shut.

*   *   *

Three days later, Dianne and I were eating lunch in the kitchen when we heard the bell. I opened the door but didn't recognise the elderly woman who stood in the porch. 'I'm sorry to intrude,' she said, 'but I'm a neighbour from down the far end of the road and I've just heard the sad news about Ronnie. I wanted to bring you a little card and these – they are from my garden.' She handed me a bouquet of roses.

I thanked her and asked, 'Did you know Ronnie?'

She looked surprised. 'Oh, yes. Didn't he tell you? I've lived on my own since my husband died. A couple of years ago, Ronnie saw me struggling with my bins and helped me get them onto the pavement. Every Thursday evening since then he has come to my house and taken them out for me. Unless he was away, he never missed. Even during lockdown, he did it for me and he would wave at me through the window. Sometimes he would get me things from the Co-op. He was a very special man.'

'He was indeed.'

'I won't stop, but I wanted to make sure you knew of his kindness to me. I thought it would bless you.'

'Well, it has. Thank you.'

When I went back into the kitchen, Dianne wasn't there. Then she shouted down the stairs, 'I'm up here. I've got to be at the undertaker's at two.' I walked into the bedroom; she was looking in the wardrobe. She turned as I went in. 'Who was it?'

I explained. Dianne sat on a chair at the dressing table. She spoke as she gazed out of the window into the distance. 'It's amazing. I'm only just beginning to realise what a total enigma he was. Do you remember the second night he was with us, and you asked me if I wanted you to put a chair under the handle of our bedroom door like we did the first night?'

I laughed. 'I do. And you said no.'

'But why did I say no? He had only been with us for a day, yet I remember thinking that he would never harm us. I felt that we had already seen the real him. But now I think there was so much we didn't know. Last night I couldn't sleep, and I just lay there, thinking, "Who were you, Ronnie? You were almost like a visitor from another world. You never spoke badly of anyone, you loved to give more than get, you were kind and reliable, solid and trustworthy, but you were broken. You were terribly broken."'

I rubbed my eyes. 'I know people say we were kind to him, and we were. And I know that you bore so much of the fallout from the hard times, and there were plenty of those. But in so many ways I think he was a gift to us and the kids. Think of it: they have never known a life without Ronnie, and they loved him. I never saw the tiniest bit of resentment from them; no murmurings of, "Why are we the weird family with the homeless guy?"'

Dianne got up to go. 'Of course, there wasn't. Ronnie was part of our family, and he still is.'

*   *   *

I got up early on the morning of Ronnie's funeral. It was still dark as I opened the door to his old room and made my way to the armchair that he used to sit in to watch television. The small square of carpet in front of it was worn and scuffed.

I sat down, laid my head back and closed my eyes. In some ways I was feeling his death more keenly than that of my parents.

I could hear Dianne moving about in our bedroom next door. She is now quite well, but every once in a while feels the worry that the good times won't have the stamina to last.

So much had changed in our lives. When Ronnie first knocked on our door, I was a lawyer working with John Loosemore and glad he had passed the interview with my parents. John had left the legal practice shortly after me, but we went on doing the seminars together for many years. We still see each other regularly, tell stories from the old days and smile at the story of Charlie Watts' wife, the Rolling Stones and the Blue Jets. The charity that Dianne and I agonised over starting has grown to levels I could never have dreamt of. We have almost a hundred employees, two hundred volunteers, and offices across the United Kingdom. Since that day in the reclamation yard, Care for the Family has gone behind tens of thousands of front doors to help families – single parents, those with children with additional needs, those who have lost a child or a partner early in life, myriads of parents facing the multiple challenges of bringing up kids, and couples who are trying to decide if it is possible to go on loving when there is no paint at all on the shoes. In 2012, I was invited to Buckingham Palace to receive an award that recognised what the team at Care for the Family has done over the years. As my conversation with the Queen was coming to a close, my mind went back to my asking my father, 'Do you ever get bored just sticking letters through doors?' I only just stopped myself from telling her 'My father used to deliver your letters.'

As I looked around Ronnie's room, I saw a photograph of him holding a huge certificate. It declared that in his time as a volunteer with Care for the Family, he had packed over ten thousand pieces of post. He was so proud of that photograph. No caller to our home could escape being ushered up to his bedroom to see its wonder. I walked across the room to look at it more closely. His smile beamed out at me, and I reached out and touched his face. I mused, 'Who were you really, Ronnie Lockwood? If you had been able to talk more easily, perhaps think more quickly, what would you have told us of yourself?'

Suddenly the door opened, and Dianne was standing there. She came in and sat on the edge of Ronnie's armchair next to me. The light was beginning to come through the curtains.

*   *   *

As the hearse pulled up outside our front door, there was an early-September chill in the air but it was sunny – the kind of day that nudges rather than pushes us into autumn. As I opened the door, I could see a number of neighbours lining the road. I remembered Ronnie telling us of the small crowd that waved him off to the children's home when he was eight.

Because of the Covid restrictions, only fifty people could

attend the funeral, and yet so many people wanted to be there – members of the football team he managed, homeless people he had helped, colleagues from the bin round, not to mention the myriads of those from church whose keys he had hidden over the years. Tickets for it were hotter than for a Coldplay concert and those who couldn't be there sent cards – over a hundred of them. I have never experienced such an outpouring of affection from people from all walks of life.

Norman Adams, the church leader who had prayed with me in the darkness that night all those years ago when Dianne was so ill, led the service. He spoke warmly of Ronnie and how he had done so many jobs so well at the church, volunteered at Care for the Family, and given himself to helping every week for years at the homeless centre. As Norman came to the end of his talk, he spoke again of the incredible value of all that work and read a passage from the New Testament.

Then the King will say . . .
I was hungry and you gave me something to eat,
I was thirsty and you gave me something to drink,
I was a stranger and you invited me in,
I needed clothes and you clothed me,
I was sick and you looked after me,
I was in prison, and you came to visit me,
. . . 'Lord, when did we see you hungry and feed you,
or thirsty and give you something to drink? When did

we see you a stranger and invite you in, or needing clothes and clothe you? When did we see you sick or in prison and go to visit you?'

The King will reply, 'Truly I tell you, whatever you did for one of the least of these brothers and sisters of mine, you did for me.'

(Matthew 25: 34–40, NIV)

It was time for the cremation, and I squeezed Dianne's hand as the curtain began to wrap itself around Ronnie's coffin. And then he was gone.

The undertakers ushered people towards the exit with Dianne and I leading the way. As we got outside, I blinked – a mixture of tears and the sun – and Dianne whispered to me in the brief moment that we were alone, 'Do you remember the night he asked us that question: "We three will be together for ever, won't we?"'

I smiled, 'I do.'

'And do you remember what you said?'

'I said, "Yes, Ronnie. We'll be together for ever."'

Dianne's voice caught in her throat as she spoke. 'Well, you were right.'

We weren't alone for long. Katie and Lloyd joined us, and soon people were milling around giving their condolences and occasional memories of Ronnie. Funeral services were pretty backed up over the Covid months and even as we were still talking, people began arriving for the next one. We said our goodbyes and walked hand in hand towards our car.

As we got to the car park, I looked up through the trees into a blue and cloudless sky. I stood gazing up for a moment and then I started smiling. Dianne said, 'Well, that's a surprise. I thought I might never see you smile again.'

'I was thinking about what you said about being together for ever. I started imagining Ronnie arriving in heaven and I suddenly had two pictures of him there that really lifted my spirits.'

Dianne screwed up her eyes. 'Come on – don't keep me in suspense.'

'The first was the Archangel Gabriel saying, "Has anybody seen my keys to the gate?"'

She laughed out loud. 'And what was the second one?'

'St Peter in a headlock.'

Postscript

On Thursday 1 December 2022, Mark Drakeford, then First Minister of Wales, opened the Lockwood Centre – a new £1.6 million wellbeing centre attached to Glenwood Church, Cardiff. It serves one of the most deprived areas in Wales. Before he spoke, I was given five minutes to talk about why the building had been named after Ronnie. I told the story of a man who had never known a real family of his own but who, in this place, had found a family larger than he ever dreamt possible. I told how he used to put the chairs out every week and then pack them away again, wash dishes in the homeless centre, and how he treated everybody the same – both professors and plumbers ended up in his headlocks.

As he listened, Mark Drakeford was visibly moved by Ronnie's story, and during his speech he said something that perhaps hit upon the key to what changed Ronnie's life: 'I've always thought that there can be nothing more dispiriting than to be constantly the object of other people's benign concern. In the story that we just heard about Ronnie and the jobs that he did here, he wasn't just the object of other people's interest, he was somebody who gave something himself.'

As I looked at the sign 'The Lockwood Centre', I felt proud of Ronnie. I thought back on our lives with him and how remarkably his life had changed. And yet the past is strong, and it was heartbreaking to see how firm a hold it had on him and how deep were the effects of his childhood experiences in care. I often feel that I can still hear him saying the phrases he used over and over. 'I haven't done a bad thing, have I?', 'I'm always getting things wrong.', 'I didn't offend you, did I?'

Thirty-seven thousand children are taken into the care system every year; the outcomes for many of them are so very poor and I wondered whether anything could be done to change that. There is no doubt that most in the social-work arena do their very best for those in their care, and yet for many children there is little improvement from Ronnie or Lemn Sissay's time. I've recently read Chris Wild's book *The State of It*. Wild was in care as a child and his book, published in 2021, catalogues his experiences and those of the many others he has spoken with. The subtitle is 'Stories from the frontline of a broken care system'. Like Ronnie, he was left to fend for himself on leaving care. He writes, 'I was left to run riot and despite the fact that I was still a child, a heartbroken, damaged and lost child, the authorities washed their hands of me. I was abandoned by the system.'

But Dianne and I also had the privilege of seeing Ronnie change over the years; slowly his narrative of 'I'm rubbish' was replaced with 'I'm brainy, I am' and 'I'm good with babies'. I realise that our experience with him is not easily replicable or probably desirable, nevertheless I can't help but wonder if there was anything we did with him – probably by accident, as we were not experienced enough to have done it by design – that could possibly make a difference in the lives of other children who are in the care system or have passed through it.

When Ronnie knocked the door on that Christmas night, he didn't only embark on a journey in which he changed, *he changed us*. As I have already said, a quarter of people on the streets have a background in care. It's easy for any of us to be judgemental, but I have never forgotten an incident that occurred shortly after Ronnie came to live with us. I was on the subway in New York; it was a freezingly cold December day.

At Central Park Station, a man entered our carriage. He had a dirty brown mackintosh that was tied with string at his waist, and trousers that were thin and torn. His woollen hat was yanked down to his ears. The scarf around his neck was pulled up high so that little of his face could be seen, but what was visible looked red and raw. At first glance he appeared old, but at a closer look, perhaps nearer 30 – as if life had etched too many years into his face for the birthdays he had known. The streets above us were icy on this winter's day and he looked pinched by the cold.

He began to shuffle along the carriage asking for money. I looked around and watched as passengers sunk their heads low into their newspapers. As he got near to me, I dropped my eyes to my book. The only person to give him anything was an elderly lady who handed him a dollar bill. As the train pulled in towards the next station he made for the doors, but just before he reached them, he stopped and said in a loud but gentle voice. 'Ladies and gentlemen, I haven't always been like this, and you should all know that anything can happen to anybody.' The train stopped at 125th Street, the doors opened, and he was gone. In the carriage there was absolute silence; we looked at each other; some quickly went back to their reading, but a few of us sat staring ahead. We knew only too well what we had just experienced: we had seen our own face behind the scarf.

As the building work was coming to an end on the new wellbeing facility, the builders discovered that an adjoining roof needed to be upgraded at a cost of just under £40,000. It was almost to the penny the amount that Ronnie had left the centre in his will.

In Loving Memory...

Ronald George Lockwood

6 MARCH, 1945 - 3 SEPTEMBER, 2020

Acknowledgements

A Knock at the Door was written as part of a PhD thesis. My supervisors were Professor Anthony Caleshu and Professor David Sergeant. Their criticism was incisive, their wisdom invaluable and their encouragement constant. I honestly believe I could not have written it without their advice. I am grateful to them and the University of Plymouth for giving me the opportunity to embark on such a programme of study at this stage of my life.

My agent, Jo Bell of Bell Lomax Moreton has been a constant support from the first day she rang me and said, 'I've just finished your manuscript. You made me cry – let's find a good home for it!' Every author knows both the highs and lows of writing and Jo has been there for me in both. I am deeply grateful to her.

Eddie Bell was the first person to read the manuscript and from the moment he did I have benefited from his incredible wisdom and encouragement. It wouldn't have happened without him.

I am grateful to each of the publishers who wanted to take on my book, but of course I am especially grateful to Myles Archibald, Publishing Director at William Collins for his warm welcome to me. Thanks also to Eve Hutchings, Kate Quarry and the whole team there. Thank you also to Bengono Bessala – for believing in me.

Many people have given advice and encouragement along the long road of writing this book, and none more so than Debbie Campbell, Meg Chester and Sheron Rice. Thank you.

Thanks also to Steve Williams, Robin Vincent, Katharine Hill, Paula Pridham, Drew Firth, Kate Hancock and the Care for the Family team.

Jody Jones my PA has been by my side since the start of this project, and I wouldn't want to think of having attempted it without her. Only she and I know both her skill and her patience.

Katie and Lloyd. You had a different family life to most of your peers and never once complained. But more than that, in every way you let Ronnie know that he was loved.

Thank you, Dianne. I have dedicated this book to you because the truth is, none of it – not its story or its writing, would have happened without you.

And finally thank you to Ronnie – a remarkable man, who made our life richer and taught us what really mattered.